Relentless

Relentless

Unleashing a Life
of Purpose, Grit, and Faith

JOHN
TESH

NELSON
BOOKS

An Imprint of Thomas Nelson

Published in Nashville, Tennessee, by Nelson Books, an imprint of Thomas Nelson. Nelson Books and Thomas Nelson are registered trademarks of HarperCollins Christian Publishing, Inc.

Thomas Nelson titles may be purchased in bulk for educational, business, fund-raising, or sales promotional use. For information, please e-mail SpecialMarkets@ThomasNelson.com.

Unless otherwise noted, Scripture quotations are taken from the New King James Version®. © 1982 by Thomas Nelson. Used by permission. All rights reserved.

Scripture quotations marked KJV are from the King James Version. Public domain.

Any Internet addresses, phone numbers, or company or product information printed in this book are offered as a resource and are not intended in any way to be or to imply an endorsement by Thomas Nelson, nor does Thomas Nelson vouch for the existence, content, or services of these sites, phone numbers, companies, or products beyond the life of this book.

ISBN 978-1-4002-0873-9 (eBook)
ISBN 978-1-4002-0871-5 (HC)

Library of Congress Control Number: 2019955086

Printed in the United States of America

20 21 22 23 24   LSC   10 9 8 7 6 5 4 3 2 1

Dedicated to my Concetta.
And to my beloved readers.
I wish that your soul might prosper
through the words in this book.

Contents

Contents

Introduction

In the halcyon days of *Late Night with Conan O'Brien*—before all the Conan-vs.-Leno *Tonight Show* controversy—I had become a regular guest on the show.

Mine was an unlikely presence, but in some ways I was also a natural fit. Conan and I were two oversized, geeky beanpoles who, somehow, found themselves hosting national television shows.

In those years, I think we were also doing each other a bit of a good turn. Finding guests to fill the hour was no small feat for a show that came on at 12:30 a.m., after the last of the sensible grown-ups had gone to bed. A-list guests were regularly commandeered by Jay Leno and David Letterman for their much bigger shows an hour earlier, and with Conan filming in New York while the center of the entertainment industry was in Los Angeles, the pool of potential guests was already limited by who was in town. That left Conan with people like me and other B- and C-list guests to pull from on a nightly basis. (I won't name my fellow Bs and Cs. Their publicists and managers may be offended.)

Conan, of course, went on to become hugely popular and soon had full access to all the A+ level guests for his couch. But he stayed loyal to me and the rest of his Bs and Cs, and so anytime I had something to promote, he was right there for me (sometimes it was with him, other times it was with him and his pal, Triumph the Insult Comic Dog). One night, following our interview about the inexplicable success of my first PBS special, *Live at Red Rocks with the Colorado Symphony*, Conan was wrapping up when he waited a beat, smiled, and spoke to the camera. At the time, his words felt like they captured the totality of my unlikely life, but now they pretty much sum up everything you're about to read in this book:

> If the guy who used to read the celebrity birthdays on *Entertainment Tonight* is now playing piano and millions of people are lining up to buy his music, then we all need to get our clarinets out of the attic and start practicing because, seriously folks, anything can happen.[1]

Conan was right. Anything can happen. For better or for worse. I am living proof. And this book is a testament to that fact. In this book there is a love story that I nearly destroyed, but with persistent pursuit it rose from the ashes and now flourishes in marriage, twenty-eight years later. You'll hear about a death sentence, handed down to me by high-level physicians and surgeons in Los Angeles. But with a deep faith in scriptural and science-based warfare, here I stand, cured. I'll tell you about being homeless at twenty years old, living in a North Carolina park, unsure of my future or true purpose, until three years later I was anchoring nightly newscasts at WCBS in New York City. I'll take you on a journey through my fledgling music career that had me selling fifty cassette tapes per week out of my garage (ten years later my wife and I sold our record company to Polygram for $8 million). You'll hear the story of how my family and I created a self-syndicated radio show that initially debuted on only six radio stations but twenty years later is heard on more than three hundred stations worldwide.

As I began writing those stories for this book, my publisher, Matt Baugher, offered some encouragement by way of reminder. "When people read a memoir," he said, "they very often see not only you. They also see a part of themselves in your journey." It's so true. It happens to me when I read a memoir, especially, but it also happens when I read any book. When I read fiction, the protagonists are usually wielding swords and they are always the underdogs. When I read books on personal development, I gravitate toward authors who take me inside the lives of artists and performers who have not only persevered but who have developed a unique process for achieving excellence. Leonardo da Vinci,

Introduction

Harry Houdini, Benjamin Franklin, Wolfgang Mozart, Ted Williams, Lin-Manuel Miranda. I read their stories and I think, *Can I duplicate their process? What of them can I find within myself?*

Those very questions, in fact, have been baked into my approach to life and to work for as long as I can remember. Even before it became a popular life hack, for instance, I was always decoding greatness this way. This desire arose in me because I felt I was not naturally talented and there were no life coaches to tell me otherwise. There was no Tony Robbins. No Tim Ferriss or Oprah. No way to study the masters like we can today on YouTube. Instead, back in the Paleolithic era of the Digital Age (also known as the 1970s and 1980s), I recorded hundreds of other artists' concerts, motivational speeches, sermons, and radio and television broadcasts off the air on my Walkman and my Betamax video player. I studied these recordings. I learned from them. I emulated the performers. Newscasters. Sports play-by-play announcers. Pianists and composers. Pastors. Coaches and athletes.

As a professional journalist since 1973, I have enjoyed the privilege of interviewing thousands of high achievers: at the Olympic Games, in the recording studio, on Broadway, in the Oval Office, and on movie sets. Along the way I realized how much these humans are just like the rest of us. They have sleepless nights. They war with the same types of insecurities we all face. The difference is, they have learned how to outwork and outlast their competitors. The one common thread in their process is *they are relentless.*

I was mesmerized, fascinated, and encouraged by men and women at the top of their game. I studied the habitual approaches of Michael Jordan and LeBron James, the rituals of author Stephen King, the video visualizations of Michael Phelps. Their unspoken mantra? "You will not outwork me." Keyboardist Rick Wakeman from Yes, sportscaster Al Michaels, *60 Minutes* correspondent Mike Wallace. Olympic announcer Jim McKay from ABC Sports, singer and songwriter Billy Joel, swimmer Diana Nyad.

There was a time when I thought that I had, indeed, acquired the art of relentless pursuit. I had, if only from a distance, been mentored by those I had scrutinized for so long. I believed the ability to be relentless would be with me forever—that I finally held the treasure map that would lead me to success in perpetuity.

Then on May 23, 2015, the world on which my blessed life was spinning spun off its axis. I was diagnosed with a rare and aggressive form of cancer; my book of life suddenly included a final chapter. Survival required a withering mix of surgeries, chemotherapy, and muscle-wasting treatments that, over three years, reduced me to a puny shell of myself—physically and spiritually. The excruciating pain, nausea, and depression left me with barely enough energy to beg God for help. I felt like I had descended into hell, and I lost my will to continue. The relentlessness of the cancer had surmounted my own.

It was then that my wife, Connie, stepped out of her own life to care for me, full time, and showed another kind of relentlessness I did not even know existed. She studied my disease and treatment options so diligently that surgeons and RNs were certain she was a health-care professional. She became my advocate for each and every treatment. She personified unconditional love wrapped in humility, in empathy. She put flesh on Jesus. And she covered our entire family with a healing scripture that was more powerful than my disease. It was a promise right there in the Bible, and it was one I had missed.

> For assuredly, I say to you, whoever says to this mountain, "Be removed and be cast into the sea," and does not doubt in his heart, but believes that those things he says will be done, he will have whatever he says. Therefore I say to you, whatever things you ask when you pray, believe that you receive them, and you will have them. (Mark 11:23–24)

That verse was life to my flesh.

My wife's faith and advocacy had brought me back to life and I'm anxious for you to hear more about my Connie—a woman who laid down her life to save her dear mother of ninety years and then used her bold faith and intelligence to stand in the gap for her husband. To save his life. And here I am. Transformed.

I'm grateful you've picked up this book. I devour books like this every day. Life stories. Personal journeys. For it's in the journey, ours and others', that we are transformed.

As the author of my own story, I've tried to write the book that I would want to read. While I describe my childhood and younger days in school, I've included them only so that you may gather a deeper understanding of some of my life decisions—decisions that give some context to my journey and reveal a process that is both universal and uniquely my own.

I organized this book in the way I like to read a memoir: by the key moments that have defined me. Because of that, if you don't feel like joining me in my high school garage band then, by all means, jump to the chapter where I was homeless in a park or the one where I recorded the beginnings of the iconic NBA theme song, "Roundball Rock," on my answering machine or the chapter where I detail the creative process of composing music for the Tour de France—a process I still use today. It's all okay by me, because I am not recounting my life as a running diary of catharsis, as a list of examples of bravado, or even as a stroke to my ego. Instead, I am unpacking the pivotal moments in my journey in the hope that I can do for readers what other authors have done for me.

This book is an invitation for you to take a look at my collection of inexplicable successes (and failures) and to find something in my personal road map—as unplanned and haphazardly drawn as it was at times— that can offer you guidance toward the kinds of outcomes I have been fortunate enough to enjoy. Even if the specifics of my life do not resonate at all with the particulars of your hopes and dreams, I still believe there is something in this book for you. I wouldn't have written it otherwise. As I write this, I could be in the pool with my three grandkids, but I want to share this roller-coaster life of mine with you because, somewhere in these pages, I believe you'll find a piece of yourself. In fact, I'm sure of it.

Let's begin.

Visit JohnTeshRelentless.com for photos and
videos related to stories in this book.

Prelude

Persistence

I've been in an accident! My voice is destroyed.
—AUGUST 4, 2015

The first sound I hear is a rhythmic, loud beeping that seems to be coming from a far-off place. My trapezius muscles on either side of my neck are on fire. The stabbing pain is excruciating and as I open my eyes and attempt to speak, the voice that comes out of my mouth is two octaves lower than my own, with a timbre that resembles someone with severely damaged vocal cords.

Oh my God, I think. *I've been in an accident! My voice is destroyed.*

My heart is pounding in my throat. I'm a communicator. An entertainer. My voice has been my livelihood for forty years.

The beeping is faster now. I feel a warm touch on my left arm.

"John? John? It's me, honey. You're in the recovery room. It went very well. You're okay."

I recognize Connie's voice, but I cannot see her. There's a film over my eyes that prevents me from focusing. It feels like trying to take a picture with the camera lens pressed against a screen door. Nothing but foreground noise and fuzzy shapes. *Where am I?*

I try to speak again. This time I'm aware that I'm talking through a mask, and I sound like Darth Vader after two packs of cigarettes.

"Mr. Tesh, are you in pain?" This is another voice now. It's a nurse. Her words are the first I fully register, and they draw my attention away from what is going on around me and back into myself. I take a quick inventory of my body. Big mistake. The disorientation that was in my brain now resolves itself into a kind of clarity that my eyes still cannot achieve: *Hell yes, I'm in nothing* but *pain.*

I nod my head. Although I'm not successfully communicating with my vocal cords, my furrowed brow must be telling another story because the voice announces that she is going to give me a shot—Dilaudid, I would find out—to make me feel better. *Why are my trapezius muscles on fire?*

"Where am I?" I manage to squeak out a few words. This time the Darth Vader Marlboro Man has ridden his horse out of town and left one of the old Muppets characters in his place. "I'm . . . I'm so thirsty."

And then, finally, I see Connie's face. She looks concerned but then, forcing a smile, quickly reminds me why I'm lying in a hospital bed with a mask on my face. "You're just out of surgery," she says. "You're going to be fine, Pop Pop."

"I have to pee."

"Go ahead," Connie says, now with more of a playful smile on her face. "You have a catheter."

My worst fear is now realized because what goes up must come down, what goes in . . . will eventually have to come out. Before the fear has time to turn into terror, the shot of Dilaudid has reached my brain and produces within me an intense urge to sleep.

The beeping seems like it's outside now. Connie's voice joins it, as her face dissolves into gauzy obscurity once again.

This is cancer.

Chapter 1

Mentors in Persistence

Music, Movies, Machines, and Mischief

I was an impulsive kid and, like anything, this impulsivity had its upsides and its downsides. On the positive side, I was continually interested in new mind-expanding, horizon-broadening rabbit holes, the first of those being technology.

At age seven, I wanted to find out how everything worked. I recall the day my parents bought a new Magnavox stereo at Korvettes. We listened to the Bert Kaempfert Orchestra for five days straight. Then I decided I needed to disassemble the unit and enhance the sound. I removed all the electronics from inside the piece of furniture in which the stereo resided and drilled holes in the chassis so the sound had more places to come out of.

In my defense, throughout history successful inventors and explorers have embraced this timeless process of testing, failing, retesting, and more failing. Thomas Edison famously said that he had never actually failed, he had just found ten thousand ways that wouldn't work. And just like Edison, I found many, many ways that didn't work, discovering in the process that there is also a certain amount of pain and suffering one must endure as a result.

The suffering, in my case, came from the business end of spankings by frustrated parents. The pain came from a far more unforgiving master: physics.

During what I now refer to as my exploration phase, I took apart numerous kitchen appliances, radios, and just about anything else in the house that was plugged into an outlet. The only problems I encountered came when, in my hyperhaste, I forgot to unplug a device from the 110 volts of alternating current pumping through it before beginning disassembly.

If she were alive today, my mom would tell you that I frequently experienced serious electric shocks during my wonder years, and after consulting her personal copy of *Grey's Anatomy*, she became quite certain that during that time in my life I suffered several auto-electroconvulsive episodes. She would also tell you that at no point did any one of these electric shocks dissuade me from taking apart the next machine I could get my hands on. My desire to know how things worked, to understand why, muted any adolescent misgivings I may have had and thwarted any attempts she might have made to keep things with plugs out of my reach. Paradoxically, while my quest for deeper understanding drove me to persist on my Edisonian voyage of household discovery, none of that seemed to translate to schoolwork. I should note here that my mom always used to blame those electroconvulsive episodes for my absence from the honor roll.

After technology, there were film and music. By first grade, it had become clear to me that my future would be as either a director or a composer. The light bulb went off the moment my dad walked in with a brand-new 8mm movie camera. His plan was to document an upcoming family road trip to Yosemite. My plan was to be Hitchcock. Or Fellini. Or H. G. Wells. My first motion picture, however, would be more of an homage to Rube Goldberg.[*]

I had no actors. No sets. No lighting director. I had my dad's 8mm camera, two rolls of unused Kodak film, fishing line, my Sears Silvertone Chord Organ, and Tippy, the family cat. I began storyboarding my concept with a genius-level idea of taking coat hangers and constructing a flying harness for Tippy. I attached the fishing line to the harness; affixed

---

[*] Rube Goldberg is best known for cartoons that depict complicated gadgets whose sole purpose is to perform simple tasks in the most convoluted ways possible. His cartoons are where the term "Rube Goldberg machines" comes from.

the harness to the clothesline; set up the home movie camera on a stack of my mom's cookbooks; and then, at the last minute, I slipped Tippy into the harness. I then carefully pulled the harness with the fishing line. (Spielberg will tell you that fishing line is mostly invisible while using 8mm film stock.) My special effects setup made it look like Tippy was flying through outer space.

When I'd completed principal photography ("filming" in Hollywood-speak), I sent off the exposed film for processing and waited for what felt like a lifetime for its return. When it finally arrived, I secretly screened my masterpiece in the privacy of my bedroom and then set out to complete what I would later learn is called postproduction. Sitting in my room, playing my Sears Silverton Chord Organ, and making some creepy sounds with my mouth, I fired up my dad's reel-to-reel recorder and microphone and recorded the film's soundtrack. It was, to my young mind, a cinematic tour de force. It was incredible. And very scary.

A few days later, I screened the finished product—*Tippy Goes to Mars*—for my mom and dad. Knowing how much work I had put into the project, my mom watched the screening with great reverence. Dad, however, roared the way he laughed when he was watching *The Three Stooges*. I was mortified. I had considered myself a serious filmmaker, so I thought he was diminishing all my hard work by laughing at it like it was a slapstick comedy. It was one of those moments that, I now realize as an adult, has the potential to derail the dreams and define the trajectory, at least in part, of any child. It certainly did for me. As a sensitive, empathic boy, I did not have the tools to persist through that kind of parental negativity. I didn't know what I wanted to do and be yet. I didn't know how to let that kind of stuff roll off my back. I was seven. Mom tried to whisper encouragement when we were alone, which helped for a little while, but when Dad discovered I had used his vacation film, he made me pull weeds all weekend to pay for it. That was the end of that. Looking back now, though, I appreciate my dad's review. The film was pretty darn hilarious.

My moviemaking career had ended, but my interest in production and performance had only just begun. When I was nine, I fancied myself a producer of live theater. Our home included a built-in intercom system.

One Halloween, I ripped out one of the intercom speakers, because of course that is something I would do, and I placed it in a hollowed-out pumpkin on our front porch. I positioned myself by the remaining speaker in the kitchen, and when the young trick-or-treaters approached the house, I drove them away in tears with evil howlings that emanated directly from Mr. Pumpkin.

It wasn't long before I graduated from public broadcasts to clandestine recordings of my sisters. Whenever one of their boyfriends came over, my parents would order me into another room, giving my sister a little privacy, while my parents went to their bedroom. (The suitor was told he had to keep both feet on the floor while on the couch.) I had already figured out a way to connect an external microphone to the intercom wiring, so I placed the microphone under a pillow on the couch. Then I connected my dad's reel-to-reel tape recorder to the other end of the intercom and recorded the lovebirds' conversations while I listened through the intercom. I still have those tapes somewhere, and I've gotten great mileage over the years holding those recordings for ransom.

All of these shenanigans and flights of curiosity were great fun. That was the upside of my undirected impulsivity: it was never boring. The downside was that it was ultimately purposeless. And when I lacked purpose, I found mischief. The surreptitious recordings of my sisters, fright night with Mr. Pumpkin, even rigging up Tippy with fishing line—all of that had some degree of mischief driving it. It would have persisted well into my teen years, and probably my twenties, had not two mentor-type figures interceded to show me the potential consequences—and probable accomplishments—if I could just channel it toward something purposeful.

I learned about consequences from my father's father, Grandpa Percy Tesh, son of Romulus (no wonder I ended up with a Klingon cameo on *Star Trek*), taker of no guff whatsoever. He and Grandma Tesh lived outside of Rural Hall, North Carolina, on a huge farm less than fifteen miles north of Winston-Salem.

Each summer, our family drove down from Long Island to visit. The trip was two full days of driving, split in half by a night at a

Howard Johnson's along the way (honk if you ever had a HoJo Cola!). I would catch up on the latest issues of *The Amazing Spider-Man*, *Uncanny X-Men*, and *Sgt. Fury and His Howling Commandos* before jumping in the motel pool and bobbing up and down, doing my patented "find a friend" dance, slowly approaching other kids until one of them got creeped out enough to exclaim, "Hey! Who *are* you?" Boom . . . friends! (It must be innate because I've also seen my daughter and granddaughters do it.)

The Howard Johnson's layover was our last bit of lighthearted fun before we got to the farm, where my grandparents raised chickens and pigs; grew beans, sweet potatoes, and lettuce; and generously doled out chores to yours truly. Among my daily chores were collecting the eggs from the henhouse, slopping the hogs (if you haven't had the pleasure of working on a farm, slopping hogs means flinging a mess of leftover food to giant animals steeped in mud), and hiking down to the well to pump enough water for the day. This was among the simplest yet more important tasks delegated to me because Grandma and Grandpa had no electricity. When Grandma washed clothes, she did it in a cauldron-like container that held the water I'd hauled from the well. She dried the clothes by running them through a hand crank and hanging them on a clothesline. When she wasn't doing the cleaning, she was getting her hands dirty, teaching me salt-of-the-earth stuff like how to kill and clean chickens, and how to kill, clean, and cure hogs. Needless to say, life on the farm was backbreaking work, the kind that can sap the energy and even the mischief out of impulsive young boys—almost.

Exhausted near the end of my chores one day when I was eleven years old, I was leaning up against the barn with my Red Ryder BB gun and, for nothing but grins, I sighted and shot a chicken in the backside. I figured the velocity of a BB was unlikely to kill anything, and I was right, but what I had not accounted for was that the chicken would go berserk and start squawking bloody murder. It jumped straight up in the air, sending the whole henhouse into a frenzy. The commotion quickly registered on Grandpa's radar, and it didn't take long for him to discover the cause of the hens' hysteria.

Let's start with how Grandpa Tesh did *not* handle the situation. He didn't say, "You're a cute kid, Johnny, but you made a mistake by shooting the hen with your BB gun. I'm not happy right now. Please don't let it happen again."

Grandpa wasn't interested in applying some touchy-feely, liberal-hippy, preschool technique to the situation or working any sort of clinical child psychology exercise. I had screwed up. Grandpa Tesh was going to provide me with a lesson and memory that I would take with me forever.

"Johnny, I want you to go into the woods, cut a switch, and bring it back to me," he said. I was from Long Island. To me, a switch was that thing on the wall that turned on the lights. I had no idea what he was talking about. Grandpa was happy to explain that picking a switch meant cutting a branch off a tree so it could be used to administer punishment.

Being a rookie switch-picker, I picked a small, thin branch off a young tree. (Wouldn't you?) But Grandpa Tesh would have none of it.

"That's not big enough. Go get another one."

The next time I brought back a bigger branch, and for about two minutes, he beat me with it as he explained, between swats, that I had upset the henhouse and hysterical chickens don't lay eggs for weeks.

"When you do stupid stuff like that," he said, "you cost me money."

I got the message. I had learned my lesson.

. . .

Growing up on that farm, my father had learned about discipline. Sun comes up, you go to work. Sun goes down, you have a hard day's work to be proud of. Most every day that the sun set beyond the horizon in the west, it closed the curtains on a day of purpose. My dad was strict. Farmer strict. Southern strict. Baptist strict. And military strict.

Dad had been a navy man, serving in the Pacific Theater during World War II, and he was convinced that he could toughen me up using the only experience he had in that area: naval basic training. If you've ever seen Robert Duvall as Bull Meechum in Pat Conroy's *The Great Santini*, then you get the idea.

Principal Dacus to Ben Meechum: All your dad is doing is loving you by trying to live his life over again through you. He makes bad mistakes but he makes them because he is part of an organization that does not tolerate substandard performance. He just sometimes forgets that there is a difference between a Marine and a son. Did he give you that shiner?[1]

After the war, my father had taken a job in the mailroom of the Hanes corporation in Winston-Salem, North Carolina. He soon climbed the ladder until he was promoted to vice president and moved my mom and two sisters to Garden City, Long Island. He was working in the Empire State Building when I was born on July 9, 1952.

A typical weekday had Dad arriving at the Garden City train station from work in Manhattan on the 6:20 p.m. train. Mom would pull up at the station in the family T-Bird holding two fingers of Johnnie Walker in a perfectly chilled lowball glass. She would hand Dad the glass as he took the driver's seat, and he would sip from it in his left hand as he drove home using his right.

While my dad worked tirelessly at Hanes, and at administering his brand of basic training to his only son, my mom's role defaulted to managing other people's perceptions of our family. Fearing discovery of Dad's out-of-control drinking and late-night wars with my sisters, Bonnie and Mary Ellen, Mom worked to create a fiction that our family was not at all unlike Wally and Beaver's Cleaver clan. She and Dad were professional socializers. Dad was often decked out in a yellow or pastel red sport coat with a white belt, and he always wore an entertainer's personality. People loved him for it.

Our family attended Westbury Methodist Church on Long Island twice a week, every week, no excuses. I dutifully memorized scripture, learned all the kids' Bible stories, and attended church camp every summer. My dad was one of the church's leaders, if not the strongest leader beneath the pastor. Yet I remember at least once a month that same pastor would answer Mom's desperate call and arrive at our house to try "Christian counseling" when Dad drank too much whiskey and initiated loud, contemptuous arguments with my sisters that sometimes put them on the receiving end of his physical abuse.

We forget: In life, it doesn't matter what happens to you or where you came from. It matters what you do with what happens and what you've been given.

—**Ryan Holiday,** *The Obstacle Is the Way*[2]

My mother had been a surgical nurse before she'd met my dad, and she brought her natural tendencies to nurture and encourage to our home. But she also was a taskmaster about my studies and music, which partnered well with my music teacher at Stewart Avenue Elementary School, Dr. Tom Wagner. He had been named New York State Teacher of the Year, and under his leadership, Stewart's programs were recognized nationally as they were easily on par with what you would find in a conservatory, Ivy League preparatory school, or a performing arts academy.

Dr. Wagner directed two choirs, an orchestra, a marching band, a dance band, and a jazz ensemble, as well as a theater program. He worked his own unique, meticulous process each day, without fail, to help his students improve. Parents never heard him say, "If your child doesn't 'feel' like studying music, that's just fine." In Dr. Wagner's world, music was serious business, and every student took one of his classes. If we didn't select the choir, then our other choices were band or orchestra. His procedure for placement was equally inflexible: we listed our top three preferred instruments and then took what we got.

Hoping for an instrument that Chuck Berry might have in his band, my list was drums, drums, and guitar. I ended up with a trumpet. I was presented a beautiful 1959 Conn Director B-flat trumpet, a 10C mouthpiece, valve oil, and a leather case along with a document to sign, declaring that I would care for, and travel on the bus with, my instrument or I would face detention. I was a skinny seven-year-old, so my instrument and case were just shy of one-third my body weight. This was a recipe for bullying and back problems, but none of that mattered once I actually started to play.

There was something indescribable about that first day, sitting in a room with my classmates, *almost* making music. Dr. Wagner moved through our ranks like a whirling dervish as he demonstrated fingerings, explained dotted eighth notes, and showed us proper embouchure.

Three months later, my fellow bandmates and I found ourselves somehow wondrously transported to the school auditorium where we performed songs from Aaron Copland's *Our Town* in front of our parents and grandparents for the first time. Their stunned expressions told us we weren't half-bad. It must have seemed like magic to those in attendance.

What is clear to me now, though, is that Dr. Wagner's magic was not magic at all. His process was consistent and dependable; he never departed from his mission and purpose. Our ensemble would snap to attention with the baton *tap-tap-tapping* on his giant, wooden music stand. Then he would announce "posture," followed by "hand position," and then "articulation!" We'd learn a phrase. Then a full measure. He'd yell, "Tempo" and "Try vibrato!" Often, without warning, he would flash his signature grin and give us an extra dose of loving guidance and encouragement.

He fostered a safe environment that cheered on risk. He'd shout, "*Risk!* Take a chance, ladies and gentlemen," and "C'mon, let's make some mistakes!" Even when we made an absolute mess of a beautiful piece of orchestral music, he wouldn't leave us as long as we were following his process, persisted in our attempts to create the music, and took his direction.

No one laughed at blown notes or flat solos because Dr. Wagner fostered a camaraderie among us that no one beyond the walls of our rehearsal space could understand. He lifted all of us up as a musical family, all of us connected by vibrato and crescendos. We were learning a foreign language, and he was our translator. Back then, and without the opportunity of clairvoyance, I had no way of knowing that Dr. Wagner was coaching us through more than music. He had created for us a communal experience buoyed by our teamwork. It was the quintessential mix of groupthink and individuality. Even more than that, it was a proving ground for what was possible when you focused the efforts of curious, excitable, impulsive little kids.

Often, after one of my shows, a mom, dad, or grandparent will ask me, "Mr. Tesh, when should I start my child on piano?" My answer is always the same: "As soon as they can find their nose with their index finger." But then I qualify my answer, channeling Dr. Wagner as I speak: "Solo instruments are wonderful, but there is nothing like the life experience your child or grandchild will receive playing in a band or orchestra. Find a place for them to plug in . . . and please, please don't ever let them quit. Because it's never about just the music when you are playing in a group." I emphasize that it's about the work. More specifically, it's about respecting the process and staying disciplined as you relentlessly work that process.

Dr. Wagner provided me with my first true exposure to deep work and focused, intense practice, and I take it with me today. He showed me what was possible with persistent effort toward a specific goal, whether that was perfecting a piece of music or mastering an instrument. If my directionless impulsivity had cost my grandpa chickens who wouldn't lay eggs, consistent, directed effort was clearly—according to Dr. Wagner—the goose who laid the golden eggs.

And although Dr. Wagner did not have the benefit of the proliferation of today's books devoted to strategies for "hacking" ourselves into mastery and greatness—*The 5 Second Rule, The Obstacle Is the Way, The Power of Your Subconscious Mind, The War of Art, Deep Work*, and thousands more—I take some solace in knowing that he had beaten them all to market. It just so happens that his market was an elementary school music room through which multiple generations of children passed, and his bestseller was an almost Paleo-esque process that was extraordinarily unsophisticated in design: "Practice, practice, *risk*! Make some mistakes, people! We are working the process!"

Chapter 2

Deadly Paradigm

June 2015

The word *paradigm* comes from the Greek *paradeigma*. It was originally a scientific term, but today is more commonly used to mean a perception, an assumption, or a frame of reference. I was first introduced to this term as nothing more than one of those annoying SAT words with a silent *G*. Then I came across one of my now favorite books, *The 7 Habits of Highly Effective People* by Stephen Covey. Reading it for the first time years ago, I was taken with Covey's description of how our paradigm, at an individual, human level, is really the way we "see" the world—not with our eyes and ears, or our taste and touch. It is through a particular framework built in our minds that we perceive and understand things, and it is through that framework—that paradigm—that we come to possess the beliefs that guide our lives. It is through the changing of that paradigm that we grow and evolve.

Covey described it this way:

> Many people experience a fundamental shift in thinking when they face a life-threatening crisis and suddenly see their priorities in a different light, or when they suddenly step into a new role, such as that of husband or wife, parent or grandparent, manager or leader.[1]

If you had met me prior to 2015, you would have encountered a stable, disciplined, and focused sixty-three-year-old man. My syndicated radio programs with my wife, Connie, and son, Gib, were thriving on three-hundred-plus stations. We owned and directed the expansion of our *Intelligence for Your Life* media brand. I was performing an average of twenty-five live concerts a year. Our adult children were thriving and we had just welcomed our second grandchild. We were enjoying creative and financial freedom. We were physically and emotionally content.

In January 2015, Connie's eighty-six-year-old mother, Ann, broke her hip in a fall in Palm Springs while visiting her son. Following the surgery to repair the fracture, she suffered a stroke. This eventually led to a full-body infection, emergency gallbladder surgery, and a dire prognosis. Several doctors predicted that she would never come off the ventilator when she came out of the operating room. They were convinced this would be the end of her.

It did not turn out that way. Three months later she walked out of that hospital on her own two feet. The doctors were stunned. But not me, because I had the privilege to bear witness, as Connie's wingman over the course of the entire ordeal, to the paradigm shift she underwent as Connie fought with everything she had to save her mom and to prove the doctors wrong. I saw what could happen when the way you looked at the world suddenly changed, through no fault of your own.

Con and I slept at the hospital for weeks on end. Her mother's three-month convalescence tested the limits of Connie's patience, the foundations of our faith, and the resilience of my spine after consecutive nights in hospital lounge chairs. But with my wife's perseverance, inspired by her role as advocate and caregiver, Ann, our spartan matriarch, was back in her senior living facility in Los Angeles, enjoying her recovery, before even the most optimistic among her doctors could have ever imagined. It was a true miracle and an inspiration to many of the professionals on the hospital staff.

Before long, Connie and I were right back in lockstep with the normal cadence of our daily lives. It was our first time back home in Los Angeles in months and we were anxious to catch up with our deferred business obligations, client meetings, and routine health-care appointments. One of those appointments was my yearly physical, which I'd been putting off because of Ann's out-of-town accident and, frankly, because I was being lazy. Now my checkup was six months overdue, and that was far too long for Connie's liking especially.

I set an appointment with our family physician, Dr. Steven Galen. I was in no *real* hurry, since this was just the standard affair—blood test, chest X-ray, and, no one's favorite, the prostate exam—so I set it for as soon as was convenient to my schedule. And thank goodness I did.

"Hey, wait a minute," said Dr. Galen as he concluded the prostate exam.

"What?"

"I don't know. It could be nothing. But your prostate just feels different."

"Different how?" I asked.

"Get dressed. Let me look at your last PSA results."

What Dr. Galen found in my history of blood work was that my PSA (prostate-specific antigen) was an average of 0.4 over the last five years and the one from that day was a 0.5, which, depending on the doctor, might have been considered only slightly elevated. But in general, those results revealed that I had a healthy prostate gland and what he had felt with the digital (gloved hand) exam was nothing to be worried about.

What transpired in the next month revealed that there was actually plenty to worry about. Dr. Galen sent me to a urologist. The trip to the urologist became a trip to the ultrasound technician, then a trip to the surgeon for a biopsy, and that trip eventually would lead to the Johns Hopkins cancer ward in Baltimore, where I had surgery.

My diagnosis was dire. I could see fear on the face of each member of my family. I was terrified. And in my terror, I became a different person, transported into a new paradigm. How do you explain a feeling like this? To your spouse, to your children and grandchildren, to anyone, really? Here's how I'll explain it to you:

While playing lacrosse at North Carolina State University in the early 1970s, I encountered a savage practice drill called *man/ball*. You stand with your lacrosse stick, facing two defensemen who are ten yards away from you. They are, ostensibly, on the opposing team. Then the coach tosses a lacrosse ball over your head. When it lands on the field between you and the defensemen, it's up to you to sprint to the ball and scoop it up and pass it up the field. The two defensive players are trying to work together to beat you to the ball. One of them is trained to yell "Ball!" The other yells "Man!" The player who yells "Man!" is supposed to take you out with a full-body check. His partner can then, without challenge, scoop up the ball because you, down on the ground, have been taken out of the play. However, sometimes in the heat of battle, both of the defensemen will mistakenly yell "Man!" Since you are required to focus only on scooping the ball up into your lacrosse stick (like a receiver in football focusing on the ball in the air), you cannot protect yourself from the impending onslaught.

On the day this happened to me during practice, I don't recall anything after hearing "Man!" and "Man!" I was told later that I was carried off the field by the team doctor. I spent the night in the infirmary, suffering from a concussion that left me feeling disoriented and dazed. Those were the same sensations I was experiencing now. I had stepped out of my comfortable paradigm (husband, father, grandfather, musician, radio host) and into the new, unwelcome dark world of cancer. I was looking at it through new eyes as well. The eyes of a cancer patient.

Connie's view of the world had changed as she faced her mother's health scare. She'd managed it with the same kind of strength and grace and equanimity that made me fall in love with her all those years ago. Now I only hoped I could handle my own paradigm shift half as well.

Chapter 3

True Grit

In junior high school I was never one of the kids who stayed outside playing stickball until the streetlights came on. Instead, I spent at least half of every day either taking music instruction or practicing an instrument. I practiced classical piano and trumpet for ten to twelve hours each week; I was a member of the orchestra, band, jazz band, and marching band. I also sang in the church choir on Sundays. The closest I ever really got to coolness was when I joined a rock band with my buddy David Koenig. The guys and I rehearsed loudly every weekend in my garage, and we played at most of the junior high and church dances.

Though Dr. Wagner had put the joy of musicianship in me early on—no one plays *that* much music if they don't like it—my mom put the fear of God in me if I ever failed to meet her daily piano and trumpet practice quota. This had a very limiting effect on my ability to get comfortable in my rangy body and to prepare for the rigors of high school social status displays, where athletic achievement trumped all.

I entered Garden City High School as a six-foot-six ninth grader, 150 pounds dripping wet. I resembled Ichabod Crane. Or a sandhill crane. Or a whooping crane. Take your pick of cranes. I fit in naturally with no one—not the greasers, the stoners, or the jocks. I also reeked of Clearasil. And with eight ounces of barbed wire and cement in my mouth (1960s orthodontia), I wasn't number one on any girl's Sadie Hawkins dance list. Even if, in theory, I got as far as "the kiss good night," I risked sending the girl to the ER with a life-threatening mouth wound. To my mother's delight, this dearth of girlfriend opportunities in junior high meant I had plenty of extra time for practice. Whether it was because she saw the future for me as a performer and a composer, or she realized that I was the only thing in her life over which she had any control, she had decided it would be her mission in life to turn her son into Van Cliburn, or at the very least, Doc Severinsen. Mom seemed to proceed instinctively, which I suspect came from her early experience as a young tennis prodigy and her focused study habits leading to her nursing degree. She'd place her Minute Minder egg timer on our upright piano and set it for two relentlessly long hours of *tick-tick-ticking*. And there I sat: me, the spinet piano, the *Hanon Handbook: 60 Exercises for the Virtuoso Pianist* (volume 1071), and that timer. The rule? I could go outside and play when the egg timer buzzed. No exceptions. *Tick-tick-tick-tick-tick.*

In 1960s Long Island, the true currency of coolness was the letter jacket. In *Godfather* parlance, if you had one of these jackets, you were a made man. I'm not even sure if the letter jacket is still a thing today, but in the late 1960s it was *everything*, and you could get one only if you had accumulated enough playing time in a varsity sport. With each additional sport, and with every additional year playing that sport, you got a new letter.

The Garden City High jacket was maroon and gray, our school colors. The body was wool. The sleeves were leather. You wore your varsity jacket at school, on the bus ride to and from school, to school dances, to the Saturday football games. Anyplace where signaling your coolness, where spending some of that currency, could produce real value. If you were serious about a girl and asked her to go steady, she typically got an ID bracelet with your name on it, but if your preference was a display of maximum devotion, she got your letter jacket. When the student body saw a girl wearing one of these varsity jackets, four sizes too big for her, with JOHNNY stenciled on the front, it was supposed to be Kryptonite for other boys. It was not at all cool for a guy to be caught talking to your girl by her locker if she was wearing your letter jacket. If this dynamic doesn't feel familiar to you, I'm sure you've seen one of the bird-of-paradise mating rituals on *Planet Earth*.

The male birds strut and preen for the attention of the most attractive female. It was like that.

If I was going to get one of these letter jackets, I was going to have to work my tail off to make the varsity team in whatever sport could use a persistent beanpole with a bottomless reservoir of energy and a very high tolerance for practice. At Garden City High, that meant soccer and track and field. I embraced the long stretches of monotonous, joint-aching, bone-grinding practice. Training for me never ended when we walked off the high school soccer field or I finished my last high jump at track practice. I was just not good enough for that. In the fall, during soccer season, the moment the afternoon bus dropped me off at home after our two-hour team practice, I set about kicking a soccer ball against our white wooden garage door. When the ball caromed off the garage, with unpredictable velocity and random trajectory, I defended against the ball as if I were on the field of play. *Boom, boom, boom.* The sound of the ball hitting the garage door echoed like a shotgun down Seabury Road. When my mom pulled out of our driveway to fetch Dad at the Garden City train station, she would show me a raised eyebrow and then I knew I had twenty more minutes before I had to shut it all down. This kind of noise, and the potential for defacing Dad's garage door paint job, would have thrown him into a cocktail-infused-post-railroad-commuter rage.

So there I was, with even more tempo now—in old-school workout mode. A ball and the garage. I was like Rocky Balboa, punching out that slab of beef in the walk-in freezer. I'd lean over my right foot and kick the ball using my instep for more accuracy. I was on offense. The ball slammed into the upper right quadrant of the garage, high and outside enough so my imaginary goalie couldn't get a hand on it. In an instant I'm a defender, as the ball, spinning with "English," exploded off the garage door headed for my left foot. *Boom*, back at the garage. It only took a couple of minutes of this to generate a soaking sweat and burning lungs. This I did for an hour each day after my mandatory music practice. It paid off. The time spent defending myself against the garage eventually landed me a spot as a fullback (defender) on the varsity soccer team, which earned me a letter jacket.

In the spring, during track-and-field season, my extra practice routine was similar but the motivation was a little more self-directed, because the field events were the antithesis of a team sport like soccer. No one was yelling "Jump, Johnny! Jump!" during my high-jump competitions. High-jumping is a lonely pursuit, requiring a whole lot of self-motivation. Most of the time you look like a crazy person, walking in circles, talking to yourself, rehearsing the bottom movements before a jump. Indeed, the field events were as much a mind game as anything else. There was very little team camaraderie. No huddles. No cheerleaders. It was mostly you against the measuring tape and a white chalk line on the ground: run toward the bar, take off on one leg without touching the chalk foul line in the process, lift your torso into the air, and clear the metal bar, trying not to rupture yourself on the bar on the way down.

Yes, rupture was a real danger. High-jumping included the potential for what we jumpers called "a full groining." You make it halfway over the bar and, without enough forward motion, your body stalls in midair. Gravity does the rest as it joins your groin with the bar and ultimately the ground. Not the way you want to spend an afternoon, a full groining.

My practice routine for the high jump took place in our backyard. I couldn't hide this from Dad like I could my soccer drills. This one needed his approval since it required that I dig a trench for the jumping pit. He surprised me by not only approving the idea but by also sketching the build-out. We filled the trench with sand and used a long piece of bamboo for the bar. The bar stretched across two wooden stanchions that Dad built using eighth-inch dowels to adjust the height of the bar. The sand came from several pail-and-shovel journeys I made to nearby Jones Beach. Contraband sand. My left wrist was in perpetual sprain from the hundreds of hard-sand landings. The high-jump pit at the high school was made of rubber shavings, which made for a softer landing.

This relentless practice with bamboo and sand during the spring semester and the garage door in the fall ultimately paid big dividends for me. I was now winning medals in track-and-field meets. I even got my name in the school newspaper after breaking a Nassau County high-jump record. I was playing at least half of every soccer game—Mom in the stands during each and every one of them with cut-up oranges and Lik-M-Aid candy for the whole team. (The team presented her with a trophy at the end of our senior season.) And by the time I graduated, I'd earned three varsity soccer and four varsity track letters.

Just to be clear, those letters in no way equaled even one-third of a varsity *football* letter. I mean, seriously? But for a beanpole like me, it was today's equivalent of an awesome online-dating profile photo. Even more than simply being a status symbol or a token of devotion, though, my letter jacket was recognition of accomplishment. To receive a varsity jacket and to earn the letters that would adorn it was to wear the proof of having set goals and achieved them, and I had created a process for achieving those goals that worked for me. Thankfully my new sports-infused identity established my social standing in high school, but more importantly, I learned the value of hustle and grit and focused practice.

There is a YouTube video with Grammy Award–winning musician and Oscar-nominated actor Will Smith that has inspired thousands of us grit-devotees. I always imagined Smith as an effortless performer, born with exceptional talent. Well, not according to him:

"I've never really viewed myself as particularly talented. Where I excel is ridiculous, sickening work ethic," Will said. "The only thing that I see that is distinctly different about me is: I'm not afraid to die on a treadmill. I will not be outworked, period. You might have more talent than me, you might be smarter than me, you might be sexier than me. You might be all of those things. You got it on me in nine categories. But if we get on the treadmill together, there's two things: You're getting off first, or I'm going to die. It's really that simple."[1]

Will Smith is talking about grit.

Author and researcher Angela Duckworth, a professor of psychology at the University of Pennsylvania, has studied grit extensively. She wrote:

Grit is passion and perseverance for very long-term goals. Grit is having stamina. Grit is sticking with your future, day in, day out, not just for the week, not just for the month, but for years. And working really hard to make that future a reality.[2]

When you ask the greatest artists and business leaders about their path to success, there is a sameness to their answers. Consistent, deliberate, mind-numbing work. Deep work.

Former Lakers player and head coach Byron Scott said he once found eighteen-year-old Kobe Bryant shooting in a dark gym two hours before practice:

> I heard the ball bouncing. No lights were on. Practice was at about eleven, it was probably about nine, nine-thirty. And I go out to the court and I look, and there's Kobe Bryant. He's out there shooting in the dark. And I stood there for probably about ten seconds, and I said, "This kid is gonna be great."[3]

The elite performance coach Tim Grover, who has worked with Michael Jordan, Dwyane Wade, and Kobe Bryant as well, put an even blunter point on this message:

> People are always asking me about the secrets and tricks I use to get results. Sorry if this disappoints you: There are no secrets. There are no tricks. Ask yourself where you are now, and where you want to be instead. Ask yourself what you're willing to do to get there. Then make a plan to get there. There are no shortcuts. I don't want to hear about workouts you can do in five minutes a day, or twenty minutes a week; that's total BS. Champions get into the Zone, shut out everything else, and control the uncontrollable.[4]

I know this to be true. I knew this even back in high school. And yet there have been so many times in my life when I've tried other, more modern, trendy formulas for success. Shortcuts. Because, guess what, hard work is *hard*. Even today on our *Intelligence for Your Life* radio show we share thirty to forty "success hacks" each month. It's a booming business. The demand is definitely out there, in part because a lot of them work . . . for a while.

Search Amazon for *success*. You'll get seventy-two thousand recommendations, but none of them, to Tim Grover's point, are going to get you where you want to go, because accomplishment, said Will Smith, is very much about going the distance. When I read that as an adult, I can see that Smith was speaking directly to my teenage heart. Other athletes had better skills than I had in high school, but few could, or even wanted to, match my grit and mind-numbing tenacity. It was a formula that actually worked for me, and one that I would have to reengage with many years later if I was going achieve what felt like the most unachievable goal I'd ever set for myself: beating this cancer.

Chapter 4

"Get Your Affairs in Order"

June 2015

Attempting to control the uncontrollable was my goal and surely my only choice in late May 2015. I was sixty-three years old, staring at a "serious, stage 3-plus" cancer diagnosis.

Truth be told, if Steve Galen had not been my family physician, this story would have ended much differently for me. Dr. Galen, unlike many other physicians, never would accept as gospel the routine PSA blood test that is part of the annual physical for men. He always insisted on the digital rectal exam. What Dr. Galen perceived as "different" in my exam lead me to (in this order) a urologist, a sonogram exam, and ultimately, a targeted biopsy.

There's really no way to blunt the cortisol-laced stress response when being notified that a biopsy is on your schedule. It's even worse when it's a prostate biopsy, because you're talking about a plastic gun that fires sharp needles into your prostate gland through your anus to retrieve tissue samples. For some reason that I still don't understand, this procedure does not include anesthesia. As it turned out, though, the physical pain I experienced would be nothing compared to the emotional wreckage Connie and I would endure in the days after. Following the prostate biopsy, the urologist who performed it—we'll call him Dr. Smith— informed us that it would take a few days to get the results. In the meantime, he mentioned that he was headed for a vacation out of the country and would let us know the results by email when he received them. A few days went by. The silence was deafening. We called the hospital. They would not give us results without the doctor's approval. Dr. Smith had left no covering physician who could follow up in Dr. Smith's absence. This did not sit well with Ms. Sellecca-Tesh. She quickly sprang into action, and we email-bombed Dr. Smith on his vacation to demand the results.

Here is the email chain that ensued.

> Good Morning, Dr. [Smith],
> We were hoping to get your report on my biopsy asap. Don't worry about what time you respond. Sorry to bother you on vacation.
> Thank you,
> John Tesh

> Tumor is present, please get bone scan & staging CT, schedule counseling session asap afterward.
> Dr. Smith

> So. To be clear. Are you seeing evidence of cancer? And what is a staging CT?
> John Tesh

> Yes. Cancer. Susan will explain & arrange. It's Gleason 9 tumors.
> Dr. Smith

Dr. Smith would not be back for another week. In that time I scheduled the staging CT scan and googled "Gleason 9 tumor." The Gleason score is the rating system doctors use to judge the aggressiveness of prostate cancer. It goes up to 10. Mine was a 9, which, I learned, meant the cancer tumor was aggressive and would likely travel outside the prostate gland to other organs. Metastasize.

When the doctor finally returned from vacation, we sat down face-to-face with him. He had the test results in front of him.

"Did I do your biopsy, Mr. Tesh?" asked Dr. Smith.

Connie and I shared the same frightened look.

"Yes, you did!" answered Connie, though her exact words were a little saltier than that.

"All right then. Let's go over these results."

There were three Gleason 9 tumors and two Gleason 6s. Five cancerous tumors in all. The two Gleason 9s were so large that they were protruding outside the prostate gland, also known as extraprostatic extension. There was a good chance, said Dr. Smith, that a cancer like this would travel into my pelvis and my lymph nodes.

Then Dr. Smith said, "This is very serious. Very serious, indeed. In my opinion it could be inoperable. But if you want to talk to a surgeon, I will give you a number. It might be time to get your affairs in order. My guess is eighteen months."

The words hung in the air for a moment.

Then, ostensibly to break our stunned silence, Dr. Smith patted Connie on the back and added, "My suggestion is that you go and make lemonade out of lemons."

Huh? I'm thinking. *Lemonade?*

I'm pretty sure "lemonade out of lemons" is not in the physician's handbook of bedside manners. This inappropriate counseling surely had a profound effect on my wife and me. We quickly found the exit to the hospital, vowing to never return. Next? We took a moment to shed some serious tears and pray some intense prayers. We then got busy devouring books and papers on prostate cancer, known as adenocarcinoma.

One of the best resources I found was the 2007 book *Surviving Prostate Cancer* by Dr. Patrick Walsh from Johns Hopkins. It was written in textbook detail, which I loved. The only problem was that there was very little mention of a Gleason 9 diagnosis. The reason? At the time of the book's writing, there was no recommended surgical intervention for tumors as aggressive as mine. Terrific. I had hit the cancer jackpot. (The book has since been revised with updates.)

I knew I had to call Dr. Walsh. Cold-calling someone of his stature bordered on inappropriate. Nonetheless I googled his office number. Forty-five years of cold-calling police detectives, politicians, and CEOs as a journalist made it impossible for me to just sit around and wait.

"Brady Urological, Dr. Walsh's line."

"Hi, my name is John Tesh. I'm calling from Los Angeles, and I would like to speak with Dr. Walsh. Is he available?"

"Is Dr. Walsh expecting your call, Mr. Tesh?"

"Uh, no. But I just finished reading his book. I'm a journalist and I thought I might ask him some questions about his work on prostate cancer."

"Oh, well, you may be in luck, Mr. Tesh. Dr. Walsh only takes calls on Thursdays. And, well, today is Thursday! Let me see if I can get him on the line."

This woman was an angel.

"Hello, this is Dr. Walsh. My assistant says you're a journalist? She can schedule an interview, if that's what you're after. My schedule is full for the next month, but I'll get her back on the line and you two can work on a date and time. How does that sound?"

"Uh, Dr. Walsh, yes, sir. I'm a journalist and would love to interview you about your work but, uh, it turns out, you see . . . I'm a journalist with prostate cancer. I think you may be the only one who can help me. I've read your book twice, and I know you're the most skilled surgeon in the country."

Dr. Walsh could most certainly hear the anxiety in my voice. He suggested I email him my test results and said he would take a look. Minutes after I pressed Send, my phone rang.

"Listen, John, yours is a very serious case of cancer," Dr. Walsh began. "You have five low-PSA-producing cancer tumors and what looks like an extraprostatic extension. If you don't have surgery soon, this could spread quickly to your bones. That's what prostate cancer does."

"Dr. Walsh, I've read that you've done hundreds of the new robotic prostatectomies. Can you operate on me?"

"I'm sorry. I'm not operating anymore," Walsh said quickly. "I no longer perform this surgery."

I swallowed hard.

"John, there is one man who I believe can save your life. He treats aggressive cancer aggressively. His name is Dr. Ted Schaeffer. He's a PhD-MD who is an expert with robotic-assisted surgery using the da Vinci surgical system. I trained him myself. With your permission, I'll forward your test results. May I give him your number?"

I agreed, and five minutes later, Dr. Schaeffer was on the phone. He was calling from his car. Connie and I were glued to his voice on the speakerphone. What Dr. Schaeffer told us on that call was a true gift in a time of very deep need.

"Don't worry, John, I can save your life. This is what I do. You'll be fine. But we have to act quickly." And then he repeated Dr. Walsh's words, almost verbatim: "I treat aggressive prostate cancer aggressively."

In a matter of a few weeks, I had seen four doctors. With each visit, each phone call, the seriousness of my predicament came into sharper focus. Now it was clear that I would have to have my prostate removed through this robotic-assisted radical laparoscopic prostatectomy. Connie and I were in agreement that we would place our faith in Dr. Schaeffer's expertise and experience, so we booked our flights to Baltimore and set a course for the Sidney Kimmel Comprehensive Cancer Center at Johns Hopkins.

Chapter 5

Buried Alive

With a diagnosis like mine, depression was going to come. It's what I'd been told. It's what I'd read in countless books. There is a sense of despair that comes with words like "inoperable" and "getting your affairs in order," because they don't give you any room to maneuver. There's no ground for debate, at least not if you only focus on the prognosis instead of the diagnosis. I couldn't do that. Even if I wanted to, Connie wouldn't let me. I just had to remember the tools I learned the first time I faced down depression and then marshal them as I confronted my new paradigm.

I first encountered the specter of depression during my freshman year at North Carolina State University. Actually, that's not true. It's more accurate to say that I *arrived* for my freshman year at State with depression smuggled away in one of my suitcases, because I had been conscripted into the NC State Wolfpack by my father regardless of my own desires, and that was just how it was going to be.

My dad had been raised on Grandpa Tesh's farm. All he knew was working with his hands. Accordingly, there was never any thought of (or money to pay for) my father attending college after high school. He worked the farm with his dad like the other boys in town. By seven, the same age I'd begun to explore my mischievous performative instincts, he had learned to drive a tractor. He could kill and clean a hog by the time he was ten. In January 1942, barely a month after the Japanese bombed Pearl Harbor, he had enlisted in the US Navy and worked his way through the ranks to become a chief petty officer on the USS *Panamint*, an amphibious assault craft that served as a flagship in the Northern Attack Force during the Battle of Okinawa.

I have my dad's diary from the war. Even his description of the rigors of naval boot camp in Norfolk, Virginia, before his deployment to the Pacific Theater, are daunting.

> Today was a ten hour day of marching, calisthenics, scrubbing our clothes, rifles-over-our-heads drills and pulling oars of the boats. I believe my back might certainly be broken from loading the heavy shells into the 5 inch guns. I have not slept in 4 days.

And that speaks nothing of the acute stress of his assignment once aboard the *Panamint*. From the top of the ship, he stood lookout and called in antiaircraft fire to shoot down incoming Japanese Zeroes and kamikaze pilots whose aim was to wipe out the US fleet off the coast of Okinawa. A good day's work in his role could mean the difference between life and death—victory and defeat—for thousands of men. One wrong calculation or command and the fleet could lose a ship, possibly even the war. His job was so important that the Japanese fighters trained their .50-caliber machine guns on his perch atop the ship. He performed that duty every day for a year and a half, until the Japanese surrendered.

When I told this story as a kid during show-and-tell, the Japanese surrendered *because* of my dad. When I tell it now, it becomes that much easier for me to understand how, as a rising high school senior, my declared intention of pursuing a college education filled with courses designed to create a career in the entertainment world would have been met by my dad with alarm and even anger. By that point he'd graduated from naval war hero to vice president of sales for the underwear division at Hanes. Another respectable endeavor that could actually be quantified—now measured in hard dollars earned instead of planes shot down—unlike his only son whose plans, as best he could figure, would culminate in plate-spinning on the *Ed Sullivan Show*, or, worse, the circus. How embarrassing for him. A potential embarrassment whose wings he clipped before it ever had a chance to take flight, before I'd even entered my senior year of high school.

Young and naïve, I set out one warm Sunday evening in April 1969 to inform my father about my upcoming road trip with my high school buddies. Both my sisters had made a similar pilgrimage as high school juniors. Bonnie decided on Mars Hill Christian College. Mary Ellen, with incredible fine-art talents, selected Emerson College. And so it was time to share my vision for auditioning potential universities. I told Dad about my plans to do two weeks of college visits, mostly music conservatories and theater schools, including Berklee College of Music, Interlochen Center for the Arts, Manhattan School of Music, and more. I wasn't expecting my dad's response. It was swift and direct. He would not use his "hard-earned" money to support this nonsense and "no son of mine," as he put it, would go to college for four years to become a "trained monkey." (To this day, whenever I see a good monkey act, it makes me regret not learning how to train one myself. It would have driven my dad nuts.) Then he methodically listed all the reasons why a career in the entertainment business was not a career but a hobby.

It was then that I learned something that felt much worse than having my dreams cut off at the knees: My dad had replaced my plans for my future with his own plans. And his plans had little to do with me specifically; they were plans for the entire family, of which this major transformational moment of mine toward adulthood was merely a minor piece.

Over our pork chops and applesauce, Dad explained to my mom and me that he'd finally had enough of the rush-hour madness and working in New York City, so he and Mom were moving back to North Carolina. Since I was the last of the three children to graduate from Garden City High School, he continued, the high cost of property taxes in Garden City was no longer necessary. The plan was to move back to Winston-Salem, closer to Grandma and Grandpa Tesh, where Dad would take a lesser role at Hanes. He would leave Garden City for North Carolina when I started my senior year in the fall. Then, he would sell our home.

Mom and I would downsize into an apartment on Seventh Street in downtown Garden City, close to school, so I could finish my last year of high school.

"Wait, what?" I said. "You're selling the house? How big is this apartment? Can I have friends over?"

No response. I hadn't even begun to think about the implications for college. That was the next arrow he pulled out of his quiver.

Because of his early move back to North Carolina, he said, he would be able to establish one full year of residency that would then qualify me for in-state tuition at North Carolina State University in Raleigh. He would be able to save thousands on my education. Tuition would be $400 a semester versus $5,000. We would apply now for early admission into the textile chemistry program. Then, when I graduated, Dad would be able to secure me a job in the lab in the Hanes manufacturing plant. The day after high school graduation, Mom and I would drive the family car from New York to Winston-Salem. The rest of our belongings would follow in a moving van. He would make sure I had a summer job waiting for me in the Hanes mill.

I was now feeling faint. So many questions. Confusion. Panic. Dread. I looked down at my pork chop, now stone-cold on my dinner plate. I looked to Mom for assistance. She was looking at her pork chop. I was certain this was not her idea. *Surely,* I thought, *she'll step in, weigh in with her opinion, ask a few questions, something. This has to be as devastating for her as it is for me.* Mom had close friends on Long Island and was a leader in our church family. She had put down roots for two decades. *What about her weekly bridge game? What about . . .*

My mind was racing. My face surely resembled what I envisioned was a victim in an Edgar Allen Poe story—prematurely interred, mouth open, soundless, buried alive. Seemingly helpless to do anything to combat a fate that had been decided for me, against my will. I could think of no other response in the aftermath of this news but to rise from the kitchen table and just walk the stairway up to my attic bedroom.

No one followed me. No one called out. There would be no debate. I closed the door to my room quietly, then drifted over to my record player and lowered the turntable arm onto my favorite Jimi Hendrix recording.

I'm not sure whom I felt worse for: me or my mom. Both of us were prisoners of this idyllic suburban fiction. Empathy for my mom was something I felt intuitively from an early age. There were many times, for instance, when I would be sitting with her, doing homework, and I would stop and ask, "Mom, what's wrong?" She would smile and quickly deflect the question. As I got older, though, I realized not only were neither of us not alone in our struggle, but she was not alone as a woman, wife, and mother either.

This struggle was happening to millions of other women just like her after World War II ended and suburbia was born in earnest. Developers such as William Levitt bought up land just outside major American cities and built inexpensive, virtually identical tract houses throughout the 1950s. With a few exceptions, these homes were indistinguishable from one another. And with the GI Bill helping returning soldiers subsidize low-cost mortgages, often making it cheaper to buy in suburbia than rent in the city, young families flocked to these cookie-cutter homes with large family rooms and backyards.

But suburban life in the '50s ended up being a mixed blessing for women. Men who had thrown back a few too many at the office in Philadelphia or Chicago or San Francisco or Manhattan and who took the last train home would wander aimlessly around their neighborhoods in a futile attempt to find their address—each home a clone of the one on either side of it. This often left wives on pins and needles as evening turned to night, waiting, hoping not to have to scoop up their husbands from the neighbors again.

Looking back now, many historians and clinical psychologists believe that the baby boom and the suburban sprawl of the 1950s had a horribly confining effect on many women. In her 1963 book *The Feminine Mystique*, women's rights advocate Betty Friedan argued that the suburbs were "burying women alive." Friedan said,

If a woman had a problem in the 1950s and 1960s, she knew that something must be wrong with her marriage, or with herself. . . .

She was so ashamed to admit her dissatisfaction that she never knew how many other women shared it. If she tried to tell her husband, he didn't understand what she was talking about. She did not really understand it herself.[1]

That was right on the money. My poor mom.

Chapter 6

Walk On

_____

Many college counselors are all too familiar with the astronomical depression rates among freshmen who have been plucked from the safety and familiarity of their station in high school. I was no exception. The fall I entered NC State, I was not only feeling unsafe as a textile chemistry major who was no longer in a rock band and had no obvious opportunity to continue in sports—certainly not a position on their Division I college sports teams—but I also felt strong-armed into a life I wanted no part of. Everything I had cultivated since I was seven years old, everything that had defined me and accrued to whatever social standing I was able to create, was gone. It was a paradigm shift before I knew what such a thing was, and therefore I was, by all accounts, completely miserable.

Then I met Steve Thomas. He was a fellow resident at the Bowen freshman dormitory and was attending State on a full soccer scholarship. After hearing about my background over beers at the Jolly Knave pub, he suggested that I try out for the NC State soccer team. Convinced that this was nothing more than beer-infused madness, I deflected the idea until the next day when Steve insisted that I show up for practice after class and introduce myself to coach Max Rhodes.

"Steve, I want to make sure you know the truth here because this could be embarrassing for you. I was not a starter in high school. I lettered, but I only played half of every game. The players on this college team are some of the best in the nation. I'm not going to be able to 'walk on' to a D-I college team. You were a high school All American!"

He smiled. "C'mon," he said. "This will be great."

If it hadn't been for Steve's encouragement, I never would have even considered such a preposterous scheme. But at the moment, I hated my life as a textile chemistry student and wanted to hang out with my friend. Someone who, for once, wasn't trying to thwart me, but support me.

The next day I showed up on the NC State soccer field in a pair of high-top sneakers and Dolfin shorts, accompanied by Steve, my eager "sponsor." I was a sight to behold.

"Hey, Coach Rhodes, this is John Tesh. He's an awesome defender from Garden City, Long Island. He'd like to practice with the team and give you a chance to have a look at him. We could use some more depth on defense, right?"

I forced a weak nod in agreement, to show some kind of confidence in myself and to support my friend Steve stepping out on this shaky limb.

Coach Rhodes nodded. Then he glanced down at my size-13 high-tops, smiled at Steve, and walked away.

Memories of the grit and tenacity I had learned to embrace in my quest for meaningful playing time on the Garden City varsity squad were still fresh in my mind. I had been a soccer player by choice, and I had busted my behind to earn a spot on the field.

By now, the rest of the soccer team had gotten a glimpse of the three of us talking on the sidelines, so I felt like that new dog at the dog park, though there was no sniffing, just plenty of puzzled looks. It was in this moment that Steve gave me the best advice I'd ever received. It's advice I apply to everything I do today: "Tesh," he said (I don't think anyone knew I had a first name), "the way to be a starter is to out-hustle everyone on the field—every day. Hustle and heart will get you a spot on this team." This was a strategy I fully understood.

Steve Thomas possessed both hustle and technique. He was All-American material and he had become my cheerleader. I had, of course, played varsity soccer at Garden City High School, but this was an entirely different level. The Atlantic Coast Conference (ACC) included teams from the University of North Carolina, Duke, the University of Virginia,

Clemson, and Maryland. These teams had recruited players from literally all over the world. The majority of the NC State team was made up of American players. That meant more of a "rough and tumble" style than the elegant, precision-passing game of the Europeans, which was to my benefit. The NC State playbook was similar to the run-and-gun, fast-break kind of play you would see on a Long Island high school team like mine.

Every day before practice, the State team had a ritual of running a one-and-a-half-mile course to "warm up." Steve, as the team captain, along with another standout, Mark Templeton, led this run followed by a half hour of calisthenics. It was a full hour of conditioning before drills and scrimmaging even began. My skills were plenty rusty. My passing was woefully inconsistent, but I was often first to the ball on defense. I didn't have the skills to play offense, but I was able to disrupt many plays during the scrimmages with my sheer size and aggressive play.

On the first Friday following a week of practice, Coach Rhodes asked me to stay behind after he released the team. He told me he was impressed with my "intensity and drive" and told me to give my sizes to the equipment manager so I could get a practice uniform and some proper soccer cleats. No fanfare; no big announcement. But, holy cow! Did this just happen? It was certainly, to my mind, the biggest accomplishment thus far in my life as a college student. I was a walk-on. I was officially a member of the NC State University varsity soccer team.

For a freshman who was twisting in the wind, struggling in a college major that was fomenting depression, I had found an identity. I found my reason—my *why*—for getting out of bed in the morning. I was part of a high-level tribe, representing a major university. I had a purpose. Nothing beats back the drumbeat of depression better than a purpose.

When I got back to the dorm, Steve Thomas was smiling. He obviously had known before Coach Rhodes spoke to me. I thanked him for the gift he had so selflessly given me. Steve knew, instinctively, that the way to shoehorn me into the team was to have me focus on what I could most likely control. Hustle. Perseverance. He knew that I could improve my skills during the scrimmages, but that I needed to get the coach's attention first. Relentless hustle, true persistence—they speak any good coach's native language. Steve's compassion and encouragement are the reason he and I are still close friends to this day. He gave me a gift I'll never be able to repay.

• • •

For the first half of my inaugural college soccer season, I rode the bench. But I sat on that bench with passion and purpose. I cheered on our team. I got water for the starters. In the practices I often finished in second place to Steve during the daily mile-and-a-half training runs. Then one day after practice, I began a process that would pay huge dividends.

It was late afternoon on a Friday in October. Practice was over. Long after everyone hit the showers, I grabbed one of the old beat-up soccer balls, and I stayed behind. No one really noticed. They were all, rightly, exhausted. It was the last practice of the week. You could hear the sound of kegs being tapped all across campus. The sun began to set, and it was just me and that beat-up ball. It was time for me to reach back and resurrect a process that had served me well a few years earlier outside my garage on Seabury Road.

Completely alone on the NC State soccer field, I sprinted down toward the goal, dribbling the ball a foot and a half from my stride. I cut left; I cut right. I leaned over the ball and fired at the goal. I ran full speed to the opposite goal, 120 yards away. I screamed, "Shot! Score!" Like a crazy person I was now announcing my own moves: "Tesh, breaking left . . . now right. He's beat two defenders. No, three. He shoots. He scores!"

I checked to see if anyone was watching this mad behavior. No one. It was just me and my process, committed to improving my game.

My legs burned. My lungs were on fire. Still, I dribbled left, right. I trapped the ball with my chest, now backpedaling, faking out invisible defenders. I tossed the ball in the air . . . headed it into the goal. I crossed the ball high into the air with a corner kick. The sun had dropped below the horizon and so the lack of visibility forced me into deeper concentration. I could barely see my foot on the ball. I visualized myself defending the goal against Clemson, then UNC and Duke. I could see their jerseys. I could see their school colors and the numbers. I imagined the moves they would make and the defensive countermeasures I would use to strip the ball from them, saving goal after goal. It was real.

This, then, was a deeper, more intense version of the process I had used in high school. There was the committed, relentless grit during the day with the team. And then it was more hard work and visualization at night. Would this be what would set me apart? I had to believe it was. At the very least, it began to equalize me against the enormous pool of talent on our team.

I'm sure there were many more high school soccer stars studying in their dorm rooms at NC State. I also believe that they had as much or even more of a chance than I to walk on to the NC State soccer team. But did they ever think it was possible? Did that little voice in their heads talk them right out of it? Perhaps it was a friend, or their parents. My dad had talked me out of a music career. He couldn't talk me out of this. He had no idea it was even happening (thank God).

Every day before practice, I was having my ankles taped next to David Thompson and Tommy Burleson in the locker room. They were two of the greatest college basketball players in US history, and they were on their way to beat UCLA for the NCAA Basketball Championship a few years later. Legendary football coach Lou Holtz, who took NC State to four straight bowl games, would walk through the training room and say hello to us all. Amazing. Here I was, swimming in this pool of greatness. What's the worst that could happen? I could get cut from a Division I, ACC college sports team. To someone like me, even that sounded like the most awesome résumé booster ever!

And what's the best thing that could happen? I could succeed. I could *win*. I could take back control of a life, of a fate, that I had felt was no longer mine, that I had lost complete control over.

One of my favorite groups as a college freshman was the supergroup Blind Faith. Their song "In the Presence of the Lord" spoke to me about this each night from a piece of vinyl in my dorm room.

In high school I had opened a door with a formula that worked reliably well. Hustle. But it was blind faith and relentless hustle that really busted that door wide open and set me up, by my sophomore year at State, to be playing close to half of all our soccer matches.

I never stopped my late-evening process of chasing that ugly, beat-up soccer ball up and down the field. At the end of my second season, during the closing banquet, Coach Rhodes passed out trophies for Best Defender, Offensive Player of the Year, and High Scoring Player, among others. Finally, he held up one more trophy, explaining that it was an award that had not been given at previous banquets. He announced, "This year's Most Improved Player trophy goes to . . . John Tesh." I was floored. It was an honor to be on this team, but to have my name called in front of my team-mates, in recognition of *anything*—there really were no words.

The team gave me a standing ovation. No one smiled more broadly than my best pal, Steve Thomas. That little soccer trophy would light my path and reinforce my process throughout life. It also paid dividends for Steve, whose hypothesis had now evolved into a theory: like water that will always seek its own level, hustle, too, can cause us to rise up and on to greatness.

Nearly half a century later, in his book *Mastery*, Robert Greene wrote about Leonardo da Vinci's commitment to his projects:

> Leonardo da Vinci adopted as his motto the expression *ostinato rigore*, which translates as "stubborn rigor" or "tenacious application." For every project he involved himself in—and by the end of his life they numbered in the thousands—he repeated this to himself, *ostinato rigore*, so he would attack each one with the same vigor and tenacity. The best way to neutralize our natural impatience is to cultivate a kind of pleasure in pain—like an athlete, you come to enjoy rigorous practice, pushing past your limits, and resisting the easy way out.[1]

Mastery is hard work. It is thousands of hours of practice. There are no shortcuts. You must believe that whatever challenges you face right now, on the other side of pain is greatness. Mastery over your goals, over your circumstances, over a disease you never anticipated and that you cannot control, requires not just hustle and grit and perseverance; it demands purpose and faith. It requires a *why* and a *how*. I'd found both on the soccer field, and I would need to use them again forty-five years later in my fight against cancer.

Chapter 7

Burn the Ships!

I n 1519, the Spanish explorer and conquistador Hernán Cortés decided that he wanted to seize the treasure of the Aztecs. He took five hundred soldiers and one hundred sailors and landed his eleven ships on the shores of the Yucatán Peninsula. Although Cortés had a large army, he was still horribly outnumbered by a huge and powerful empire that had been around for six hundred years.

Many of Cortés's men believed there was little chance of success, and the terrified men tried to seize some ships to escape to Cuba. Cortés got wind of the plot and arrested the ringleaders. At that point he wanted to make sure that the remainder of his men were completely committed to his mission and to his quest for riches, so he did something that seemed nothing short of completely insane: Cortés gave the order to burn his own ships.

His men resisted, wondering how they would ever get home, but Cortés was ready with an answer: If we are going home, we are going home in their ships!

The path forward was clear for Cortés: it was all or nothing, 100 percent commitment. Do or die. And so after scuttling his ships, his thinking was that the option for failure was gone. They would either conquer as heroes, or they would die.

There was a time when I burned *my* ships, but with far less of a plan for victory than the Spanish explorer, and far less in the way of riches in my sights.

In the fall of 1973, I was a rising senior at North Carolina State University. I'd made it through my freshman depression and was now a two-sport walk-on varsity athlete and an elected officer at the Lambda Chi Alpha Fraternity, with thirty-five credit hours standing between me and a mortarboard. For most people in a similar position, with a baccalaureate degree easily within reach, the next nine months would have been smooth sailing. For me, they were anything but, because instead of strolling into Dabney Hall as a senior for my first day of organic chemistry, I was cracking concrete with a construction crew on Hillsborough Road with a sledgehammer, working for C. C. Mangum Company in the shadow of the NC State University Memorial Belltower. My fellow students, my fraternity brothers, my peers, all shared laughter and a full measure of confidence as they streamed into their classes on the first day of the fall semester. I know this because I worked in full view of them, even if I was ostensibly cloaked in invisibility as I labored with my construction crew.

Earlier that morning, and an hour before sunrise, I had crawled out of my sleeping bag, closed the flaps on my Eureka Timberline pup tent, and climbed into the pickup truck that had pulled up to the northwest corner of Raleigh's Umstead Park. With a few obligatory nods, I joined the six other men in the flatbed who sat in a storm cloud of Marlboro cigarette smoke and the putrid aroma of stale chewing tobacco. I rode in the pickup in silence, groggy from another fitful night of sleep in the pup tent, effectively homeless in a public state park.

Among the men who form this "chain gang," I am known (through sniggers) as the College Boy, but today I'm feeling more like Henri Charrière, the main character in a movie that had just come out called *Papillon*. It's about a convicted felon sentenced to live out his days in solitary confinement on Devil's Island in French Guiana with no hope of escape. Only a few years earlier, I had been reading Charrière's riveting novel of the same name in English class as a high school senior. Now, here I am, emotionally shackled to these co-workers who, I am sure, suspect there is some kind of *Papillon*-esque backstory to explain my placement amid their ranks. A twenty-year-old out-of-towner with a thick Long Island accent who turns up in Raleigh, North Carolina, with nary a trace of Red Man chewing tobacco in his cheek or calluses on his palms, isn't supposed to be available for full-time manual labor like this. It doesn't take a genius to conclude that there is something fishy going on. My crew mates may have been unfamiliar with the story of Cortés burning his ships to forge his future, but I'm certain they figure I must have burned a very large bridge of some kind to land here with them. And I had, both unintentionally and intentionally.

Growing up in Garden City public schools I had been introduced to music, and under the tutelage of my incomparable music teacher, Dr. Wagner, a spark had been lit in me that was unquenchable. As Daniel Coyle describes in *The Talent Code*, that "ignition" had shown me my identity, and my "ignition and deep practice work" together produced a "skill in exactly the same way that a gas tank combines with an engine to produce velocity in an automobile."[1]

Coyle's research led him to conclude that ignition is about the set of signals and subconscious forces that lead us to say *that* is who I want to be. My true purpose had been ignited, only to be unceremoniously extinguished by my father's dictate that I attend NC State and major in textile chemistry. That's when my spark died out and when the other, more destructive one was lit, the one that led me to that chain gang.

. . .

When I arrived at NC State as a freshman, I'd felt as though a cold blast of water from a hose had doused me. I looked down at my Monday schedule: statistics, SAF 101 (Surface Active Agents for textiles), Organic Chemistry, Calculus I, and Quantitative Analysis. No band. No orchestra. Nothing that held even a glimmer of possibility that it might fire me up. I was facing a curriculum devoid of creativity.

It was not that this course load was cognitively difficult, though it certainly was no cakewalk. I had been educated at Garden City High School with college-prep, highly technical course material. Calculus I and II. AP chemistry and physics. At the same time, though, I never thought of these college courses as contributing to my future job. Moreover, I held the opposite opinion of my high school humanities courses, which my father only considered hobbies but which I saw as a possible ticket out of obscurity.

Thanks in no small part to the efforts of Steve Thomas, my extra-curricular life was on solid footing, but my decline on the academic side was precipitous. If you graphed my first month at NC State, it would look like a hockey stick. I quickly fell behind. I cut classes, lectures, labs. Homework assignments were late or just plain missing. In a university the size of NC State (enrollment in 1970 was north of thirteen thousand) there was no parental figure hovering over you, ready to administer encouragement or threats. You were on your own. It was very easy to fall hopelessly behind.

With my academic life spiraling downward, I lived for the joy of the afternoon soccer practice. The workouts kept me engaged mentally and physically. I thrived in that structured, coached environment. Often, after workouts I would sneak an hour or two in the music school's piano practice rooms, writing songs. Then I'd eschew studying for a trip to the local pub.

In the 1970s, long before one-third of North Americans would be diagnosed with depression or bipolar disorder, I was headed for what could reasonably be described at that time as a nervous breakdown. I was ignoring my responsibilities. I was drinking to mute my predicament. I was sleeping ten to twelve hours a day. The result was self-loathing. The golden ticket in this environment was a university diploma. Nothing less could be counted as gain. And still, in my heart of hearts, I could not be made to care. My nights in the dorm were filled with nightmares. I endured this torture for five maddening semesters. It nearly ended me.

After two and a half years of suffering through the textile chemistry program, my grade point average hovered around 1.9 and was falling. I was placed on academic probation. I was faking swagger on the soccer field, trying to send a message of bold confidence, but one more semester on probation and I'd be suspended from the team. Adding to that stress was the fact that I was carrying this burden alone. I told no one. I dared not call my parents. I was living a lie.

Few people in my life at the time suspected that inside me was a locomotive already off the rails. I was consumed by the recurring vision of my future self back in Winston-Salem, living in my parents' basement, working the graveyard shift at Hanes. Forever. My own personal hell. One I'd actually had a taste of the summer before coming to Raleigh for school.

Remember when my dad said, "We will move the day after graduation"? Well, he wasn't kidding. Graduation was on a Saturday. Mom and I were in the car pointed south at 8:00 a.m. Sunday morning. Five days later I was sitting on a metal stool at Hanes Dye and Finishing Company, watching giant sheets of cloth go by on an enormous machine. When there was a hole or a tear in the cloth, I pushed a black button. The machine would stop, an alarm bell would ring, and a guy with a mouth bursting with chewing tobacco would run over and sew a patch over the hole. I would then push a large green button, one more alarm bell would sound, and the machine would roar back to life.

I was in need of a miracle. It came during a conversation with Steve Thomas.

Since Steve was the one responsible for the only present joy and purpose in my life—the soccer team—I felt I needed to confide in him about the possibility that I might get benched next semester because of my grades. He had an idea. Steve suggested that in the spring semester we both pick up a course elective called Radio and Television 101. The course was worth 4 credit hours and included a lab. This certainly sounded more interesting than matching shades of cloth, but it was Steve's big pitch that really sealed it: "It's supposed to be an easy A!"

I was in.

On the first day of Radio and Television 101 the following semester, I was, as my uncle Charlie would have said, "a blind dog in a meat house." Professor John Malcom believed in immediate and total immersion. Within the first hour of the class Steve and I were creating radio and television news programs. The course also gave us access to the production studios at the campus radio station (WKNC). We were rotated into news-reading duties on the station's live hourly news broadcasts. Steve, I think, could take it or leave it, but I fell in love. And I fell hard.

It was reminiscent of the joy (and the mischief) I found in those early years in the family basement: disassembling electronics; wiring up

Mr. Pumpkin for what were, in effect, live radio plays; assembling my mail-order Remco Caravelle radio transmitter and then broadcasting into all the car radios in the neighborhood on Halloween. There was even an upright piano in the WKNC studios where I could dash off news-theme music for my fellow radio lab students. Organic chemistry? Calculus? Wool and cotton blends? One hour in the radio-TV lab as a second-semester junior and I was done with all that. I had become transformed. It was another paradigm shift, but back toward the version of myself I actually knew and liked.

This Radio-TV course was created for someone like me. You work all day on a project and see the finished product take on form and substance right before your eyes. It was that beautiful combination of creativity, purpose, and accomplishment that I still enjoy to this day.

The next morning I stopped by the registrar's office to pick up the drop-add forms I would need to drop three of my courses and prepare the way for a new communications curriculum. I did this without my parents' consent. When I shared my passion and vision for this new world with my professors, most caught my excitement and signed my drop forms without hesitation. (I'm sure that more than one was glad to be rid of me!) My statistics professor, on the other hand, insisted that, because I was one week beyond the drop-add deadline, he would not sign the form since it would be against university policy. I pleaded. He refused and would not relent.

Back in the dorm my buddy Steve listened as I outlined my dilemma. When I was done with my sad tale, which included tears and resignation, he smiled, armed with another miracle solution.

"C'mon, Tesh, you're crazy. What are there, a hundred people in that statistics class?"

I nodded.

"The teacher is being a jerk. Everyone just drops courses when they need to. The professors don't even know. The classes are way too big to keep track."

"What are you saying?" I asked somewhat expectantly.

"I'm saying, if you sign the guy's name to the form, who's gonna know?"

"But that's forgery," I said. "Have *you* ever done that?"

"No . . . but . . . you know this textiles thing is not you, right?" Steve had expertly boxed me in. He knew the answer to his question. It was undeniable.

Don't underestimate the power of vision and direction. These are irresistible forces, able to transform what might appear to be unconquerable obstacles into traversable pathways and expanding opportunities. Strengthen the individual. Start with yourself. Take care with yourself. Define who you are. Refine your personality. Choose your destination and articulate your Being. As the great nineteenth-century German philosopher Friedrich Nietzsche so brilliantly noted, "He whose life has a why can bear almost any how."

—**Jordan B. Peterson,** *12 Rules for Life: An Antidote to Chaos*[2]

By the end of the day I had signed my professor's name to the drop form. *What's the worst that could happen?* was my thinking. *Maybe he makes me stay in the course? Maybe he fails me?* I already had a low C average. I was a stone's throw from an F anyway.

When the end of the spring semester arrived, I traveled back to Winston-Salem from Raleigh and resumed my annual summer position at the foot of the giant textile machine at Hanes. I knew that my report card from State would be forthcoming, and for the first time I was feeling no trepidation at all. According to my computations, my Radio-TV grade (A on both lecture and lab) plus the dropped Statistics would bring my GPA up to at least a 2.5. I would be off probation and I'd be impervious to suspension from the soccer team.

I needed just one more minor bit of good fortune (or subterfuge, depending on how you look at it). I needed my dad to not look too closely at my report card. I knew that the textile courses would be missing, which would be a huge red flag. I felt pretty secure that he would only look at the grades and not the course names—TX 301 or SAA 202. As it turned out, he would see neither, because he never saw a report card at all.

In late July, in the heat of a North Carolina summer, I was called into my dad's downstairs office in our home. He was seated behind his desk. To his right, next to his gold-plated letter opener, was a copper table lamp. There was the faint smell of whiskey and a stronger smell of cigarettes. He appeared as a human leviathan, seated behind that enormous oak desk. He was holding a letter, which he began reading before I could sit down. It was from the chancellor's office at NC State. My statistics professor had filed a complaint against me. He had, indeed, spotted my forgery.

My dad's voice boomed with the remainder of the chancellor's letter. I was being "suspended indefinitely" from the university for breaking the honor code. I would receive an F for the statistics course.

I did not sit down. Without looking up from the letter, my dad continued extemporaneously. He told me that I had shamed him and our family. He called me a liar and a cheat. He told me I was no longer welcome in his home, and that I had to take my belongings and leave. Immediately.

. . .

Early the next morning, I pack up my 1967 Volkswagen Fastback and drive out of the city limits of Winston-Salem on my way back to Raleigh. On the seat next to me is a brown paper bag with a sandwich my mom had handed me before I'd pulled out of the driveway. She had hugged me and then kissed me on the cheek. She had been crying. I'm feeling horribly guilty for leaving her alone, for making her life worse than it already is.

In that moment of deep shame and moral failing, I still have enough awareness of who I really am to know that I would much rather plot a course back to Garden City, to relive my life before all of this and pursue those things that Radio-TV 101 had reignited, but I barely have enough gas money to make the 110-mile trip to Raleigh.

Up front in the trunk of my Volkswagen is my vinyl record collection, a pile of jeans and T-shirts, and a few 8-track tapes. My Boy Scout pup tent and a sleeping bag are lashed to the roof. There's a strong smell of burning oil as I sequence through the manual gear shift and merge onto Interstate 40. I have no plan. No family. No future.

My 8-track tape player pauses to switch tracks, and for a brief moment I'm left with the unmistakable whine of the VW engine calling for a new gear. The solenoid in the 8-track clicks over to channel 2.

Two hours later, I find myself back in Raleigh, parked in Umstead Park, untying my tent and sleeping bag, preparing to forge my way in and set up my "home" for the night. Or nights.

Fortunately, the experience of crawling into a sleeping bag in a pup tent is not unfamiliar to me. I am an Eagle Scout, after all. I have spent many summers at Boy Scout camp and have my Operation Igloo patch from a week of winter camping in the mountains during a blizzard. Still, pitching a tent in a public park without promise of a merit badge is quite different. I think it wise, for instance, to make camp near a pay phone, in case my mommy calls.

. . .

When I was living in New York and didn't have a penny to my name, I would walk around the streets and occasionally I would see an alcove or something. And I'd think, that'll be good, that'll be a good spot for me when I'm homeless.

—**Larry David**[3]

As comfortable as I was in a tent, I had no grand plans to stay in that park for longer than was absolutely necessary. And while the camping fee was negligible, without the weekly allowance I was getting from my parents as a student, I would not have enough cash for food. That meant finding work. I already had connections at College Esso, where I had pumped gas part time during the school year. I figured I could pick up some hours there, but ultimately I ended up with a Monday through Friday gig working for a construction company called C. C. Mangum.

Since I had no experience operating a front-end loader or with carpentry work, I was hired as "utility." A utility worker did a little bit of everything—breaking up concrete with a pickax, hauling trash, making runs to the liquor store for chewing tobacco.

Other industries have this type of role in their hierarchy as well, just under different titles: assistant, runner, gofer. The only difference between my job and all of those was that by the time my day was done and my construction crew buddies had dropped me off at the southeast corner of the park, I was usually too exhausted to join them for a beer.

Alone at night with the crickets and my Coleman lantern, I tried to visualize a future. Perhaps I could get trained on the backhoe loader. Perhaps I could work my way up to construction foreman. Then I laughed. If I hadn't wanted to manufacture underwear, why was this now an option? No, if a passion for being a musician or broadcaster had put me in this tent, then I needed to somehow manifest that.

The next morning I called my friend Howard Stanis at WKNC Radio, the campus radio station. This was the studio where we had our Radio-TV 101 labs with Professor Malcolm. From the park pay phone I explained my predicament and my desire to use the campus facility to produce a demo tape. I pleaded with him, outlining why I needed only a few hours in the studio to produce the tape. I knew that if I was going to try to get a job at a local radio station, my only chance was to go in with something more than an empty résumé.

"But how are you going to produce a demo tape if you've never been on a commercial radio station?" said my friend.

"Please, can you just get me into the studio after school hours tomorrow night? You could meet me there and let me in. I'll lock up before dawn when I'm done."

There must be something about getting thrown out of school and being forced to live in a tent that softens people up, because Howard agreed to help if I promised I would be out of the studio before 6:00 a.m. when the cleaning crew arrived.

Obviously, since I was no longer registered as a student, this was highly irregular. It was definitely trespassing. And since I was using their tape, it might have even been theft. But since I had already been "convicted" of forgery, what was a little more criminal activity to add to my growing rap sheet? Howard let me in the following night.

. . .

In front of me in the WKNC college radio studio is an Ampex reel-to-reel tape recorder, an Olivetti manual typewriter, an Electro-Voice RE55 microphone, and an old Wurlitzer spinet upright piano. Finally in my element, I grab the nearest sheet of paper and jot down the news copy for my demo.

With the recorder rolling I play three syncopated notes, in octaves, on the piano: G-E-C. It is the NBC News theme. (That should get someone's attention!)

> This is John Tesh, WKIX 20/20 News.
> *(Typing on the Olivetti, creating the sonic illusion of a teletype machine.)*
> This is all the news you need to hear at twenty minutes before and
>   after the hour. Today, Dr. Henry Kissinger told reporters that
>   he thought we would finally see peace in the Middle East.
>   Correspondent Maurice Ghindi has more from Cairo.
> *(Holding my nose and with an awful imitation of the CBS*
>   *correspondent.)*
> This is Maurice Ghindi in Cairo. Today, Secretary of State Henry
>   Kissinger had this to say about the possibility of peace in the
>   Middle East.
> *(Now with an even worse imitation of Kissinger.)*
> I think there is a possibility of peace in the Middle East.
> *(Pinching my nose again.)*
> This is Maurice Ghindi in Cairo. Back to you, John, in the studio.
> *(Typing again as I continue my "broadcast.")*
> Thank you, Maurice. Now let's get a check of traffic with our eye-in-
>   the-sky reporter, Captain Johnson, in Skycam 5.
> *(Now I'm beating my chest with both hands to simulate the sound of a*
>   *helicopter. I speak with a touch of a southern accent.)*

Well, John, traffic is quite heavy on Interstate 40 with a fender
bender at Hillsborough Road. We'll keep an eye on it for you.
Back to you in the studio.
(Typing again.)
Thanks, Captain. Up next . . . President Richard Nixon faces more
impeachment proceedings as we update you on the Watergate
Hearings. I'm John Tesh, WKIX 20/20 News.

I reach for the piano . . . G-E-C.

On the tenth take, I've got it. I rewind the demo tape, box it up, and lock the studio door behind me. My goal is an entry-level radio job, so I assume that my best shot is to drop the tape off at the station I had mimicked in the demo: WKIX.

. . .

WKIX-AM radio was my favorite station in town. It was saved on my first radio button on the Volkswagen. The 20/20 News was incredibly stylized and unique. I enjoyed the music (Rick Dees in the mornings) but tuned in for the newscasters. Scott White and Bill Leslie were the lead newsmen. When they came on, they would shout—with intense drama—one-word teasers and then play the commercials.

"Watergate? Nixon? Guilty? I'm Bill Leslie. Details next on WKIX 20/20 News."

I arrived at WKIX two days later, tape in hand, wearing flip-flops and hair down to my shoulders. Fortunately, the receptionist was not put off by my appearance. She was wearing a tie-dyed tank top and had a neck tattoo featuring her boyfriend's name. So when I told her that I had created a demo tape for Mr. Scott White and that I was looking for my first job in radio and that I was living in a pup tent in a park because NC State had thrown me out for forging a professor's name . . . she was instantly Team Tesh.

I could tell from her expression that I had just become the scraggly-haired shelter puppy that no one would adopt. She promised she would get the tape to Mr. White. I handed her a piece of paper with my phone number on it. It was the number of the pay phone in the park.

Two weeks later "my" phone rang. On the other end was Scott White. He asked if I had done all the voices and production on the tape. I wasn't sure what the right, best answer was, but deceit had landed me in the tent I was trying to hustle my way out of, so I opted for the truth. It worked.

The next day I was in Scott's office, reading copy for him and taking direction. He told me it was tough to hire someone with no experience but that he felt I had some potential and would like to train me. In the meantime, he could only offer me four hours of work on Sunday mornings, playing the religious tapes. That was fine with me. I had my foot in the door. And when that door gets cracked open, opportunities are often what come through next. Someone leaves. Another gets promoted. Within a few months, Mr. White's training and providence, along with the support of WKIX program director Ken Lowe, combined to land me a job as the weekend newscaster on WKIX radio, which was my ticket out of Umstead Park and off the C. C. Mangum construction crew.

To this day I can still remember the weeks of irony, triggered by the *Papillon* movie marquees along the drive from Umstead Park to our construction site in Raleigh. The C. C. Mangum project was my own Devil's Island, and my decision to lie and cheat in contravention of my father's wishes was the crime that sent me there. The marquees were staring back at me as a grim reminder of my own self-inflicted exile; the result of the worst decision since they decided to fill the Hindenburg with hydrogen.

And yet, here's the rub: if presented with the same set of circumstances again, and the same choices to pick from, I'm not sure I wouldn't make the same decision, because I'd found something that many people in this world spend their entire lives looking for and never finding: I'd found purpose, passion, and direction.

Does that justify my lying or cheating or violating the university's honor code? Of course not. But it does highlight the importance of finding purpose and then working relentlessly in service of it.

When you have your *why*, you can endure any *how*. And when you've renewed your mind to eliminate external doubt and resistance, all that is left is vision and purpose. "Do not be conformed to this world, but be transformed by the renewing of your mind, that you may prove what is that good and acceptable and perfect will of God" (Rom. 12:2).

I also now have revelation and even a measure of respect for the decisions my dad and my statistics professor both made. They were, at their core, acting honorably. I respect that. And I believe it made a man out of me.

Chapter 8

Is This Flying or Dying?

August 4, 2015

The metal railings on the sides of the recovery room gurney are chilling to my right hand. The beeping is back. I can also make out what sounds like the *clack-clacking* of shopping cart wheels. The ceiling is moving like a fun-house tunnel and I have to close my eyes to make it stop.

I feel as if I am flying . . . an imaginary aircraft banking left, then right. This film is playing in my opioid-infused brain. Where have I seen this image before? Oh yes. The last scene in the movie version of *The World According to Garp*. Garp is coaching wrestling and then Pooh shoots him at point-blank range. He's being airlifted by medivac helicopter to a trauma center. He's dying but he believes he's flying in an imaginary airplane—he's flying!—right before he dies.

Holy hell! No! I'm flying—but not dying! My words come out as a desperate shout: "I'm not dying, right?"

I am terribly afraid. My left hand suddenly feels very warm. I open my eyes once more. It's Connie. My partner. She is holding my hand. I squeeze it. She squeezes back.

The vision vanishes. Garp is gone and I relax into another deep sleep.

August 6, 2015

For some ludicrous reason, I was actually looking forward to this surgery when it was first scheduled. It's hard to sleep knowing that evil cells are dividing within you. There's something about seeing cancer inside of you—actually being able to look at pictures of the tumors inside your body on a CAT scan—that makes you want to grab a scalpel and just get it out yourself. It mutes much of the trepidation you might have about general anesthetic or going under the knife. And in my case, the rest of the fear was addressed by reading dozens of articles about the actual procedure I would be receiving.

Back in the medieval days of prostate surgery (which lasted until at least 2001), removing a cancerous prostate gland usually included horrific collateral damage to the thoracic region of the patient's body and resulted in permanent incontinence and lack of sexual function. This new, laparoscopic, robotic surgery avoids both of those complications and the recovery process is quicker and easier than ever before. Most patients are able to resume normal activities within two to three weeks of the surgery and are able to go home within twenty-four hours after surgery. So the thought of being instantly cancer-free while enjoying a few days with some great drugs was, strangely enough, enticing.

I was an idiot. Seventy-two hours after my surgery, I was still in the hospital and things were not going well.

Within twenty-four hours of the surgery, the doctors and nurses wanted me to walk around. It's considered required therapy; it gets the blood and the bowels moving and avoids complications. Unfortunately, each time I tried walking through the hospital's corridors, one small, labored, shuffling step at a time, I would be overcome by nausea. The result was a frighteningly loud and uncontrollable retching that triggered an urgent response from nurses who would come running with plastic buckets to catch whatever might come out while I resisted the urge to fall down.

Once they were confident I wouldn't topple over, the nurses would escort me back to my room and work together to get my large six-foot-six frame into my hospital bed, like Lilliputians carting Gulliver into their capital city. They would fuss and rearrange things until I was sufficiently comfortable, all the while talking to each other in whispered tones that were not at all comforting. It turns out, the powerful anesthetics I'd been given had worked so well that they not only numbed my pain but they also paralyzed my intestines.

This was not good. Our intestines are about twenty-eight feet long. This means the foods we eat have a long way to travel before they're fully digested or excreted. Our intestines complete this job by moving in a wavelike motion known as peristalsis. The muscle contractions move our digested food forward. However, if something (opioids, for example) slows down or blocks this motion, the result can be a blockage in the intestines. The medical term for this lack of movement is an *ileus*. An ileus can lead to an intestinal obstruction that prevents food material, gas, or liquids from getting through. Without treatment, an ileus can perforate or tear the intestine, which can lead to bowel contents, which have high levels of bacteria, leaking into your abdomen, which in turn can lead to sepsis.

This can be deadly.

This was why everyone around me was whispering in loud voices.

This was why I was paralyzed with fear.

Chapter 9

Dream and Become

In July of 1973 I finally departed Umstead Park and left the ranks of the homeless tent-dwellers, but not without considerable effort. I'd joined Bill Leslie, another WKIX newsman, who was two years my senior, as his roommate in the Meredith Village apartment complex. Bill had studied communications at UNC and had already developed a solid reputation at the radio station. I was taking over the spot in the apartment that had been vacated by the one-and-only Rick Dees.

Dees had left WKIX to work in Memphis, where he not only ruled the AM airwaves but also scored a number one hit with his song "Disco Duck." I shared the three-bedroom apartment with Bill and another disc jockey, J. J. Towry. I struggled every month to pay my part of the rent even though I was working weekends as a part-time newsman at WKIX radio, so I supplemented my income by busing tables on weekday mornings at a delicatessen in Cameron Village and pumping gas at College ESSO in Raleigh in the evenings. Then, once a week, I played jazz piano at Cameron Village Underground for tips.

By the end of every month, I had enough money for rent, but barely enough for food. The bulk of my meals were cheese hot dogs (without the bun), which I had learned how to prepare while still in school, thanks to an engineering major in my fraternity who had perfected an ingenious and frugal process for avoiding starvation when your monthly beer expenditures exceeded your parental allowance. At the risk of inflating my insurance premiums, I will now outline the extremely dangerous and patently unsafe method of cheese-hot-dog-meal-making that electrical engineering sophomore William Huddelston jotted down for me on a yellow legal pad in 1971:

How to Create a Cheese Hot Dog Using House Current

1. Go to the Piggly Wiggly and purchase a pack of hot dogs and cheddar cheese slices.
2. Cut the plug off a lamp cord or the power cord of an old stereo that no longer works. (Do this while they are not plugged into the wall.)
3. Strip the two (2) ends of the cord and attach the bare wires to two (2) open paper clips.
4. Slice the hot dog, length-wise, down the middle, and insert strips of the cheddar cheese.
5. Insert the plug into the wall socket. The moisture contained in the hot dog should provide enough conductivity to cook the dog, but not so much as to arc the current, potentially blowing out the fuse box.
6. Watch the hot dog closely and pull the plug when the hot dog flesh begins to show blisters (approx. thirty seconds). Do not touch the hot dog until the plug is out of the wall socket. The heat from the process will melt and then cook the cheese, filling the crack in the hot dog with gooey goodness.

This hot-dog-house-current hack was a common practice among starving students in the 1970s. It was the impetus for Ron Popeil's patented Hot Dogger (though his was UL approved). And based on what I know today about alternating 110-volt house current, not to mention the effects of large quantities of nitrite-infused deli forcemeat, I'm lucky to be alive.

I bring this up not as some ingenious accomplishment that others should laud and follow but rather as an illustration of the things I willingly endured back then to make this weekend radio job at WKIX work.

It gave me relevance. It also kept me off the stools at the Jolly Knave pub during happy hour.

I lived this way—three jobs and cheese dogs—to support my weekend gig at WKIX for five months, and I likely would have continued in this fashion for quite a while longer if I'd witnessed any improvement to my schedule at the radio station. Alas, in all my time there I was never on the WKIX clock for more than eight total hours per week, and I was at the bottom of the food chain when it came to experience and seniority. My only chance for future advancement would come if someone moved on, creating an opening for me to step into, much the way Rick Dees's departure opened a spot and all of the disc jockeys moved up the ladder by a rung. The problem was, the staff I joined was young and happy, and no one seemed primed to move on. It might take years to move into a full-time slot.

With little hope of returning to school to finish my degree and the specter of possibly clearing dirty tables, washing dishes, and doing oil changes while I rode the weekend news desk into my forties, I knew it was time for another Hail Mary.

The inspiration came at the deli while in a dishwashing-induced trance (or delusion, depending on your point of view). I had taken, and enjoyed, the Radio-TV 101 course at NC State less than a year earlier, so, my thinking continued, why not apply for a job at the local TV station in town?

As I think back on this, I don't know what led me to make this leap with such confidence. Or why I'd even stopped there. Why hadn't I just entered the space program while I was at it? No experience. No training. The chances were probably about the same.

I'm guessing the only reason I didn't immediately abandon this absurd idea was because I believed I'd already done the stupidest thing I was ever going to do by forging my professor's name. I'd also grown tired of my cracked, soapy hands bleeding into the sink and the rest of my body reeking of gasoline and motor oil. Besides, I was the guy who thought Napoleon made the right choice to invade Russia, so if being laughed out the front door of a TV station was the worst thing that ever happened to me, I would still be ahead of where I'd been six months earlier. I'd also be *way ahead* of Napoleon.

Elbows deep in soapsuds and slimy dishes, I decided right then that the following Monday I would march right into WTVD, Channel 11, and ask for a job. I had a purpose, I had persistence . . . and I had no practical experience. Who wouldn't want to hire me?

When I arrived at the reception desk in Durham on Monday morning, I carried no actual TV news demo tape, just a pair of fake TV newscasts I'd created during my Radio-TV course. I did, however, introduce myself with boyish insouciance to the receptionist as a "news reporter for WKIX radio." This, to my astonishment, got me an audience with Max Powell, the WTVD news director, who told me the station just had a key employee leave the station.

They had an opening!

"NewsFilm processing assistant." That was the title of the position. Mr. Powell asked if I had any experience in film processing. I thought for a moment and then mentioned my stint as photo editor of the Garden City High School yearbook. Surprisingly, that was enough for Max. I had my first full-time television job, at $1.60 an hour. Minimum wage. I would soon be able to quit the deli and gas station jobs. My daily personal aroma would transition from dish soap and gasoline to the more pungent film-developer-fixer chemical smell of a darkroom.

This was, of course, before the age of digital. Music was on vinyl and moving pictures were on acetate (film). When a television news reporter got assigned to cover a fire or other breaking news story, the cameraman or the reporter (who was often a one-man-band in smaller markets) would capture the scene with a Bell and Howell Filmo 16mm movie camera. The Filmo was standard equipment for US military combat cameramen from World War II through Vietnam, and it was the workhorse camera for the vast majority of TV stations from the 1950s through the 1970s, WTVD included.

Both of our cameramen carried a Filmo camera for their news gathering. When they rushed back to the station with their exposed news film, which was black-and-white and silent, it was my job as the "NewsFilm processing assistant" to get the film into the chemical processing "soup" so the director could put the film on a projector and then on air for the six o'clock news.

It wasn't long before I figured out why there had been an opening for "NewsFilm processing assistant." First of all, assistant? To whom? I was the only guy. Moreover, within just a few days of getting my bearings at the station, the gig showed itself for what it truly was: a high-speed, high-pressure position on a perpetually ticking clock with very little margin for error that had managed to burn out the guy who came before me.

The reason for this was that film processing was the singular choke-point in a news broadcast. Unlike a TV news car that could break the speed limit while rushing the film back to the station, or the reporter/cameraman who could sprint it down to the basement, news film processing time was fixed. It could not be rushed. It usually took at least an hour from the time the film arrived back at our newsroom until it was ready to be broadcast. If you increased the speed of the processor drum and attempted to accelerate the process, the film would be underexposed and unusable. If the director demanded that I pull the film from my processing tanks before it had dried, there was a good chance the projector would tear the film apart as the sprockets grabbed the wet acetate.

Film editing, which came after processing, was similarly stressful. It was done by hand and since we had a tiny staff of four (not counting the anchorpeople), everyone, out of necessity, had to learn how to edit the news film. The editing process required counting the words on the news script and then cutting the film into 3.5-second segments per line of script. (For Don Shea, our awesome, fast-talking, histrionic sports anchor, we counted only 2.5 seconds.) Then the segments of film were spliced together using film glue. A common problem was film breaking during the newscast because editors didn't use enough glue or it had not yet dried and then jammed in the projector.

Welcome to the halcyon days of local news. They were glorious and wholly unglamorous.

For me, WKIX radio and WTVD television were my first experiences with the world of true apprenticeship, of working with purpose as opposed to strictly for profit. I'd found something I really liked and I wanted to get better at any and every aspect of it. But make no mistake, there was something very romantic about hustling to get my foot in the door and then, in the case of the TV staff, finding myself in league with a group of broadcasters, with water right up to their noses, just trying to survive producing two live newscasts a day. The beauty of this challenge for me was that I was, on any given day, required to jump in on tasks for which I had no formal training. It was sink or swim. I had, of course, been trained to process news film for my primary job, but I had to be a quick study for everything else. I soon became proficient on film editing, operating the Bell and Howell Filmo cameras during breaking news events, running the studio cameras for the local nightly newscasts when someone called in sick at the last minute, even standing in front of a camera (called a "stand-up") reporting on a local fire.

There weren't some bigwigs in a conference room deciding these job-sharing moments. I did what was necessary to get the show on the air. It all just happened in real time. This jack-of-all-trades hypertraining continued for five or six months. You've heard that the best way to learn a language is total immersion. This was that. It was an intense, high-stakes, trade-school-like trial by fire, and through it all, I didn't just grow up. I also caught a 20/20 vision for my future. I could imagine the natural progression of the path I was now traveling. I knew I was apprenticing with the critical tools and habits I would take with me forever.

With this strong wind at my back, I now began a nightly ritual. Before I dropped off to sleep and again in the morning when I opened my eyes, I would recite the Lord's Prayer out loud and then verbalize my future into existence.

After the prayer, I would say something like this: five years from today, I am sitting at an anchor desk in New York City, reporting the nightly news.

Simple, direct, and I swear I could see it. I could see the color of the suit I was wearing. I could feel the script I was holding at the desk.

Dream lofty dreams. And as you dream, so shall you become. Your vision is the promise of what you shall one day be. Your ideal is a prophecy of what you shall at last unveil.

—**James Allen,** *As a Man Thinketh*[1]

On any given day, when I wasn't praying, visualizing, or up to my neck in news film, I was rehearsing. Little did he know, my roommate Bill Leslie had been modeling his techniques of focused, intense training for me for as long as he'd allowed me into his presence. It was awesome—and impossibly difficult. I drilled myself with his method of memorizing newspaper articles and then "broadcasting" them into the bathroom mirror each morning and evening.

The idea was to take a five-hundred-word article, read it once, and then quickly condense it into a one-minute stand-up report. It was an ad-lib without supporting notes. Bill knew that White House reporters, for example, were tasked to do this following a press briefing. They had to absorb the information, understand it, and turn what could be a complex issue into a story that people at home could easily comprehend—and do it in one minute, max. Bill is, to this day, one of the best at the stand-up ad-lib I've ever seen.

In my formative years, Dr. Wagner and Mrs. Andriani (my piano teacher) had created habit-loops for my musical practice on the trumpet and piano, respectively. These teachers and mentors had spoken the theory of deliberate practice into my life long before my nascent radio-TV broadcasting career. They'd helped me develop habitual behaviors that served me well. And now, with the addition of Bill Leslie's tutelage, I'd refined a full set of skills that I would need for my dream job in New York City, which my subconscious mind believed was already mine.

Chapter 10

Be Found Ready

I tell every young person who asks me for career advice the same thing: "Find the thing you want to do, or even the broad area where you'd like to work, choose the path of least resistance, and plot a course for your way in."

For me, circa 1973, the *thing* in "find the thing" was a job in broadcast media, and the path of least resistance was a small-market TV station. It didn't feel small at the time, mind you, but I realize in retrospect that were I to have attempted to break into the business at the very top (aka big-city TV market), I would almost certainly have been met with failure or, at the very least, stagnation. Going in at the top of any high-power, high-status industry, you run the real risk of being trapped with no chance of advancement. In the case of broadcasting, you end up going for coffee for the experienced superstars, while the station manager hires experienced broadcasters out of the small and medium markets. When it comes to breaking in anywhere, you're better off turning the bombastic conventional wisdom on its ear and, instead, going small.

The small-market "farm team" training I was getting in North Carolina was energizing, and I cannot stress this enough for anyone serious about breaking into the world of television news broadcasting in particular: plot a course that begins in a small town, because what happened to me is what can happen to anyone in a smaller market television news operation.

It was five o'clock on a Thursday when word quickly spread through the corridors of WTVD-Raleigh/Durham that news anchor Chris Key would not be doing the news that evening. In fact, effective immediately, he would no longer be working at the station.

> **Max Powell (News Director):** Tesh, do you have a sport jacket?
> **Me:** Yes, sir, I do own one, but I don't have it here.
> **Powell:** Well, grab one of Skip's jackets [Skip Carpenter, the weatherman] and get ready to go on the air. You're anchoring the news tonight.

I was about three months into my daily job developing the WTVD news film and infrequently filling in for cameramen and reporters. I had never anchored the news before. I had never even been on the news set. I was in shorts and sneakers. And now—actually, in fifty-eight minutes if I was being precise—I would be delivering the nightly news, sitting between veteran sportscaster Don Shea and weatherman Skip Carpenter.

What happened? Rumors were flying, but there was no time to indulge them. Chris was gone, and in less than an hour I had to figure out how to act like Walter Cronkite—those were the only two things I knew as facts. I remember very little about what happened when the red light went on over the camera at 6:00 p.m. that night. I do remember how soaked with sweat Skip Carpenter's spare coat was when I handed it back to him. And when we signed off the broadcast, I don't remember any balloons being released or confetti in the air. Sportscaster Don Shea simply said, "Well, you got through it, kid."

When I returned to the newsroom to grab my car keys, the room was empty and Max Powell's door was closed. I imagined he was scouring a drawer full of résumés and demo tapes from potential anchormen. When I returned the next morning to start my film-developing duties, Max asked if I had brought my sport jacket.

"Uh, no," I answered. "I wasn't sure that—"

"Well, go back home and get it!" he bellowed with a tone I'd heard my dad use when I left a wet towel on the bed. "Marni will start the film processor."

One week went by. Then two. Three. I was still anchoring the news, but I definitely felt like I had a target on my back. Fortunately, I had some experience reading the news on WKIX radio, and I was still working the Bill Leslie "fake it in front of the mirror" live stand-up rehearsal technique every day. The biggest challenge for me was not looking like I was frightened to death. That day and over the next several, I also dug out old scripts from the station archives and worked on emulating their style. Then, for the live broadcast I had to memorize each news story so that I kept my head up and faced the camera, instead of looking down to read the copy. Since we were live, I knew I also had to learn the time cues leading into the Cronkite national news. For the first four nights I got cut off midsentence while trying to say, "For Skip Carpenter and Don Shea, I'm John Tesh. Please join us aga—"

* * *

Captaining the anchor desk in Raleigh was a classic example of being in *the right place at the right time.* If I hadn't had my foot in the door at WTVD, processing the news film and filling in as needed, this enormous break never would have materialized for me. When the coach called my number, I was ready to play. I had been "found ready" in the darkroom.

Years later, while teaching a course in television production at the New School in New York City, I would retell the WKIX and WTVD stories to illustrate what I call the street-smart technique of being "found ready." This concept of training oneself into readiness has always been popular in the Broadway theater world and has been the plot for a number of classic films where a chorus member is suddenly called up into action as a last-minute replacement for the ailing star of the show. No one has any idea that she has learned all of the leading lady's lines until she steps into the role and shines. There are many folks who believe they can interview for a job and then the company will train them. It's wrong thinking. I believe that the moment we dismiss the thought of starting small, of leaning into apprenticeship—no matter how experienced (or proud) we regard ourselves—is the moment we begin to shrink from advancement and growth.

You must never disdain an apprenticeship with no pay. In fact, it is often the height of wisdom to find the perfect mentor and offer your services as an assistant for free. Happy to exploit your cheap and eager spirit, such mentors will often divulge more than the usual trade secrets. In the end, by valuing learning above all else, you will set the stage for your creative expansion, and the money will soon come to you.

—**Robert Greene,** *Mastery*[1]

Whether it was the prayer, the visualization practices to manifest my purpose, or raw persistence (or a combination of them all), what happened to me in the thirty-six months following my first night anchoring the Raleigh TV newscast was what one journalist later described as "an unparalleled flurry of advancement and success in the world of broadcasting." It began with a change in the tide that was disrupting the entire local news landscape in the United States.

In 1973, a trend had emerged in the world of broadcast news to have news teams *present* the news, rather than just read fifteen minutes of news headlines from behind an old wooden desk. Major national networks were spending tons of money on glass and stainless steel anchor desks, symphonic news-theme music, logo design, and promotion. Pricey consultants were hired to conduct market research and, based on that research, station directors often demanded that their anchor teams project a friendly and even funny demeanor. It was all very show-business focused. It even had a name among industry insiders: "happy talk news."

The relationships and banter between news-team members became crucial to developing a relationship with the viewers. So, for example, viewers would sit down to watch the local six o'clock newscast and would see the anchorman poking fun at the weatherman for missing a forecast; the weatherman taking a jab at the sports anchor for his goofy tie; and the sports anchor jabbing the news anchor about his lousy golf game. If this sounds a lot like the cast of the movie *Anchorman*, there's a reason for that—the film was set in 1975 and drawn from the real-life 1970s local-news world.

The challenges this presented to station directors were many. Not only did they have to fill twice as much airtime as they used to, but now they had to find a pipeline to "presentable" on-air personalities. In the mid-1970s, news teams were a veritable cast of *performers*. There were news anchors, weathercasters, sportscasters, investigative reporters, consumer watchdogs, and entertainment reporters. In some of the larger markets, stations were pouring millions of dollars into hiring this talent, building them flashy studios, and purchasing billboard advertising to promote them.

This free market for broadcasters spawned as many opportunities for growing mid-tier markets as it created problems for stagnating local ones. The William Morris Agency created an entire division devoted to representation of local news anchors. Headhunters sprang up as well. One in particular: Sherlee Barish.

Sherlee Barish was a gravelly-voiced, tough-as-nails broadcasting industry headhunter based in Manhattan. In the summer of 1973, I came across an interview with her ("Honey, I know where all the bodies are!") in *TV Guide Magazine*, and I made a mental note that if there was ever one person who could get me to where I wanted to go, and if I had the means or opportunity to get in contact with that person, she was it.

Never one to shy away from potentially getting too far out over my skis, once I had been on the air at WTVD for about four months, I made the bold (and what turned out to be fateful) decision to mail Sherlee a VHS tape of my work. The tape was a gross collection of news reading, banter with Don Shea and Skip Carpenter, and a couple of two-minute reports on local fires and car chases. I had no idea if it would reach her, or if it would end up on one of those notorious slush piles that agents often talk about, but two weeks after slapping a wall of stamps on the envelope containing my WTVD demo tape, Sherlee called.

"Hello, John?" The voice was a Broderick Crawford whiskey-and-Marlboro rasp.

"Uh, yes, this is John. Who's speaking please?" And then in one long, run-on sentence, it poured out.

"John, this is Sherlee Barish. Listen, I received your tape, which is very raw and you don't have much experience, and why did you write a résumé all in lowercase? Anyway, there's a station in Orlando called WFTV that is looking for an anchorman and reporter and they like you and want to pay you $17,000 a year to come work for them, they need an answer by tomorrow 'cause they are looking at some other people so call me back tomorrow morning with your answer 'cause they want you to start in two weeks."

Click.

I was making $7,280 a year, so this was a huge raise. But the decision was not about money. It was about more opportunity.

Max Powell was not surprised when I gave my notice. He was a member of that old-school breed of broadcasters who slept next to three police scanners. He never arrived at a local fire after the fire department. He put a hand on my shoulder and said simply, "Go get 'em, Tesh. We knew you wouldn't be here long."

When my last day arrived at WTVD-TV, I was so anxious to start my new position in Florida that I rented a U-Haul trailer, packed up everything I owned, and drove six hundred miles straight through the night from Raleigh to Orlando. When I arrived, exhausted, in Orlando ten hours later, I left the U-Haul locked to the car with a bicycle cable lock and crashed at the Howard Johnson near the WFTV-Orlando studios. Twelve hours of sleep later I ventured out of the motel for a fresh change of clothing. There was no U-Haul. My first thought was that the kind people at the front desk had moved my trailer to the rear parking lot to be out of the way. What I soon learned was that they had done no such thing.

When I called the local police to tell my tale, I was informed that I had, regrettably, arrived in town in the middle of a U-Haul trailer crime wave. Twenty-two travel trailers had been stolen in Orlando in the previous ten days. Terrific. The next day I borrowed a hundred bucks from the WFTV news director and bought a jacket, shirt, and tie. Detectives never recovered the contents of my U-Haul. Most notably I lost all of my prized Jimi Hendrix and Led Zeppelin albums, plus about a hundred 8-track tapes. Yes, Emerson, Lake and Palmer, King Crimson, Blind Faith, and more. All gone. A greater crime, I know not.

Compared to WTVD in Raleigh-Durham, Orlando was the big time. Disney World had opened two years earlier and the population in Central Florida was exploding. Even more impressive as far as I was concerned, Orlando had a teleprompter and four cameras. That was one prompter and three cameras more than WTVD. I mean, seriously, a teleprompter? That I got to use? Up until this point I had been memorizing the nightly news and doing a bad job of it. Reading a teleprompter took a little practice—the first week I resembled a deer caught in the high beams—but after a few weeks I became proficient enough that I was also able to master the "fake look-down" that Walter Cronkite used every night and made America believe he knew everything.

This was broadcasting heaven. John Chancellor and David Brinkley were on NBC; Walter Cronkite was on CBS; Harry Reasoner and Howard K. Smith were on ABC; and I was on . . . WFTV Orlando. To celebrate, I took my first WFTV paycheck ($325—that's $1,921 in today's money) and bought two shirts and three ties. That was two shirts and three ties more than what I had after a night at the Howard Johnson. It wasn't taking me long at all to settle into my new digs.

Then, four months into the Orlando gig, the phone rang for me in the newsroom following the six o'clock broadcast.

"Young man!" came the deep, refined voice of a man who sounded eerily like Charles Emerson Winchester III from *M*A*S*H*. "You're coming to work for me!"

"I'm sorry, who is this?" I glanced around the newsroom.

"This is Irving Waugh, president of WSM Television in Nashville, Tennessee."

Whoa. In 1974, WSM-TV was the dominant newscast in Nashville. Unlike most stations in North America, WSM ran a full hour of news at 6:00 p.m. and a half hour at 11:00 p.m. Nashville was also one of the first markets (along with St. Louis) to shoot their news footage with electronic video cameras instead of film cameras (this was known as ENG—electronic news gathering). These state-of-the-art news-gathering tools created an enormous amount of competition between stations in every market for live on-the-scene reporting. It was also a key element in the discovery and rise in popularity of Oprah Winfrey, who was, at that time, a nineteen-year-old street reporter in Nashville for rival station WLAC. She was reporting live on everything from brush fires to garden parties (and she could ad lib for hours). If you subscribed to *Broadcasting* magazine, you knew about WSM-TV.

"I've been watching you," Mr. Waugh boomed through the phone. "I'm in town for a conference and I spied your work on the Channel 9 News. Give me the address of your station, and I'll have my secretary messenger over a plane ticket. Is next Tuesday good for you?"

"Next Tuesday?"

"Yes, Tuesday, Tuesday. You'll fly to Nashville on Tuesday morning and I'll have you back in Orlando by Wednesday evening. It's a short flight. You'll be fine. You'll meet our other anchors and our news director and we'll see what's what. I look forward to it."

Click.

What just happened? Why does everyone in the news business hang up without saying goodbye? I had so many questions, namely because this did not feel like a request from "Irving Waugh, president of WSM Television in Nashville, Tennessee;" it felt like a command. Delivered like something out of *Ice Station Zebra*: *LAUNCH COUNTERMEASURES!*

I looked around the newsroom again to see if anyone was cracking up. Newsrooms were notorious for their elaborate phone pranks. I detected none of that now. One hour before the 11:00 p.m. broadcast, the WFTV security guard handed me an envelope labeled "Personal and Confidential." Inside was a plane ticket (dated Tuesday) and instructions regarding the car service that would meet me upon arrival at Nashville Airport (it would take me straight to the station).

. . .

WSM was Nashville's leading newscast because of its news team, led by uber-popular anchorman Dan Miller and weatherman Pat Sajak. Miller was the embodiment of what TV news executives called the "quintessential anchor." He was a performer way beyond his pay grade and current standing in Nashville. He was that rare combination of good looks and a voice that would rattle the television set. He had just enough southern in his baritone to leave you warm and fuzzy while simultaneously delivering even the most harrowing, sanguine breaking news stories. He also had a reputation for being kind to his fellow broadcasters. Dan was able to provoke thoughtful answers from his interview subjects, who would often forget they were in the middle of an interview. He was smooth.

Watching the team broadcast the Tuesday six o'clock news from the WSM control room with Mr. Waugh, I was mesmerized. My first thought was simply, *Why am I here?* It was the most perfect news team I had ever seen. In this mid-size market these were serious, polished broadcasters who could banter back and forth with ease. Miller was rock solid. Sajak was hilarious. It was clear why this was the number one news program in town. So again, why was *I* here?

The answer came soon from Mr. Waugh. All three network news divisions (NBC, CBS, ABC[2]) had been chasing Dan for the past two years. They had all been screening his tapes and using them for focus group testing. He consistently scored off the charts in likability and trustworthiness. Dan had turned down huge money offers from Chicago, NYC, Philadelphia, and Miami because he loved his life and work in Nashville. He was a single parent, raising two young daughters who were happy and comfortable. But like the star quarterback in high school, Dan Miller was being heavily recruited, and everyone has a price. Irving Waugh, news director Mike Kettenring, and the entire news organization knew it was only a matter of time before the right deal came along. They were constantly in danger of losing their WSM-TV News franchise signal caller and they currently had no backup quarterback.

Mr. Waugh introduced me to the makeup artist. "Slap some pancake on this young man, Barbara, and let's see what we've got here."

I was not prepared for an audition. Silly me.

Miller and Sajak were wrapping up the newscast. The stage manager escorted me toward the WSM "Scene at 6" news desk. Miller jumped to his feet with a broad smile.

"Hello, John Tesh. We've been waiting for you! Please take a seat. Irving wants us to talk for a while and the guys in the booth will record some of it. Let me introduce you to these crazy camera people. Also, say hello to Pat Sajak!"

Pat trotted over for a handshake and quick hello. I felt my pulse climb into fight-or-flight mode. Cortisol ripped through my bloodstream. It wasn't like I was meeting Walter Cronkite. Why was I so nervous? Perhaps it was because nine months ago I was developing news film and getting coffee for reporters at a Raleigh-Durham TV station. Maybe it was because a little more than a year ago I was living in a pup tent in a park, smashing concrete with sledgehammers.

Dan sensed my nervousness, so when the tape rolled, he guided me through the process. This was no direct-to-camera teleprompter performance. Irving and Mike would say later that they wanted a look at my ability to *have a conversation*. Dan and I spoke in front of the cameras for a half hour. He was wonderful. When it was over, I felt nothing but relief and an overpowering urge to return to my proper place as the fledging anchorboy in Orlando.

Instead, I found myself with Mike and Irving in Irving's palatial office. Irving explained that Nashville viewers were incredibly loyal and that it took them a very long time to warm up to new on-air personalities. Mike only wanted to know about my experience with field reporting. He had just been hired out of his New Orleans news director position and brought with him dozens of accolades and awards for local news coverage and investigative reporting. It was clear that Irving was serious about his news operation. I could learn a lot from Mike; that much was clear just from this brief interaction. He had *mentor* written all over him.

My flight was scheduled to depart for Orlando in two hours. People kept sticking their heads into Irving's office to say hello.

"John, say hello to Bob O'Connor. Head of sales," Irving said by way of introduction.

"Get in here, Huell! John, this is Huell Howser. Huell does our Happy Features segment. I guess you could say Huell owns this town!" Laughter all around.

Huell's voice sounded like something out of *Hee Haw*. I would later learn that his features were the most popular segments on the nightly newscast. Even more popular than fires. His features were also usually the longest. (My favorite was his twelve-minute report on a pig who rode on top of a pickup truck.)

Huell would go on to host the *California's Gold* television series for PBS. Pat Sajak would leave for a Los Angeles station in 1977, then for *Wheel of Fortune* in 1981.

In a single moment, a person can choose to change everything. Change doesn't have to take a long time, it happens *the instant we decide.*

—**Benjamin P. Hardy,** *Slipstream Time Hacking*[3]

What I thought was an impossibility a year earlier when I walked into WKIX, or nine months earlier when I stumbled into WTVD, or even nine *hours* earlier when I'd gotten on the plane in Orlando, had, in fact, already occurred. It was becoming very clear that I already *had* this job. This parade of warm hellos that Irving had ushered through his office wasn't good old-fashioned southern hospitality, strictly speaking. It was the Welcome Wagon.

It was now up to me to appear as normal as possible as Mr. Waugh kicked everyone out of his office and got serious, just him and me. Man to potential anchorman. Irving did not mince words. They needed a three-year commitment. They would offer me $34,000 a year to co-anchor the six o'clock news with Dan and to be a field reporter on Mike Kettenring's news team. This was double my Orlando salary. More importantly, it was an opportunity to swim in a much larger pond.

. . .

How do you tell your current boss, who hired you out of obscurity only four months ago, that you are "leaving to pursue other interests"? (Yes, that's what I said.) How you do it is, you walk into your general manager's office, tell him to his face, and then sit there for as long as they want to keep you so you can hear all about the investment they have made in you and how you are betraying everyone at the station by leaving after only four months. And you sit there and say nothing, because they are right.

I sat there and endured a litany of character assassinations and threats of legal action. I felt like a jerk. I *was* a jerk. But I had not signed a contract with the Orlando station. There was little they could do. I gave two weeks' notice.

I was a pariah. Had Orlando station owner Walter Windsor not plucked me out of obscurity in Raleigh, Irving Waugh never would have seen me on that television in his hotel room, and this job in Nashville never would have existed. It was dishonorable behavior. It felt ungrateful. It was also the right decision, both in the moment and in retrospect, because it aligned with the purpose that guided me out of my pup tent and the persistence that kept me out of it for good.

"Young man, you're coming to work for me." Those eight little words had just manifested in a stunning piece of good fortune. One that would set into motion, within a couple of years, both my broadcasting and music careers, on a scale I only ever dreamed of but never thought truly possible.

Chapter 11

Fight or Flight

August 6, 2015

From my propped-up position in my oversized hospital bed (at six-foot-six, I could not get comfortable in a bed made for normal human beings), I was presently "Live in Concert!" with two rows of doctors and nurses in front of me.

What an audience! Standing room only. Lots of bright spotlights. Someone hand me a piano, please.

A portable X-ray machine was being wheeled in to my right. With its giant feet and head, it resembled one of the all-terrain scouts in *The Empire Strikes Back*. It was there to determine if the nasal gastric tube (NG tube) that the doctors wanted to insert through my nose in order to clear the ileus in my intestines made its way properly into my stomach.

And yes, it's as awful as it sounds.

The tube was six feet long. Its job was to suction out the extra air and material that I may otherwise vomit because of the backup in my intestines. In its packaging, the NG tube looks innocent enough, like a French horn made out of flexible PVC tubing. Out of its packaging, though, and in the hands of a licensed health-care professional intent on inserting it into your nose, it looks like something out of the *Saw* movies.

Fight-or-flight hormones started flooding my brain. I imagined Michael Crichton punching up this scene for an episode of *ER*. Or, more aptly, that scene from *Rosemary's Baby* where Mia Farrow exclaims, "This isn't a dream! This is really happening!" The doctors weren't helping either. They wouldn't give me drugs for my anxiety because that would make the bowel paralysis worse, and if I continued to wretch from the nausea, I would likely rupture the surgery sutures inside my abdomen and bleed internally. I began to panic again. My senses were on fire. I was now hyper-aware of my predicament.

The pitying look on the RN's face as she approached me with the NG tube spoke volumes.

"Try to relax, Mr. Tesh," she said. "Please keep swallowing. You need to swallow the tube."

Connie's voice cut through the chaos in my mind. "Just look at me, John. Keep your eyes here. I love you, honey." I searched her face. Had I forgotten that her eyes were this green? They looked tired from all the nights sleeping on that tiny couch by the window, but right then they were so brilliantly green. I recalled the hours and hours of her reading Scripture to me. It reminded me that I wanted to live, and that I had to fight.

It was a beautiful moment of serenity. But it was short-lived.

My fear response was in overdrive. I reached up to yank out the tube. Someone held my arm down to stop me. I fought with them. The heart rate and telemetry monitor seemed to be ear-splittingly loud. Blood was pouring from my left nostril where the NG tube had pierced my nasal passage. And then the room seemed strangely bright. Everyone seemed to be moving much slower now. The loud beeping from the monitors was barely audible. It had been replaced by a rushing sound in my ears, like the sound you hear as a kid when you put that big shell up to your ear.

"Do you hear the ocean?" my mom would ask.

Before I could answer, I was back in the moment, bleeding, gagging.

Through tears, I mouthed the words to my loving partner that neither one of us will ever forget: "Kill me. Please, kill me."

Chapter 12

Homeless Once More

Anchoring the news for WSM-TV in Nashville with Dan Miller and Pat Sajak was like being on TV with your family. Dan was eleven years my senior, and he made it easy to follow his lead. I was comfortable subordinating myself to his elder statesmanship and avuncular style, and he seemed comfortable in the role of mentor to me. Dan and I also shared a passion for music. I discovered this one night between the six and eleven o'clock newscasts. I usually spent those hours banging on an old upright piano in the WSM production studios, practicing and composing music. One night Dan walked in holding a vintage Autoharp, also known as a zither. He strummed the thing like he was Pete Townshend from the Who. Our jam sessions ended up becoming a nightly ritual. Dan taught me Merle Haggard songs; I taught him Beatles tunes.

When I wasn't on the news set with Dan and Pat, I worked under the direction and instruction of our news director, Mike Kettenring. Kettenring was exacting, merciless, and he suffered no foolishness. Each morning he would meet with the reporting staff, distributing written critiques of the previous evening's newscast. He would then play a VHS recording of the broadcast, all the while commenting, gesturing, and scribbling his reviews on a giant whiteboard. Every reporting, interviewing, writing, and editing technique I use today has come from the tutelage of Mike Kettenring.

In 1975, he coached me through an investigation of the Nashville

...e codes. The city had been plagued by fatalities following numerous fires in newly constructed apartment complexes. The builders were allegedly creating fire hazards in the crawl spaces joining the apartments in an attempt to save money. Our reporting began with clandestine, Watergate-like "deep throat" tips from inspectors inside the fire marshal's office, hinting that the building approvals were being signed off on without the proper inspections. When our series of reports began airing, WSM received threats of legal action, demanding that we reveal our sources. Kettenring was steadfast in his support of protecting my sources, even under enormous pressure from station management to back down, and like always, he was right.

Ultimately, under pressure the fire marshal stepped down, the Nashville fire codes were rewritten, and the series won the station and me an Associated Press award for Investigative Reporting. Indeed, Mike Kettenring's unyielding dedication to the importance of investigative journalism and his unflinching persistence throughout the story lifted WSM-TV News into a realm reserved for the likes of *60 Minutes*, and it opened the door a year later for the next chapter in my career as a correspondent for WCBS News back home in New York.

Whenever I reported or produced a story at WSM that I believed might be exceptional, I archived it on three-quarter-inch tape. It wasn't that I was unhappy with my job in Nashville. Working with news director Mike Kettenring was transformative. However, I still felt the constant pull toward even more. I had my sights set on a top-ten news market.

Broadcasting magazine frequently published stories about award-winning news operations. One of them was WCBS-TV in New York City. In the story the writer singled out the news director, Ed Joyce, as a force of innovation and journalistic excellence. I couldn't tell you exactly why, but I knew that I knew that I knew that I would, somehow, get an interview with Mr. Joyce. So one Friday evening, when the WSM staff had gone home for the weekend following the 11:00 p.m. news, I stayed behind, grabbed three of my three-quarter-inch archival videotapes, switched on the CMX editing deck, and began piecing together a compilation of my work. Before dawn, I had a new six-minute demo tape.

On that tape were excerpts of my investigative reports; snippets of me anchoring the news with Dan and Pat; and live interviews with politicians during election coverage. (Oddly enough, the video of the election coverage included me reporting from Republican headquarters with a nineteen-year-old Oprah Winfrey seen over my shoulder, filing her own live report for rival news station WLAC-TV.) I typed out a personal letter to Ed Joyce, shoved the demo tape and the letter into my backpack, and pointed my Datsun 240Z back home to my apartment in Bellevue. Within three weeks of sending off the tape to New York, I received a letter from Ed Joyce.

I was very familiar with form rejection letters. They always started out the same way. You could tell your name was inserted using a different typewriter, or even a ballpoint pen. Except this was different. This appeared to be a personal letter from Mr. Joyce himself. In it, he mentioned how much he enjoyed the tape and suggested that we meet at the broadcast center in New York City at my earliest convenience.

What?! This was not a rejection letter.

I reread the letter from the beginning. This was not just a friendly meet-and-greet either. This was an itinerary! Mr. Joyce's assistant would take care of my travel arrangements. I should be prepared with proper attire to do what he called an "audition" on the news set at WCBS in New York. I would spend three days with Mr. Joyce, general manager Neil Derrough, assignment editor Donna Ziede, and several producers.

The audition went remarkably well and on August 4, 1976, I walked through the CBS Broadcast Center security desk in New York City wearing my CBS personnel badge for the first time. It was my inaugural day as a correspondent for WCBS News. I was barely twenty-four years old, and the youngest reporter in the building. If I had known then what I know today about the scope of the job I had signed on for, I am confident I would have run out of the CBS building like my hair was on fire.

This was CBS's flagship local news operation, after all. They employed *famous* reporters, with names my parents recognized. There was John Stossel, the decorated consumer reporter, who would become my close friend and who would soon advance to ABC's *20/20* news magazine with Barbara Walters. There was Dave Marash, veteran print and radio journalist. Marash was a musician and jazz music aficionado whom I soon bonded with as we sat front-row center in after-hours jazz clubs after the news. There was legendary WCBS anchorman Jim Jensen, known for his booming, authoritative voice, whom I used to watch from our TV when I was a first grader on Long Island. And now I would be working on the same news team with them? The bullpen of news reporters, anchors, writers, and producers was no less formidable. It was a who's who of remarkable talent.

If you were fortunate enough to catch HBO's *Newsroom* series, then you can imagine this scene. In the first moment when the news director, Ed Joyce, introduced me around the newsroom, there's no better way to describe this experience than to just say it was like "Welcome to Fido's first day at the dog park!" At the sight of Mr. Joyce, everyone looked up from their typewriters, acknowledged their boss, scanned me, sniffed the air for the scent of fear, and then got back to business.

I bonded easily with another recent hire, newswriter Andrew Heyward, who was two years my senior. Heyward graduated from Harvard College in 1972 with a BA in history and literature and was elected to Phi Beta Kappa. Not all that long out of a pup tent, I decided to keep my résumé to myself for a while. Heyward would go on to become president of CBS News, but not before he, like Nashville's Mike Kettenring, would closely mentor me as a newswriter and reporter-producer.

I began my employment at WCBS at the nexus of what was known as "participatory journalism"—a bit of an oxymoron—where reporters were encouraged to insert themselves into the story to add more drama to the broadcast and perhaps a more powerful connection to the viewer. The trend created giant news personalities. One of the most successful was Geraldo Rivera, a local reporter at rival WABC-Eyewitness News.

Geraldo's exposé on the Willowbrook State School shocked New York City—and the world, for that matter. Willowbrook housed over six thousand intellectually disabled people despite having a maximum capacity of four thousand. In early 1972, Geraldo conducted a series of investigations at Willowbrook uncovering deplorable conditions, including overcrowding, abhorrent sanitary facilities, and physical and sexual abuse of residents by members of the school's staff. Parents who watched the exposé had been unaware of what was happening to the children they'd admitted to Willowbrook. They had placed their family members at the school to receive care that they could not provide. Now they were watching along with television viewers as Geraldo and his camera crew marched through the halls of the school revealing unspeakable atrocities.

The exposé, *Willowbrook: The Last Great Disgrace*, garnered national attention and won Rivera a Peabody Award. He later appeared on the nationally televised *Dick Cavett Show* with his film of patients at the school. As a result of the overcrowding and inhumane conditions, a class-action lawsuit was filed against the state of New York by the parents of five thousand residents of Willowbrook in federal court on March 17, 1972. The political reaction to this report led to the enactment of the Americans with Disabilities Act.

Geraldo continued to build a reputation as a champion of the people. He was famous for "going in rolling," and he and a film crew regularly ambushed landlords, street vendors, and politicians, browbeating them with a barrage of questions while his camera crew recorded their awkward, and at times violent, reactions. By the time I began my work at CBS, Geraldo's persona had grown to near absurdity.

I recall one afternoon when all of us television, radio, and print journalists were rushing to the scene of a hostage crisis only to find the perpetrator screaming for Geraldo from a third-story window. Much to the dismay and horror of the local police detectives, the hostage-taker invited Geraldo up to interview him. Geraldo did the interview and then walked the criminal down to the waiting officers. All of us journalists acted horrified, too, although I remember it more as jealousy if I'm being honest.

. . .

Not to be outdone, my fellow TV news reporters and I inserted ourselves in more than a few news stories during this trend in the late 1970s.

When a landlord in the South Bronx was accused of limiting steam-heat to his renters, I went and spent the night with one of the families in the building. The next day I proudly demonstrated on camera how I couldn't brush my teeth because the toothpaste was frozen solid.

I ran the NYC Marathon carrying a camera and broadcast my run live. Painful.

I got shot at during a nine-hour siege covering the JFK bus hijacking story in July of '77.

Later that month, I covered the legendary blackout of 1977, whispering my reports into a microphone from the bathroom stall of a Western Auto store, my cameraman risking both our lives by recording the rioting and looting through a crack in the bathroom door. Over three thousand people were arrested, and the city's already crowded prisons were so overburdened that some suggested reopening the recently condemned Manhattan Detention Complex to accommodate them.

Then there was my "Con Man Cabbies: A Special Report!" with camera crew Steve Jackson and Howard Raymond shooting video through one-way glass in a white van. I posed as a Swedish businessman; I had been a Swedish exchange student in high school, so I knew a few Swedish words. We began our investigation on a tip that some New York City cab drivers were weighing their passengers halfway through the trip from the JFK Airport into the city. Rumor had it they would pull their cab over somewhere in the middle of Queens, open the trunk, take out a bathroom scale, and then weigh the passenger while the passenger held their luggage. The crooked cabbies then created some cockamamie formula for the fare increase, based on the number on the scale. No cab driver had weighed me, but nearly one-fourth of the cabbies did overcharge me once they heard my fake Swedish accent. After we ran the three-part series, I couldn't get a taxi for six months. I was a marked man.

One of the biggest stories I covered was the Son of Sam manhunt (when we began our coverage, he was called the .44 Caliber Killer). David Berkowitz killed six people and wounded seven others between the middle of 1976 and July 1977, before being arrested in August. As the number of victims increased, Berkowitz was able to elude the biggest police manhunt in the history of New York City. He left letters that mocked the police and promised more killings. The killing spree terrorized our New York City viewers. One of his attacks occurred not far from where my crew and I were covering another story. The police scanner in our news van erupted with the news that the .44 Caliber Killer had struck again.

. . .

I am now on the two-way radio with the assignment desk at CBS. Nightshift editor Andy Meppen is relaying the location of the attack. It's less than a half mile away from our location. Cameraman Dennis Drinnon is already strapping on his battery belt and pulling the giant Ikegami news camera onto his shoulder. My heart begins to race as I realize we are the first news team to arrive. It looks as if there are a hundred police cars on the scene. Officers are running everywhere, ostensibly trying to find the trail of the killer. Out of the corner of my eye I see a young man sitting on a ledge. His head is in his hands. He is covered in what appears to be blood. I motion to Dennis to roll the camera and switch on his light.

Dennis looks at me with surprise. He's clearly uncomfortable. "Uh, hey, John . . ."

Too late. My hand and the WCBS microphone are in John Diehl's face. I make a spinning motion with my arm, cueing Dennis to roll his camera. I can barely get my questions out, consumed by the adrenaline in my bloodstream. This is a huge scoop. I am the first reporter on the scene, interviewing a victim of the .44 Caliber Killer! John Diehl is now sobbing as I pepper him with questions—about his girlfriend, about his first thought when he heard the gunshot, whether he saw the killer, whether he was frightened. His hands are bright red. There is blood and human tissue in his lap—pieces of his girlfriend's skull. He's now crying so hard I can't understand his answers. And then there's a hand on my arm. It's Dennis. He's doused the blinding Frezzi light on his camera. He has stopped recording. Over my shoulder I see two very angry detectives hastily approaching. One is a woman. She shakes her head at me in disgust as she wraps a blanket around John Diehl's shoulders and begins to comfort him.

"Leave, now. This is an active crime scene."

Like a slap in the face to someone in uncontrollable hysterics, reality sets in. Here is where a paradigm shift becomes painfully real, particularly when it occurs in the context of doing what you think you were put here to do. If I had just taken a deep breath and reacted to the pause cued by my cameraman, I might have acted responsibly. I would have seen this man as a human being, suffering horribly. Instead, I am consumed by self-inflicted shame. In a crucial moment where I had an opportunity to act with compassion, I let pride and selfish ambition rule my decision.

On Jan. 29, 1977, in the brick plaza in front of the Forest Hills Inn, Christine Freund, 26, sat in the car with her boyfriend, John Diehl, 30. They had just seen a movie up the street and now a pudgy guy with a wool watch cap on ran up to the car and held a gun out in both hands and fired three shots through the passenger window and into Christine Freund's head. She died. [John survived.][1]

. . .

Dennis and I drove the interview tape back to the broadcast center in silence. The interview aired on the newscast, and I was congratulated for my aggressive reporting work. But at what cost? As I write this, the memory plays like a movie in my head. It's easy to understand why that awful decision has remained with me for these forty-plus years. It was one I worked to rectify, both personally and professionally.

The year 1977 was not the ideal time to be living or working in New York City but it was the perfect time to be a street reporter. The city and its people were coming apart at the seams. It was painful to watch but plentiful to report on. "Slow news day" was never heard in our newsroom. My fellow reporters and I were filing at least two stories a day, seven days a week. There was the massive financial downturn. There was rising poverty and inequality levels, paranoia about the Son of Sam murders, and the debauchery of Studio 54. In the summer of 1977 fires burned down much of the Bronx. Then hip-hop music began to rise from the ashes. The looting of music stores during the blackout allowed people who couldn't afford turntables and mixers to pick up the equipment they needed to become DJs. All of these things took hold of the city and, in lockstep with high crime rates, a widespread belief emerged among its people that New York City was in irreversible decline.

By the end of the 1970s, more than a million people had left the city. *Fled* is a more apt verb. This ultimately became a population loss that would not be recouped for another twenty-five years. To quote Jonathan Mahler, the author of *The Bronx Is Burning*, "The clinical term for it, *fiscal crisis*, didn't approach the raw reality. Spiritual crisis was more like it."[2]

This miasma of circumstances also made it a very bad time to be a homeless person in New York City. (Is there ever a good time?) Out-of-work white males in particular, often in very bad health and many with alcohol and drug addictions, made up a big part of the growing homeless community. There were more than fifteen thousand people in the city's shelters by the end of 1977, but most of the homeless were confined to "skid rows," with the Bowery as New York's homeless hub. In the Bowery, men would be found sleeping in the streets, the subway, or tiny, windowless, ninety-cents-a-night hotel rooms. Police stations also became the shelter for hundreds of homeless people on any given night. And to make matters even worse, the city's financial predicament meant that there was little money available to expand any meaningful services to the homeless.

This story needed to be told and I felt the need to be the one to tell it.

I pitched my idea to the news desk. They were, of course, familiar with the data and agreed to a two-part series in the dead of winter in 1978. Andrew Heyward, now an associate producer, had what was, at the time, a novel, radical idea, even for this era of participatory journalism. Cameraman/documentarian Steve Jackson and soundman Howard Raymond would join me to film *John Tesh: Homeless in NYC*. We would take the audience on a vérité trip through the plight of the homeless by spending three nights in subzero temperatures with some of those unfortunate enough to have missed out on one of the limited number of shelter beds.

It took three hours of makeup and many tubes of glue and charcoal to apply my homeless disguise—beard, ratty wig, and tattered clothing—but eventually, and with Jackson and Raymond once again recording behind the one-way glass of a van, I began walking the streets of the Bowery. There was only one problem, at least in the beginning: I had no acting experience, so my first attempt to wander the streets was laughable. Even the homeless men shook their heads at me: a shivering six-foot-six, 210-pound man with good posture. They were readily able to spot my masquerade.

Jackson: Tesh. You look like a friggen tight end for the Jets!

This all changed, however, once I purchased a pint of rot-gut Mad Dog 20/20 wine and chugged half of it before pouring the rest over my clothing. I now stumbled, smelled, and spoke in character. As I shuffled through the Bowery, my appearance and "walking dead" gait were horrifying to anyone who dared look in my direction. I begged for cash. People changed sides of the street. I attempted to enter one of the shelters. No room. Full.

The footage we took to document my every step was both enlightening and disturbing. For the first time the WCBS audience would see homelessness through the eyes of the homeless. It was also heartbreaking personally, as I befriended dozens of homeless men and women on the streets, knowing that I would soon be returning to the warmth and safety of my Upper West Side apartment. I was fully aware that, in this withering cold, at least one of them wouldn't make it through the night. I bought more MD 20/20 and shared it with my new friends. The burn of the alcohol generated warmth, if only for a moment.

It's hard to find a hero in a news report like this. But one showed up nonetheless. I'm sorry I cannot remember his name or his badge number. He knows who he is. After I got turned away from two shelters, I walked up the front steps of Manhattan's Seventh Police Precinct, Lower East Side. I was a mess. I smelled horrible. By now I was exhausted and nearly frostbitten. The temperature was three degrees. As I approached the front entrance of the station, the sergeant raised his hand, motioning for me to stop. With my wireless microphone hidden inside my coat, Jackson and Raymond recorded my conversation as I told the officer how I was turned away from the overcrowded shelters, and I asked him if he could find me a warm place to lie down. If not, I would surely freeze, I told him.

Without hesitation, the police sergeant acted with compassion. He told me he would find a space for me in his precinct house to spend the night out of the cold, if only for one night. He reached out to take my hand. I hesitated. Instead of taking his hand, I held mine up in protest, then motioned over my shoulder for the crew to open the sliding door of the van, revealing their presence. I explained to the officer that our goal with the hidden camera and personal immersion was to reveal the true plight of the city's homeless population.

The officer agreed to answer a few questions. I spent the next forty minutes recording his answers, which were both forthright and chilling. He was risking a reprimand from his superiors—offering opinions to a TV news crew was way outside an officer's protocol—but his honesty and concern added gravity to the pictures we would broadcast later that week. They also reinforced how I had come to feel over those three frigid days, and they helped to make me feel just slightly less ashamed about the way I'd treated poor John Diehl in service of my own unrelenting personal ambition.

The homelessness series, complete with a music score I composed in my home recording studio, won an Emmy award for me and WCBS, but most importantly, it raised awareness for the epidemic of lost, suffering souls in the city. The series also became part of a new conversation in city hall about the lack of homeless shelters in the Lower East Side. Still, since my news report in 1978 the homeless population in New York City has only gotten worse. By early 2019, there were more than sixty-three thousand people sleeping in the New York City municipal shelter system—up 43 percent from just ten years earlier. Nearly four thousand more sleep on the street, in the subway system, or in other public spaces.[3] It's a problem that is not going away.

My most poignant remembrances of my evenings on the cold Manhattan sidewalks were the times when I felt like a dead man walking. Not human. It was the way people looked upon me. When eyes met, it was only for a moment. But that was enough. No one should feel that. I was transformed by those nights in the Bowery. To many I was a ghoulish figure to be avoided at all costs. To my "peers" on the street I was a brother in suffering.

Chapter 13

Guerrilla Television

The Tour de France

It's 1981, 11:00 p.m. WCBS news producer Andy Meppen yells across the newsroom, "Hey, Tesh, the president of CBS Sports is on the phone for you. Where do you want it?"

"Send it to the wall phone," I say.

I had stumbled through reading a few sports scores on the Sunday evening local newscast. Did I get a score wrong? Why is this guy calling me?

"Hello?"

"Hello, John, it's Van Gordon Sauter. I'm the new president of the CBS Sports Network. I'm here with our executive producer, Terry O'Neil. We'd like to talk to you about maybe coming over here with us."

"I'm sorry. You mean sportscasting?"

"Something like that," Sauter says somewhat coyly. "We are putting together a new team here, and we'd like to hire some folks with journalism credentials and really go after ABC's *Wide World of Sports* with some bigger World Championship–type events. And besides, you've been at WCBS for almost six years and you're looking a little bored on the air lately; maybe you'd like a fresh challenge."

Excuse me? I don't know what bothers me more, that he thinks my broadcasts are boring or that he can see something I cannot. Bored? Me? I am in New York City!

O'Neil clears his throat and immediately jumps in.

"Listen John, we love your work and we think you'd be great at doing some sideline reporting for CBS Sports and perhaps some of our event coverage."

"Uh, thanks, Terry, but you should probably know that I know very little about sports reporting. I can't name three NBA teams."

O'Neil laughs at this. "I get it," he says, "but the events we are talking about are usually very unfamiliar to TV audiences. We've watched quite a few tapes of your live interviews, and we think this could really work. What if we at least sit down and get to know each other. How is tomorrow? Tenth floor at Black Rock?"

Black Rock was the headquarters for most of the CBS network brass. While the production studios, where I was, were in a low-slung brick building on West Fifty-Seventh Street over in Hell's Kitchen, Black Rock was a shiny tower down on Sixth Avenue in the heart of midtown.

"Uh. Okay," I said.

Click.

Why doesn't anybody in the business say goodbye?!

I didn't know it at the time, but aside from owning the broadcast rights to a number of major sporting events—pro basketball, golf, US Open Tennis—much of CBS Sports' other programming was an embarrassment for the network. While ABC, with Jim McKay as host, covered figure skating, skiing, and gymnastics, CBS was broadcasting World's Strongest Man, Mr. Universe, and Major League Fishing (not that there's anything wrong with fishing).

Terry O'Neil had been hired away from ABC Sports to revamp the programming and change the CBS reputation. Terry knew that I did not have experience doing live play-by-play sports announcing, but he felt he could add some gravitas to the sideline reporting and to the events themselves if he hired guys like me and Pat O'Brien out of the news reporter ranks. His vision for what I could add personally to the anthology events was far beyond anything I could have imagined for myself. Terry and CBS Sports president Sauter had obviously had a sidebar conversation with my superiors at WCBS before coming to me. It was all in the family.

In the middle of all of this, my dad was diagnosed with stage 4 lung cancer. Two weeks prior to the meeting with Terry, test results confirmed that the cancer had spread to his lymphatic system. I had been flying to North Carolina each weekend trying to help my mom, and now Terry was talking about a job that would send me all over the world. I remember a strange conversation with my dad when we were alone in his hospital room. I was crying pretty hard and he put a hand on my shoulder and said these words: "Don't worry, Johnny, you won't catch this."

It's not at all what I had been thinking. Nonetheless, what a strange (albeit false) prophecy.

In any case, during the next four months I was an emotional, unstable wreck. My dad succumbed to the cancer at the age of sixty-three and I began my new professional life, traveling to a new country every other week, and I rushed into a proposal and then marriage to my on-again, off-again girlfriend.

I had said yes to the job offer when I met with Terry that day at Black Rock for several reasons. First, I was taken by Terry's experience, intelligence, and vision. Next, if you're looking at a career ladder in the world of broadcasting, the CBS Network is right at the top. Terry also seemed interested in my background as a music composer and saw it as an asset in the assignments he had in mind for me. And finally, Sauter was right, sort of. I was getting bored—of reading the news, of racing to fires, of covering murders. These things had satisfied my performative streak, and they quenched my thirst for being in the center of things, live and in person, but fundamentally I wasn't creating anything. I was just catastrophizing. And when that happens, two things are possible: either it gnaws a hole in your spirit, or you become numb to it. I was becoming numb, which from the outside looks very much like boredom.

. . .

But Terry O'Neil's most masterful move was not his sales pitch. It was pairing me with incredibly talented producers for whom creativity was the rule, not the exception: John Faratzis, David Dinkins, Ed Goren, David Winner, and David Michaels. I found out later how much Terry fought for us, particularly Michaels and me, when the old-school producers and directors at CBS rolled their eyes at our documentary-style approach to sports broadcasting, but O'Neil was no fool. He somehow knew that the match of Michaels and me could produce groundbreaking television.

There was never a time during my five to six years at CBS Sports when I wasn't challenged, when I wasn't stretched beyond my abilities. One weekend I'd be covering downhill skiing in Wengen, Switzerland, the next I'd be broadcasting the World Speed Skating Championships in Karl-Marx-Stadt, East Germany. There was the Ironman Triathlon, World Figure Skating, World Gymnastics Championships, and the US Open Tennis Championships. I put in hundreds of hours of research, not only learning about the athletes, but also trying to make sense of the rules. I felt like I was studying for the SAT each weekend. But no event was more challenging than the legendary Tour de France bike race. It was where Terry O'Neil's belief in me as a writer, announcer, and especially, later on, as a composer was put to the ultimate test, and where it began to mightily reshape my life anew, once again—this time back toward music.

• • •

It's 2:00 a.m. We're in Bordeaux, France. In the corner of my eye I can see four giant reel-to-reel, one-inch videotape machines spinning wildly back and forth. They are searching for in-cues and out-cues of cycling footage sent to them by the CMX video-editing console. The smells of coffee and stale French cigarettes are punctuated by the body odor of a half-dozen men who haven't slept in days. This is the CBS editing truck. A truck like this is normally parked outside an NFL football stadium or a golf match. Today the truck is perched in the center of a centuries-old cobblestone square in Bordeaux. We are at the halfway mark of the 1982 Tour de France bike race, and it is the job of the men inside this truck to produce what amounts to a two-hour documentary about the previous week's racing.

Our makeshift broadcast compound here in Bordeaux is ringed by handcrafted shoemakers, elegant boutiques, tea cafés, and countless bars and restaurants. The quiet of the town is presently being shattered by the persistent chugging of our power generator. Our white truck, with the giant CBS Sports logo, presents as an alien spacecraft that has crash-landed in an unsuspecting French village. From my position inside, in the far-left recording booth, if I stretch my neck I can see a small piece of the cobblestone street outside that we are blighting. It's much easier to see the video output of the master recording machine that is showing me a video recording of hundreds of miles of French countryside with cyclists snaking through it. On this monitor I can view the edits and hear sound effects and the music score I composed on my synthesizers to accompany these riders' arduous journey.

My eyes are bleary, but I can still see that this week's coverage has begun to take shape. When the program is fully realized, it will be transmitted from our truck in Bordeaux to a satellite. That signal will then be relayed to another satellite, which will send it to a giant dish on the roof of the CBS Broadcast Center on Fifty-Seventh Street in New York City. In seven and a half hours, Master Control in New York will lock on to our signal and ultimately turn over the entire network of CBS local stations to this smelly van full of ragtag, exhausted humans.

As I scan the men and the equipment to my right, I feel like someone should call New York and tell them to have a movie rerun ready to go. I'm certain that we have little chance of having even one hour of Tour de France programming completed by 3:30 p.m. eastern standard time. The stress is showing on producer David Michaels's face. It would be awfully simple to use the French video coverage of the race, dub over their footage to our machines each week, and then have me and fellow announcer Phil Liggett do some cursory play-by-play announcing. We would just tell the audience who was in the lead and who the key athletes were, and call it a day. Boom. Done. Simple. Red wine for everyone.

• • •

That was not something Michaels was going to do. He was a documentary filmmaker at heart and the crew he had assembled for this event, including me, revered him as one of the best storytellers in the sports world. And Le Tour, as it is called by the French, is a heck of a story. For years, it has been described by American journalists as "the Super Bowl of Cycling," but that's just a cute little euphemism that disguises this monster of a race. In actual fact, the Tour de France in 1982 was twenty-three Super Bowls contested over twenty-four days. It included seventeen six-hour races with seventeen different finish lines, interspersed with six separate twenty- to sixty-minute sprint races at breakneck speeds. It was 2,200 miles of racing, all of it staged during the month of July, in the French summer heat. The only thing that's been able to stop the Tour de France since its founding in 1903? Two world wars.

When CBS vice president Peter Tortorici and executive producer Terry O'Neil purchased the US broadcast rights to the Tour, they had a vision for how CBS could bring that story to life and elevate the sport of cycling to something Americans would be interested in watching—and not just for the whizzing bicycles and crashes involving athletes no one in the US had ever heard of. The challenge for those of us in the trenches wasn't so much finding the story that Tortorici and O'Neil (and Michaels, to his credit) knew would change Americans' perceptions; it was turning six days and more than eighty hours of weekly race footage into a two-hour movie each week for four straight weeks. It was a daunting task.

Fortunately, I had David's unique formula for covering the Tour de France to follow. His approach, while straightforward and later emulated by broadcasters at all of the sports networks, was incredibly difficult to execute. David's process opened up numerous creative possibilities for me on the music composition side. Instead of merely "following the leader" during the race, Michaels wanted to find the Rocky vs. Apollo Creed story each week. He wanted to find the tortoise vs. the hare, the Cain and Abel within a given team, the man vs. the mountain, the little engine that could, the dark horse.

"Who is the underdog?" David would ask. Why did we want him to win? What were the stories in the *grupetto*, the back of the pack? Each of these stories had a different tone, a different pace, a different feel. The music required to convey the appropriate emotion to the audience, to make them understand, was wildly different from story to story, rider to rider. It was heaven for a composer. David Michaels's approach—up close and personal—was originally made popular by Jim McKay and ABC's *Wide World of Sports*. It was a boon for my creative side, but it was a nightmare for my practical side. Applying this storytelling technique to the Olympic coverage is one thing—you literally have years to shoot those personal background pieces—but in a race that unfolds before you each day in France, you have only hours to create biographies for the key figures. The enormity of it all, jammed into such a tiny temporal space, made your head spin.

. . .

Before David Michaels edits each of the twelve- to fifteen-minute television segments of the Tour de France, he writes out an outline. Then, without music or narration, he edits the video segments, going through in his mind what the story, narration, and music (tempo specifically) will be. With associate director Victor Frank and his tape operators listening intently, Michaels calls out the shots he needs to tell the story, and the team frantically scans their notes to see which cameraman or helicopter pilot has recorded those shots during the race coverage. On most days, Michaels is on the back of a motorcycle, shooting with a video camera so he knows what has transpired during the day's competition. In a perfect world, armed with that firsthand knowledge, David and his team would complete the video edits for the weekly show twelve hours before broadcast. Then he and I could sit and watch the rough cut ("spot it") while he offered copywriting suggestions and I took notes.

During this time he would also switch "creative languages" and go on to describe the styles of music he wanted. David was an orchestral bass player in high school and had great facility speaking musical language:

"I hear a big orchestra hit here!" he would say.
"I hear a haunting cello line just as Greg LeMond comes out of the
     Pyrenees fog during the uphill climb."
"Make it a 'devilish symphony.'"
"Can we just do some ostinato piano notes that match Bernard
     Hinault's pedaling tempo when he is chasing down Greg?"

This is moviemaking, and although most writers and composers get more time for production than a rapid-fire conversation over a rough cut, David would say, "It is what it is. We're making movies here."

I certainly would've loved to have twelve hours to do my work—what a gift that would've been—but that was not going to happen that day. We were far behind schedule. I knew full well that if I waited for the video team's rough cut, I'd be dead in the water. I knew that if I didn't somehow outthink David, the fate of the entire broadcast would, at the eleventh hour, fall squarely on me. Of the four essential production elements that go into a documentary approach to filmmaking—pictures, writing, narration, music score—three of them were my responsibility.

This challenge was overwhelming at times, but David's faith in me was a powerful elixir.

. . .

Right now I am writing this chapter on a souped-up MacBook Pro laptop computer. On this computer I have the Logic Pro X music application loaded with seven hundred gigabytes of sound samples from three different orchestras, including a massive orchestral percussion library. I can import video directly into this laptop and in fifteen minutes I can create a realistic symphonic score, perfectly synchronized to picture. I can even email it to you, if you'd like. Then I can plug my Sennheiser 416 dialog microphone into this computer and add narration to that picture and score. While I'm watching and mixing in Logic, I can use Google Docs to write the narration. As I type, that narration will simultaneously appear on my iPhone, which I can then read from while I'm using the laptop to record and mix. In 1982 none of these futuristic tools existed.

. . .

Before me in the truck in Bordeaux are two giant E-MU systems keyboards known as emulators. They are the very first generation of sampling music keyboards that can emulate acoustic instruments. I have emulations of orchestral brass and stringed instruments as well as drum kits, basses, and guitars. The challenge, however, is that the emulator can load only one sound at a time from a floppy disk, and each one takes two to three minutes to load. That waiting time adds up quickly.

To my left is a four-track reel-to-reel recorder. I load it up and start composing with the emulators. After I lay down tracks to each piece of music, I mix the music down in one pass and transfer the audio to the video team.

Then I grab a chair next to Michaels in the control room and start writing my narration for the first three completed segments while keeping an eye on the other segments he is currently working on. The control room is now an ear-shattering cacophony of spinning tape machines, shouts of time cues, and music cues in rewind. It is 7:30 a.m. in France, but the clock above the video switcher is set to eastern time in the US. It's 2:30 p.m. The feed from our truck is "Live!" in exactly one hour, and we are nowhere near close to finishing the program.

Because of my twelve years as a local news anchor and reporter, I am familiar with breaking news in a live situation. There were many times on WCBS when I'd be reading a news story on live television. The producer would hand me a piece of news copy just off camera while the other anchor was delivering a story. Typically, I'd have sixty seconds to read the story "cold," trying to look far enough ahead so that I wouldn't be tripped up by a typo or say something that could be libelous.

After three or four of these per broadcast, I learned how to go into a kind of trance, slow down my delivery, and use an economy of words. It's clear that I will be calling upon all of my guerrilla TV training to provide the live narration and music cues (along with the live audio mix) to the satellite.

Right now I'm trying hard not to fully embrace the enormity of what's expected of us all in this TV production truck, thirty-six hundred miles from the CBS Broadcast Center in New York. When CBS throws the switch in New York, connecting our truck to its network of two hundred local stations, we will control all of the network's programming for a full two hours. In theory, we should finish all of our taped segments, transmit them to the broadcast center, and then they can simply be played back like a normal, two-hour television program. But because we are still editing the last two segments, it's apparent that those won't be ready until it's time to play them live-to-air from our truck.

This is not an ideal scenario for a sports television network, and there was a good amount of screaming on the other end of our phone by the producers in New York who are being stressed out mightily because we are cutting it so close.

Anything could happen from a remote location like this. We could have a power failure, the satellite feed could fail, or I could faint from exhaustion. As the World Clock ticks down toward the 3:30 p.m. eastern debut of our program, Victor Frank counts down our tape operators: "Five, four, three . . . ," then shouts, "Roll video machine one! . . . two, one!" Segment one is now transmitting from our truck to the network. I glance out the tiny window in my booth and see two security guards standing at attention on either side of our power generator. There is a small crowd of locals gathered around a TV monitor that our guys placed outside for them so they could see the coverage. They are holding wine glasses and gesturing wildly as they watch.

As the French revelers look on outside, inside we still have thirty minutes of new program time to complete before 5:00 p.m. eastern. Michaels is giving out more time cues for the final two segments. As he makes each edit, I scribble down ideas for my narration. I've left three long pieces of music cued up in my recording booth. I've tested the microphone signal and I have labeled the audio mixing console.

Michaels is now a ship's captain in a storm, stitching the storylines together for the final segments.

It's almost time. Michaels has completed the video edits for the last two segments. He now transitions from producer to live-TV director. I have my production headset on. In my right ear I will hear my voice as I read and ad-lib the narration while at the same time mixing the music score underneath. In my left ear will be Michaels, counting me in and out of each transition as the shots change. He will also be whispering ideas into my headset as he leads me through the storyline. With a stopwatch in my left hand and a pen in my right, I'm rehearsing with my notes: adding a word here, placing two Xs where I need to remember to stop talking and bring up the volume of the music track.

Michaels is speaking into my left ear now: "Thirty seconds until we're live to air, Teshman. Deep breath. I'll be with you all the way. If you get stuck, just pause and I'll lead you through it. Fifteen seconds.

I'll cue you, first to roll music and then to start your narration with the opening helicopter shot. Ten seconds!"

One more reflexive glance out my window. The crowd on the cobblestones, sipping wine and watching our coverage, has doubled in size. They look so calm and relaxed. I want to be there. I want to feel like that.

"Five seconds, Tesh. Good luck, everyone. Four, three, two, one. *Cue music. Go John!*"

> *I roll the reel-to-reel tape with my music, lift the volume fader on the mixing console, and lean into the microphone.*

Me: Still eighteen hundred miles until they reach Paris. *This* is the race that will tease and torture its world-class competitors until it finds a champion. I'm John Tesh. Welcome back to the Super Bowl of Cycling. *This* is the Tour de France!

. . .

Today, when you attend one of my live concerts, you'll see and hear evidence of all of this trial-by-fire training in the orchestrations and arrangements I use on stage and the video we project on the giant screen behind me. They are skills I developed while working under David Michaels's direction during not just the Tour de France but the Ironman Triathlons and the Barcelona and Atlanta Olympic Games. I've often said in interviews and speeches that I will forever carry these skills I learned from David wherever I go, whatever I do. Ours was a classic creative partnership.

We had vastly different skill sets, but when combined, they worked together to create unique programming. It was guerrilla television. No job descriptions, just a mission, a common purpose. Here was yet another mentor who had developed a process. Years later this partnership that worked on sports television, that earned numerous Emmy Awards, would work to even greater effect with Michaels beside me at the Red Rocks Amphitheater, ultimately launching my music career and generating millions of dollars for local public television stations.

Chapter 14

My Worst Nightmare

August 7, 2015

According to David Eagleman, a neuroscientist at Baylor College of Medicine, when a person is frightened, an area in their brain called the amygdala becomes more active, recording an extra set of memories that go along with those normally taken care of by other parts of the brain.

"In this way, frightening events are associated with richer and denser memories," Eagleman explained. "The more memory you have of an event, the longer you believe it took."[1]

Twenty-four long hours after an army of Johns Hopkins health-care professionals had pinned me down and snaked an NG tube down my nasal passage and into my organs, the ileus that the tube was meant to clear was gone. The NG tube had done its job and had been removed at some point after I passed out from exhaustion. When I woke, Dr. Schaeffer, my surgeon, was sitting by Connie. Her face was soaked with tears. They told me I'd been asleep for a day, but if they said I'd been asleep for a week, I would have believed them.

Then Dr. Schaeffer held up a piece of paper in front of me. There was a happy face drawn on the top. It was the pathology report on my prostate from the Johns Hopkins lab. Dr. Schaeffer had been explaining to Connie that the surgery had been a success, and that the margins surrounding my cancerous prostate gland were clear of any cancer cells.

He believed I was cancer-free. Connie's tears had been tears of joy.

There was only one "minor" lingering issue that I still had to contend with. My bladder had not yet fully recovered from the procedure, so Dr. Schaeffer could not remove the indwelling urinary catheter. Connie asked how long I would have to keep it in. Dr. Schaeffer gave us every postoperative patient's favorite answer: "I don't know, we'll have to wait and see."

We were not going to wait and see in Baltimore, however. A few days later we were set to fly back to Los Angeles, with one of us sporting a catheter bag strapped to his ankle. We did not complain though. We were both shell-shocked, to be sure, but our feelings were easily eclipsed by the good fortune of the successful surgery and healing. Another few weeks catheterized was a small price to pay.

Eventually, we got the thumbs-up from Dr. Schaeffer to have the catheter removed. For that, we went to a local Los Angeles hospital, where the nurse, despite her best efforts and the best of intentions, could not get the catheter out to save her life. She tugged and tugged at the hose, but it wouldn't budge.

Yep. My worst nightmare.

The nurse called for the doctor, who arrived shortly thereafter and demanded that Connie leave the exam room. She protested. He insisted. I shared the concerned look now on her face.

"Mr. Tesh, this is going to be a little uncomfortable."

Before I could recruit my panic hormones, the doctor put his foot onto the exam table between my legs. He grabbed the catheter hose with both hands and pulled with all his might. There was a popping sound and the catheter flew out and onto the ground.

"Done," said the doctor. He smiled, then turned and exited the room. (Mic drop!)

I sat in stunned silence. No pain. No discomfort. No fainting. I was free. Free of the catheter. Free of cancer.

Chapter 15

ET Phones Home

I was very content in my job at CBS Sports. In 1985, two years into my second three-year deal with the network, every assignment still brought new challenges and unique opportunities for creative writing and music composition. I also had the freedom, along with my producers— David Michaels in particular—to operate in a sort of clandestine *Mission Impossible* scenario. We would receive our event assignments by phone or fax, we'd research and plan our mission, and then we'd hop on a plane and fly first class to some exotic locale—Switzerland, France, Austria, Egypt, Nebraska—where we would work like maniacs for a month straight covering the event before being granted a month off to recover. We rarely spent time talking to network executives back in New York, and we completed our jobs without *ever* having to physically show up at the CBS Sports offices at Black Rock. It truly was my dream job.

The freedom we enjoyed was not without its limitations, however. Covering major sporting events in the 1980s, particularly in Europe, was a study in isolation. Total immersion, in the sensory-deprivation sense of the term. No cellphones yet. No internet, and more often than not, a foreign language to deal with. Constant travel and little sleep, hours upon hours in a dark production truck where day turned into night turned into day again, without one even noticing. With an event like the month-long Tour de France there was a new finish line in a new town every day, which meant we were never in the same hotel at night, which meant trying to stay in regular contact with anyone stateside was next to impossible. In fact, the only time we got messages from home was during the weekend when we'd be connected to the broadcast center in New York by satellite phone and we could check with the office or even our answering machines. Basically, we had to be at work for a chance to connect with home. However, home for me represented the early stages of a failing marriage. I was traveling too much. I was very committed to my career and I had made the decision to propose at a time when I was losing my father to cancer and I was not emotionally available to be a good partner.

During one of those weekend check-ins with New York, I picked up two messages that had been left three days apart by a man named Frank Kelly from Paramount Television in Hollywood. He wanted to know if, upon my return from France, I'd be interested in doing a screen test with the co-host of *Entertainment Tonight*, Mary Hart, in the show's New York City studios. This was, on its face, something I was not at all interested in doing. I had heard of *ET*, but I had never seen the show, and the words "screen test" were more than a little bit foreboding. Plus, I had another year left on my CBS Sports contract, so a serious conversation—or audition, if that's what this was—seemed moot. I could not and would not break my sports contract.

But when I returned to New York that August, there was another message from Frank Kelly waiting for me on my answering machine. Mary Hart was going to be in New York in two days, he said; would I meet her at the Gulf and Western Building (the *ET* East studios) and read some teleprompter with her and have a casual chat? He explained that he and his boss, Lucie Salhany, had seen a tape of me anchoring the news in Nashville, and that they were looking for a newsier approach to their half-hour, nationally syndicated program.

That night I watched *Entertainment Tonight* for the first time. Robb Weller and Mary Hart were hosting. It was a fast-paced half hour with incredible graphics and music. It was hypnotic. Could I see myself in one of those anchor seats? The most famous people I had met to that point rode bicycles and walked on balance beams. But actors and directors? Studio heads? Where would I even begin to know how to talk about them in a way that wasn't immediately obvious to the viewing audience at home that I had no idea what I was doing?

I decided this was probably not for me, but I showed up for the meeting out of professional courtesy and curiosity. The words "Paramount Television" were intriguing. Paramount also made major motion pictures. *Hmm.* Movies need music. So do TV shows, now that I think of it. Maybe there was a side door into composing for film and television.

So a couple of days later, I step out onto the fifteenth floor of the Gulf and Western Building right on Columbus Circle without a care in the world, and it showed. I was wearing cutoff jean shorts and a tank top, my hair nearly reached my shoulders, and I had gained twenty-five pounds over the summer, courtesy of Breton buckwheat pancakes and baguettes at breakfast every morning while over in France. Needless to say, the person whom Mary and her producers met that day looked nothing like the newscaster on the decade-old Nashville news tape they'd watched.

Mary Hart was wonderfully cordial at our meeting. Producer Larry Fleece offered me a seat next to Mary on the set. She was dressed like people I'd seen walking on the red carpet during Oscars coverage. Larry politely suggested that I might like to put on a sport coat. We are close to the same size so he offered me the coat he was wearing. Larry then informed me that the "folks in LA" will be watching Mary and me on a closed-circuit satellite feed. This suddenly felt like one of those recurring nightmares where you are giving a speech but you forgot to put on your clothes. Perhaps I should have taken this more seriously? I apologized to Larry about my appearance, explaining in way too much detail how grueling it was to cover the world's greatest bike race. He was nice. But he had a job to do.

"What we'd like to do, John, is have you and Mary read some copy from yesterday's show and then have Mary ask you a few questions. This shouldn't take long. This is Cynthia. She is our makeup and hair person. You should spend some time with her now."

Very subtle, Larry. Very subtle.

I'll never forget the look on Mary's face when I sat down next to her on the news set. It was somewhere between shock and the look you get on your face when you see something weird that's washed up on the beach. Things got much worse when the cameras rolled. I hadn't read a prompter since my days at WCBS. It's not at all like riding a bike. I was rusty. I stumbled. And I was perhaps a little loud. Mary read a couple of stories about new movie releases. Then she turned and threw to me.

"John?" (That was my cue to start talking.)

I could see my face pop up on the monitor in front of us. The prompter quickly cued up a story on Bruce Springsteen. I dug in. I mean *hard*. Unfortunately for Mary, and the sound engineer, I read what was up on the prompter like I was calling the last ten seconds of a World Cup downhill ski race.

"BRUCE SPRINGSTEEN IS BACK OUT ON THE ROAD AGAIN!"

Mary began waving her arms wildly. "Whoa, whoa, too loud. Ouch!"

"Cut!" yelled Larry as he dashed out of the control room. "John, let's take it down a notch and try again."

Larry was right. This was *Entertainment Tonight*, not *Entertainment LIVE FROM KITZBÜHEL, AUSTRIA!*

The on-set interview with Mary following my epic teleprompter fail was pleasant and uneventful. Mary was a pro. Every now and then there'd be a pause and I could tell Larry, or someone, was speaking to Mary in her ear. She would pause and then ask more questions. The whole process lasted an hour and a half. When we were done, Larry and Mary bid me farewell; I returned Larry's sport coat, wiped off the half pound of makeup, and mercifully resumed my life as *not* a host of an entertainment news show. I was determined to erase this experience from my memory.

Three months went by. No call from anyone at Paramount. This did not come as a surprise. And it mattered not in the scope of things because I still had plenty of time left on my sports contract before it was time to renegotiate. I had, however, begun hearing through the grapevine that the upper management team at CBS was changing, and CBS Sports' programming priorities with it. I decided it was a good idea to be proactive and to ask for a meeting with the new president of CBS Sports, Peter Lund. I could just introduce myself, if nothing else. It couldn't hurt.

Peter represented a new guard at the sports network. During our meeting he gently informed me that in the "foreseeable future" the net-work would not be broadcasting the anthology-style sports that I was known for hosting. Yikes. He insisted that the viewers had grown tired of those events and wanted more live programming. Therefore, Lund continued, CBS would not be renewing my contract. He said they would honor the last few months of the contract but that if anything else came along, I should probably take it. All I could think was, *Perhaps I shouldn't have scheduled this meeting!* Not long after that Lund fired my godfather at the network, the man who hired me, Terry O'Neil.

The handwriting wasn't just on the wall regarding my future. There was a horse head in my bed just to make sure I understood the score. I got the message. I was done. With Lund's words—"If anything else comes along, you should take it"—I was transported back into my version of purgatory. The pup tent. Where would I go? Back to WCBS-TV news? Would they have me? What about radio? I could still do that . . . right? It was 1986. I was thirty-four years old and feeling like I was being forced into retirement.

I walked out of the CBS Black Rock offices on Sixth Avenue, into a pay phone booth, and dialed the number I had for Frank Kelly. I hated playing defense (I mean begging), but it was the only play I had. Oddly, Frank Kelly seemed excited that I had called. He told me they had auditioned a few select people for the hosting job at *ET* and they were narrowing their choices. He suggested Paramount fly me out to Los Angeles the following week for a second round of camera testing. They'd put me up at the Sunset Marquis on Sunset Boulevard in West Hollywood. I would do the audition on the *ET* set and later meet with Paramount TV president Lucie Salhany.

Had Peter Lund just done me a huge favor? Perhaps. But first thing's first. Haircut. A week in the gym. I set my Betamax to record every episode of *ET* being broadcast between now and the day I left for Los Angeles. I had to get this job. My ships were on fire once again, except this time someone else had struck the match.

For a garage-band kid from Long Island, checking in to the Sunset Marquis in West Hollywood was a supernatural experience. This was where music royalty had stayed since the 1960s. Aerosmith, Keith

Richards, Cyndi Lauper, U2, Ozzy Osbourne, Liza Minnelli, Neil Diamond, and more. I dropped my bags in the room at noon and decided I needed to get some color on my face before the next day's camera test at Paramount. I headed for the pool and spent an hour in the California sunshine. I soon found out the hard way that the West Coast sunshine produces more intense UV rays than what I remembered at Long Island's Jones Beach. The next day I showed up on Paramount's Stage 28 beet red. The *ET* makeup team was hilarious. "Wow, what have you done to yourself, young man? Let's see if we can fix your face." Let me tell you, blond hair and sunburns do not go well together. It took them an hour, but eventually they got me looking almost human.

Maybe looking like a beefsteak tomato coated in vanilla frosting was my lucky charm, because my second audition with Mary Hart went a whole lot better than the one I had punted pitifully in New York. I was very familiar with the pacing of the show this time, having watched hours of recent episodes. I was also wearing a tailored suit I had purchased at Barneys New York. Sunburn aside, I looked the part. Even Mary seemed more at ease with our banter on the set.

Following the audition, I was escorted across the Paramount lot to a conference room that adjoined the office of Paramount Television's president, Lucie Salhany. As I walked in I could see a camera shot of the empty *ET* news desk on her TV monitor. Obviously she had been watching my audition.

Lucy got right to the point. A TV-news headhunter had sent her a bunch of air checks of news readers and she had come upon the one of me anchoring the news in Nashville. She echoed Frank Kelly's line: "We are looking for a newsier approach to the show."

Then she said, "So, we are talking about a thirteen-week contract to co-host the show with Mary, Monday through Friday. You never know how these things will work out so that's as much time as we can commit to at the moment. Now, John, it looks like you've gained quite a bit of weight since your Nashville days. We would need you to lose twenty pounds or so. Can you make that happen in two weeks?"

"Uh, sure thing." I made a mental note to buy a new pair of running shoes.

And that was that. The good news? The first thirteen-week contract was quickly renewed and then eventually turned into a one-year contract—which then grew to a three-year deal as Paramount and I got used to each other and my "newsier approach" to entertainment news.

I co-hosted *Entertainment Tonight* for ten years. I told Lucie on the phone recently that her decision to hire me set an incredible course for my life. All of it. Without *Entertainment Tonight* I never would have met Connie; I wouldn't know her first child, Gib, now my son, and we never would have had our daughter, Prima. There would not have been a Red Rocks concert to catapult my music career. And I never would have interviewed Eric Clapton, Bette Davis, Gregory Peck, or Pee-wee Herman, twice.

Chapter 16

"Roundball Rock"

In 1989 I was entering the fourth year of my run at *ET* in Los Angeles, going through a divorce, when I was recruited by my old friend David Michaels to work part time for NBC Sports. He'd moved into his new position at NBC Sports a few years earlier, and he wanted me to work on the Tour de France with him again and to be a host for NBC's Olympic Games coverage in Barcelona coming up in 1992. I said yes, of course, because David is David and because this time, I'd get another opportunity to flex my creative muscles, which had gone a bit soft because of too much teleprompter time on ET.

In the middle of the Tour that year, neck-deep once again in exhausting twelve-hour TV work days, I heard through the grapevine that NBC, who had just acquired the television rights to broadcast NBA basketball for four years, had put out an open call for composers to submit demo songs for a "signature" theme to accompany their newly minted basketball coverage.

At this point in my professional music career I had very little notoriety as a composer beyond a small tribe of cycling loyalists who had heard my underscore on the Tour de France TV coverage. And while I felt certain that every composer in town would want a shot at writing the theme, since the network sent the message that they were not already committed to super-pros like John Williams or Hans Zimmer, I allowed myself to visualize what it would be like to be the guy listed on the credit roll.

Looking back, it shouldn't have felt like such a crazy idea. I certainly had a bit of an edge over other TV and film composers, what with my knowledge of the form and substance of a sports theme. I had already composed two Emmy-winning themes for the Pan American Games and the Tour de France, and I had spent hundreds of hours in sports production trucks collaborating with producers and directors to create music for an array of sporting events. This could be considered to be in my wheelhouse.

We were in the final stages of the Tour when the news about the theme song search found its way into the production truck. I had been writing nearly an hour of music a week, and I was tired, but now all I could manifest were thoughts of basketball music. *What should that sound like?*

My first hint of inspiration shocked me out of a dead sleep like a bolt of lightning. It hit at 2:00 a.m. in a tiny hotel in Megéve, France, a few kilometers down the road from the starting line of one of the last mountain stages of that year's Tour.

• • •

I'm sure you know the feeling of being jolted awake from a deep sleep with a big idea bursting from your brain. Nine times out of ten when it happens to me I just roll my groggy self back to sleep, but for some reason I can't roll over this time. Instead, I leap from the bed like a wild animal, searching my dark hotel room for a notepad—except that isn't going to work. This is an idea *for a song*. I need to either sing the melody or somehow play this thing I have in my head on a keyboard and into a tape recorder, otherwise it will be gone forever by morning.

I quickly run through my mental rolodex of options. All of my recorders and synthesizer keyboards are locked in the production truck, so that's out. Wait . . . had I spotted a piano in the lobby when we checked in? Ugh, no. There is barely a lobby in this tiny hotel, so I doubt there is a piano. My watch now says 2:15 a.m. The tune is just barely hanging on in my prefrontal cortex. If I go back to sleep and then wait until morning to use one of the crew's tape recorders, it will definitely be gone. I switch on the lamp on the nightstand in my guest room so I won't fall back asleep, which then triggers a light-bulb moment in my brain.

I've got it!

I'll use the phone to call my answering machine back in America and sing the melody into the machine. There's just one problem: France. More specifically, making an international phone call in 1989, in a very French town of only a few thousand people, from an alpine hotel staffed by people who, if they are even awake, are probably not at all interested in dealing with an overanxious American walking in circles muttering music to himself. You see, you don't just pick up the phone and dial the United States. First, you must dial zero on your room phone for the front desk. Then the desk clerk dials your number in the US (after doing the calculus for the country and city codes). When the number in the US answers, the desk clerk then puts that call on hold and has to call you back in your room to complete the connection between his switchboard phone, the international call, and the room phone (usually with those giant patch cords you saw on *Laugh-In*).

On a good day this is a labyrinthian process, but for what I need it's effectively impossible. The process is so time consuming that by the time the clerk can call me back and connect me, my answering machine will have hung up on us both and reset itself. Or I will have fallen back asleep with the melody lost in dreamland.

So here I am, looking like a lamebrained nincompoop, pacing the floor of my hotel room, relentlessly repeating a melody under my breath:

Da Da Da Da Da, Da, Da-Daaaah. Ba-Ba-Ba-Ba Baa Ba ba-ba-ba-Bask-et-Ball. Da Da Da Da Da, Da, Da-Daaaah. Ba-Ba-Ba-Ba Baa Ba ba-ba-ba-Bask-et-Ball.

I'm left with one choice. I need to go downstairs and dial the international call myself right from the front-desk switchboard. If the clerk is asleep, I'll do it myself, even if that is not technically "allowed." What's the worst that can happen? It's no more risky than using the NC State University reel-to-reel tape machine without permission, and it is certainly less audacious than forging a professor's signature.

That settles it. I dash down from the third floor, still repeating the melody softly to myself as I run.

What I confront when I get to the lobby is not promising. Behind the front desk is a swirl of switchboard wiring. There's a very real possibility that if I monkey with it too much I could cut off Megéve from the outside world. I pause to imagine the consequences: my next few weeks in a high-altitude French prison, surviving on a baguette and something less sparkling than Perrier at the hands of the local *gendarmerie*. There is no way I'm touching this tornado of patch cords.

I figure my only choice is to find a phone and just start dialing the country and city codes and hope for the best, except all I can find is a headset that looks to be from World War II and a giant rotary dial bolted to the wall under the patchbay. I start dialing. A full two minutes later, after listening to a bunch of weird tones . . . Eureka!

> **Answering Machine:** Hello, this is John, there's no one home right
> now. Please leave a message at the sound of the tone and I'll
> get right back to you. *BEEP!*

> **ME:** Hey, it's me.

> *(I know, so polite.)*
> Here is the NBA basketball theme. There are two parts and the first
> part begins like this:
> *(singing)*
> Da Da Da Da Da, Da, Da-Daaaah. Ba-Ba-Ba-Ba Baa Ba ba-ba-ba-
> Bask-et-Ball. Da Da Da Da Da, Da, Da-Daaaah. Ba-Ba-Ba-Ba
> Baa Ba ba-ba-ba-Bask-et-Ball.
> **Answering Machine:** *Beep!*

The machine cuts me off. Now I'm in a panic. I'm exhausted from the previous day's twelve hours of broadcasting and travel, and I'm fighting to stay awake so I can file the rest of this melody, which could easily end up being worthless anyway. One more flurry of wrist-wrenching rotary phone dialing.

"Hello, this is John, there's no one home right now . . ."

I skip the pleasantries this time, get right to singing the second part of the theme, and get it out with just enough time on the tape to spare.

"Buh buh buh buh buh buh-ba ba ba ba ba ba-Buh buh buh buh buh buh-DOO DOO DOO DOO!"

Done!

I leave one hundred francs (the equivalent of about twenty dollars) under the telephone for the clerk. Hush money. I've got to get some sleep. There are only three more hours till daylight and I'll once again be back in a van writing bike music.

. . .

One week later, I've arrived back home. My trusty Radio Shack sentinel is blinking the confirmation that it had, indeed, recorded *something*. My luggage is still by the front door as I scramble to unplug the machine from the telephone jack and place it on top of my piano in my studio. I hit Rewind. *Brrrrrrrrr-eep!* Play. It takes a while for me to decipher the melody. The audio sounds like it's been bounced off ten satellites and then played through two cups and a string. But I have it! With my Studer reel-to-reel tape recorder rolling, I sketch out the melodies from both messages with my right hand on the piano. Next, I set about experimenting with chord changes to support the theme. I play those on a Prophet 10 synthesizer and a Roland Super Jupiter. (You can hear those keyboards used brilliantly by composer Tom Conti on the *Rocky IV* soundtrack and of course on all of my Tour music.)

I see my basketball theme in three distinct movements. The primary movement (the first twenty-two notes on the answering machine) should repeat twice in order to establish the theme. I use my Synclavier music sampler to play that line with trumpets the first time through and then include low brass the second time through to add more energy.

The second movement of the theme (also repeated twice) will be violins, cellos, and violas with a completely different melody line (answered by the brass section). For the third movement I know that I will need one radically different, but crucial, section in the song that should feature a more syncopated feel. For that, I will use only bass trombones, bass guitar, drums, and guitar. A deep, masculine sound. This is when an announcer will break in and describe the teams and what's at stake in the game.

The arrangement for this "announcer" section is so critical that I will tell the drummer not to use high hats or crash cymbals while we are recording it because they will interfere with what the announcer is saying. This technique also speaks to the art of demo *presentation*. When the network producers first hear a demo, I never want to give them an opportunity to say, "It's great, but . . . blah blah blah." I want them to hear it fully formed (even as a demo) so they can actually put it on the air as is, if they had to.

Okay, I have my arrangement and a rough music mix. But there is one more thing to do. I know these sports executives. I know how they think. I need to add video to the music demo. I call around to my old sports buddies from CBS, locate a VHS recording of 1988's NBA Finals, and head for a small video-editing house in Los Angeles. Six hours later I have my theme perfectly synchronized to highlights from Game 7 of the 1988 Finals between the Los Angeles Lakers and the bad-boy Detroit Pistons.

At this point no one has heard the theme except me and the video editor, whom I just met. The two of us watch the demo five times. It is good, but there is something wrong. What is it?

"Well, your song is much slower than the pace of the guys playing basketball," my editor says matter-of-factly. "Wait . . . that's genius!"

. . .

He is right. When the video footage shows Magic Johnson and Isaiah Thomas fast-breaking down the court, their tempo of dribbling the basketball is significantly faster than the tempo of my song. I had been so enamored by the sheer excitement of creating the musical arrangement, I had missed the disparity.

I book a second editing session for the next day and spend that evening back in my home studio synchronizing the Synclavier's digital click track (the metronome) to the average fast-break dribble rate in the game footage. I estimate the tempo to be 132 beats per minute (slightly faster than a Donna Summer song) and remix at the new tempo. When it is matched to the video the next day in the edit bay, the effect is remarkable. The editor and I spend the rest of our session finishing the mix. When we are done, I slap a title on the tape, "Roundball Rock," along with my name and then drop the tape off at the NBC Sports offices the following morning.

They've had my demo videotape with the theme and highlights for two days when I get the call. It sounds like a room full of people on a speaker phone.

"Hey, John, it's Dick Ebersol from NBC. We love the theme!"

Just like that. One sentence.

"Wow! I mean, thank you. I mean, that's great, Dick. Thank you so much."

"Just one thing, John."

Here it comes.

"We like your arrangement and all that, but . . . would you be okay if we had a live orchestra record it before we debut it on the network?"

Silence. How does one respond to an offer like that? It's like someone *asking* if they can buy your house for more than the sale price.

"John?"

"Uh. Yes, sir? I mean . . . of course, that would be great!"

"Okay, perfect. I'll have my guys get back to you and we can work it all out. And congratulations. This is great work."

. . .

As goofy and ludicrous as the creation process was for the "Roundball Rock" theme, there was one element that I never could have predicted: the explosion in popularity of NBA basketball. The 1990s would be a golden era for the NBA, defined by the double three-peat dynasty of the Chicago Bulls and the reign of Michael Jordan. This was the decade that featured other iconic superstars beyond Michael as well: Magic Johnson, Charles Barkley, Scottie Pippen, Patrick Ewing, Shaq, and Dennis Rodman. Add announcer Marv (*yes!*) Albert to the mix, and pro basketball resembled a modern-day Circus Maximus in scope and intensity, rife with epic confrontations. In the '90s, pro basketball television audiences reached near Super Bowl proportions every year during the playoffs and finals. And with NBC owning the broadcast rights, my song was set to become the era's soundtrack.

Not that you would have known it if you were judging by its debut.

. . .

It is November 3, 1990. I'm sitting in an airport sports bar in Atlanta, bound for a destination I cannot recall. The bar is jammed. There are no fewer than ten large-screen TVs set to full volume as NBC Sports debuts their coverage of their new sports television franchise.

(From the TV)
Deep Voice Guy: Stand by! The debut of the NBA on NBC! The Los Angeles Lakers versus the San Antonio Spurs . . . is next!

At the top of the three o'clock hour all of the big screens in the bar dip to black. The NBC Sports logo bursts with shimmering brilliance onto the screens. The bar fills with a trumpet fanfare and a thunderous tympani roll as my answering machine message, now an orchestral piece, fills the room.

Da da da da da da-da-daaah—Marv Albert adds his trademark announcing style. *Yes!* And there it is. The phone call from Megéve, France, is reborn as "Roundball Rock," the signature song for the NBA.

I'm pinching myself but this is real. And it's absolutely the coolest thing that's ever happened to me. I'm grinning like a crazy person. I look around the bar. No one is looking at me. They're all watching basketball. But shouldn't they know who wrote the song? They must be curious, right?

Nothing.

After the first fifteen minutes of play, Marv throws to commercial break and the theme blasts once more through the big speakers in the bar. I can't take it anymore. I signal for the bartender.

"Refill?" he asks.

"No, I'm good right now. Did you hear that?"

"I'm sorry, hear what?"

"That music. On the TV. The basketball music."

"Oh, no, I didn't notice, I'm slammed back here, pal. You a Lakers fan? You ready for another beer?"

. . .

There are many ways to write a piece of music. Elton John and Bernie Taupin famously split the music-lyric duties right down the middle. There are artists who start with either music or lyrics first and others who will write both concurrently. I know many movie soundtrack composers who sing and/or dictate ideas for musical themes into portable tape recorders. With the advent of high-speed internet and Skype, co-writers can now collaborate from any place on earth. My trusty Radio Shack answering machine was my co-writer for what is arguably my most recognizable composition—the tune that travelers now sing back to me in airports; the melody that has been played by YouTubers on everything from ukuleles to Casio keyboards and banjos; the theme that generated a hilarious parody on *Saturday Night Live*, complete with lyrics by my fictional brother, Dave: "Ba Ba Ba Ba Ba Basketball, gimme, gimme, gimme the ball 'cause I'm gonna *dunk it*!" During those "answering machine years" ol' Radio Shack and I collaborated on hundreds of song ideas from dozens of remote locations. Most never matriculated into compositions but a few made it through to become songs. I'm proud of all of them, but none more than "Roundball Rock."

Thirty years hence, whenever I perform "Roundball Rock" live in concert, I tell this bizarre story and I always bring that answering machine up on stage with me. It still powers up and blinks when I plug it in, and I play the tape of the original message with the song demo, although the oxide on the little Radio Shack mini-cassettes is just barely hanging on.

I love this song. I fought hard for it. The story of its creation, the melody that woke me that night in France, was a "Holy Spirit moment" in my life. A big tap on my shoulder of inspiration. During my concerts, I especially love to watch from the piano as the men—who I imagine were dragged there by their wives for a romantic John Tesh concert—become galvanized and suddenly shift to the edge of their seats when they grasp the reality of the music that's coming at them from the stage.

"Wait, honey, *this* is the basketball music I listened to every week at McSorley's Old Ale House. This guy wrote it?!"

The ballads and wedding songs are forgotten as the room is now brimming with testosterone-filled memories of fast breaks and three-pointers. What a rush.

Chapter 17

Helen of Troy Riding
a Bicycle

I was midway through my ten-year run as co-host of *Entertainment Tonight*. My face was becoming somewhat recognizable, which wasn't always the most comfortable feeling but also had its fair share of benefits. Perhaps the strangest of which was that it put me on the short list for highly lucrative corporate events. Big companies love to hire comedians, musical acts, and TV personalities to host or perform at their company-wide events and retreats engineered to reward and inspire their employees. In early 1991 the IBM Corporation hired me to host two nights of their gala celebration honoring their top performers of the year. They dubbed it the IB-Emmys, complete with gold trophies and a red carpet, and they took over the ballroom of the Marriott Desert Springs Hotel in Palm Desert, California.

As the week of the event arrived, I walked off the *Entertainment Tonight* set at 1:00 p.m. on a Tuesday afternoon and jumped into a limousine with my close friend, attorney, and consummate wingman, Chuck Kenworthy. We then made the two-hour trek east into the desert. Rehearsal for the two ceremonies I'd be emceeing, the first one taking place later that evening, was set for 6:30 p.m. Once the ceremony was over, Chuck and I would then limo back to Hollywood and return for the final ceremony on Friday evening. I would have much rather just stayed the entire week, but Chuck and I had our day jobs to consider.

• • •

We arrive right around 3:00 p.m. I'm in my room for maybe ten minutes and the phone rings. It's Chuck.

"Hey, I'm down in the lobby bar. My old pal Glen Larson is here shooting his new series, *P.S. I Luv U*, starring Connie Sellecca and Greg Evigan. Come on down!"

"Wow, that's great," I say. "I'm going to hang out here. Maybe hit the gym before the IBM rehearsal. But enjoy!"

The thought of a bar full of entertainment industry people is not at all appealing to me. Besides, I am feeling more than a little unprepared for the IBM thing, and I need to use the time to come up with some snappy *ET*-like zingers for the gala. I spend the next couple of hours going over the show prep that the IBM folks have sent me and then decide that I need a little free-weight time in the hotel gym to clear out the cobwebs now occupying my brain. When I get to the gym I take one step inside and right there in the corner, pedaling away on the exercise bike, is none other than Connie Sellecca.

There is something you need to understand—or remember, depending on your age—about Connie. She was transcendent—and she still is. In the 1980s and early 1990s, she was *it*. She was the star of the hit television series *Hotel* with James Brolin, but my strongest memory of her was when she played Pam, the levelheaded attorney and voice of reason for the other characters on the kitschy superhero series called *The Greatest American Hero*, of which I was a huge fan. The show featured William Katt, Robert Culp, Connie, and a number one hit theme song I wish I had written. I've always been a big comic book devotee. I'm a sucker for anyone with superpowers even if they can't figure out how to use their new super suit and they fly into walls. Connie was stunning in her role as Pam, and in her capacity as the Greatest American Hero's love interest. Back then, did I imagine her as *my* love interest? Didn't everyone?

Connie had also been a special fitness correspondent for *ET*, and although I had never met her in person, I did end up "throwing" to her exercise report on a prerecorded video. I even tagged her "celebrity fitness report" with a friendly jab at her New York accent that slipped out during her signoff: "I'm Connie Sellecca for EN-TUH-TAIN-MENT-TUH-NIGHT." It was beyond cute, and a welcome reminder of the accents I grew up with as a kid on Long Island. I couldn't resist pointing it out on the broadcast and it played great. You wouldn't know from watching that we'd never met—at least that's how I feel all these years later, looking back.

And so, as I stand there in the doorway of the Marriott gym, I am frozen in my tracks at the sight of her. She's wearing a Sony headset over a white headband, a floral print leotard, white anklets, and a pair of blue Nike running shoes. Her incredible green eyes are laser-focused on the bike's digital display. I feel like if I keep looking, I'll turn to stone. I call on my legs to move. No response. I have just become super-geek-Johnny-Tesh, with rubber bands on my braces and dots of Clearasil on my face. My heartbeat doubles.

My first thought is that if she spots me, she will likely be furious at my cute little New *Yawk* ad-lib on *ET.* So I take a hard left in the gym and head for the chin-up bar. This is the first of a number of mistakes. I haven't done a pull-up since junior high, so when I jump up to grab the bar, instead of actually lifting 210 pounds into the air, I just hang there swinging slowly back and forth, doing a little "chin-up bar stretch" and pretending that is a thing. That's a thing, right? I look down toward my feet that are now thirty inches off the ground and notice that one of my socks is inside out and I have a salsa stain on my gym shirt. From my elevated vantage point I can now see that Connie and I are the only two people in the hotel gym. Thankfully, she is still staring at the digital display on the exercise bike and has not yet spotted me.

I drop off the bar onto the mat and head over to the sit-up bench where I think I'll be safe. Mistake Number Two. The bench is elevated, and when I lock my size-16 tennis shoes under the rollers at the apex of the bench and lean back down the length of the bench, I'm suddenly staring up at the ceiling. My body is at a 90-degree angle, and the blood is rushing to the back of my head. I know I'm in serious trouble. By now, it's logical to assume that Connie is watching all of this and reviewing her CPR training in her head. I begin doing inclined sit-ups. The sit-ups deteriorate into mini crunches. The crunches devolve into simple, feeble stretching.

I'm done for.

I am an Eagle Scout, so I am at least cognizant of the fact that in order to survive I need to save enough energy to lift myself all the way up to the rollers one last time, release my feet, and run back to my hotel room in a cramping, panicked, red-faced ball of shame. One more desperate burst of sit-up power, a thrust skyward with my arms fully extended, and I'm able to barely reach my ankles to pull myself up and out of the sit-up bench.

I'm free!

I immediately head for the exit, head bowed, averting my eyes. This could have been Mistake Number Three if it weren't for this voice coming from the corner of the room: "Ah, excuse me . . . are you John Tesh? Is that you?"

I spin around. My legs are once again granite. I'm dazzled.

"Oh, Connie. Connie Sellecca. I didn't see you there!"

With that cute little New York accent she quickly shoots back, "Well, we're the only two people in the gym."

"Yeah, you've got a point." I manage an awkward smile.

"What are you doing in Palm Desert?" she continues.

"Well, I'm hosting an event in the ballroom for IBM tonight and then again on Friday night."

"Oh, that's great," she says. "It's nice to meet you. Maybe I'll see you around."

"Well, I'll be back on Friday. Maybe we can have a drink at Kosta's right here at the hotel?"

I look around to see who said that. It is me. In a nanosecond the reel-to-reel recorder in my head goes into rewind. My brain hits Play. Yep, I just asked Connie Sellecca out on a date.

Connie continues pedaling, then says, "Okay. That sounds great," like it's the most casual thing ever.

Her answer reaches me, drowned in reverb. And suddenly it occurs to me that I just asked out the prom queen.

I hear myself say, "Okay, see you Friday," then see myself, in some kind of out-of-body experience, spin around toward the exit, slither out the gym door, and leave the presence of one of *TV Guide*'s ten most beautiful women. My head is on fire. I just spoke to Helen of Troy on a bicycle in a hotel gym and I asked her out?

I've now switched into full courtship mode and I'm pummeling the elevator button, frantically trying to get back upstairs to my room before Connie gets off the bike. Once there, I grab a piece of hotel stationery out of the desk drawer. I telephone guest services to "send a bellman to my room right away!" I pull my new Tour de France cassette tape out of my backpack. I sit down and write this note:

Hey Connie,

It was great meeting you. If you are listening to music while you're on the exercise bike, you might as well listen to music that was written for the greatest bike race on earth, the Tour de France. I'll see you Friday.

—John

The doorbell rings.

I place a twenty-dollar bill in the bellman's palm and then hand him the note and the tape.

"Please deliver this to Connie Sellecca's room right away."

"Yes, sir, and thank you, Mr. Tesh."

As the door closes behind the bellman, my first thought is that I have just made a huge fool of myself. Connie Sellecca is Hollywood royalty, and I am just one of the many reporters who cover her world. I am the tall blond guy on the edge of the red carpet, holding the big *ET* microphone, yelling questions about who designed her dress. I imagine her bemused look as she reads my note and looks at the cassette tape with bicycles on it.

"Wow, this guy composes music for bicycles. Lovely. How quaint. I must remember to have my assistant dash off a nice thank-you note right after I drop this tape into the waste basket."

Despite my typical male misgivings and a whole lot of a second-guessing, I am still smitten. My feelings are all-consuming, to the point that I barely remember the next two and a half hours hosting the IBM event. In fact, the only reason I'm sure I fulfilled my obligations is because they didn't ask for their money back and because I spend the entire limo ride back to Hollywood from Palm Springs telling my buddy Chuck about my adventure.

Chuck can feel my excitement and wants to know if he can be my best man.

"Can you imagine?" I laugh and say, "I mean, *yes!*"

But as Chuck continues to riff on "the perfect couple," my initial misgivings return, and this time they've brought reinforcements. My mood swings dark and like a Sandburg fog, dread begins to creep in. Anticipation turns to trepidation as my powers of visualization and manifestation turn on me. I begin to envision the demise of a relationship that has not even begun. What will I say on Friday? Who am I to entertain this sophisticated woman? She must have every super-hunk in Hollywood after her. This is madness.

As the Hollywood sign grows larger on the horizon, I now have this palpable feeling that, once again, I'm about to burn my ships.

The next morning I wake up with a renewed, single-minded sense of purpose. I need to know more about this Connie Sellecca. So the first thing I decide to do after I get to work and go through makeup is visit *ET*'s research department for the first time.

When I step inside Sharon Smith's research department, I'm struck by how it resembles the monolithic and historic Rose Reading Room at the New York Public Library. Yes, that smacks of hyperbole but I submit that, by both quantity and quality, it's an accurate comparison. I'm bleary-eyed but excited after the trek back to Hollywood from Palm Desert the night before, and I'm armed with a sincere ulterior motive—finding out more about Connie Sellecca.

The place is buzzing. It feels like I'm standing in the middle of *the* entertainment breaking-news mecca, because I am. Research activity abounds. Lots of it. To and fro action. The constant hum of old-school, pre-internet research clamor fills the air. Clipping articles. Checking fax machines. Reading press releases. Watching prereleases of movies on VHS video players. Transcribing interviews. The scene recalls movie versions of *All the President's Men*; *Good Night, and Good Luck*. Even better, *Three Days of the Condor*. My WCBS producer, Andy Heyward, used to call this "boots on the ground" research. To my surprise, what I'm looking at here inside this nondescript building in Hollywood is exactly what the research offices looked like in our newsroom at WCBS-TV back in my New York City days, which was what you'd expect from a legitimate, hard news operation but not necessarily from a show-biz show.

When I first arrived at *Entertainment Tonight* in 1986, I only had an inkling this research department existed because of the occasional delays, the stop-downs during show tapings, that occurred when someone yelled, "Research on the phone!" from the wings. For some unknown reason, it was always called out much like "Shark!" was shouted in Spielberg's Amity. I knew that someone, somewhere, was rechecking a fact or two, and since the call often came from Sharon Smith, I figured she was hunkered down in her command position, a good two hundred meters and another building away from *ET*'s Sound Stage 28. Every day at 11:00 a.m., she was glued to her closed-circuit feed of the *ET* taping, standing at the ready to pick up the hotline to director Ron de Moraes. Sharon and her team had already edited and approved the script for the day's program, but when Tesh or Hart would go rogue with an ad-lib, or if a creative graphic might imply someone was guilty of aberrant behavior, then she had the power to halt production immediately and double-check the facts to avoid the risk of slander or libel. Her decision to press the research panic button was not without its own consequences, of course, as that decision—or any delay for that matter—could jeopardize the satellite feed to our hundreds of syndicated stations and incur the cost of another half hour of what we called "bird time," or pricey satellite feed time.

If you are struggling, as I once did, to imagine the *ET* research department, it's probably because you're thinking that the need for a research staff for an entertainment television program is (1) laughable or (2) unnecessary, since research on movies and celebrities today is mostly gathered live on Twitter and TMZ handy-cams outside the Peninsula Hotel or LAX baggage claim. But in April 1991, before Wi-Fi and search engines, when Wiki-anything was not a thing, thankless gumshoe research from the trenches was all there was. And it was a noble pursuit. In the 1991 feudal broadcasting world, researchers were its lords while hosts and reporters labored as serfs. This wasn't reflected so much in salary or even in social standing, but certainly within the ranks of the organization itself it was an unquestioned truism. And Sharon Smith was, without a doubt, Lady of the Manor. She was revered as that buttoned-down, incorruptible protector of the realm who stood sentry over all our reputations (the show's reputation, first and foremost).

So here I am at 10:30 Wednesday morning, face caked in preshow makeup, standing before research royalty ready to make my big pitch. In my five years at *ET*, I've never been in this room before now. This is a consciousness now confirmed by all the head-snapping and puzzled looks from the research team members at their desks. I mean, what is one of the hosts of the show doing off the set and in the research office, this close to air time no less? I'm guessing it's because no one here has seen that episode of *Star Trek* where Kirk ventures down into Scotty's warp drive room. "See, Jim. I told you. I'm giving it all I've got!" The only difference was that Kirk was looking for more power, while I am looking for more information.

"Hi, Sharon," I say.

"Well, hello, John."

"Wow, this place is amazing," I say, genuinely gobsmacked.

"You should visit more often," she says, I am sure half out of politeness and half out of a genuine desire for the on-camera talent to understand how hard her team works.

"I had no idea!"

"What can I do for you, John?" she says finally, having tired of the pleasantries, I assume.

I suddenly realize that the person standing before me is most definitely sporting a bull**** meter that is, right now, pegged to 11. Plus, while scanning Sharon's "I've seen and heard everything, pal" gaze, I'm certain that the speech I rehearsed in my office will not sufficiently cloak my intentions the way I had originally hoped.

"So, Sharon . . . I wonder if you and your team have a file here on, ah, Connie Sellecca. I . . ."

"Oh, are you interviewing Connie?"

Oh no, she's on to me. I've made a terrible mistake.

"Well, no, there's no interview scheduled, as such, but I'd really like to get a little background information on Connie."

Most of the clipping and transcribing and faxing sputters to full stop and Sharon's squad members are all swiveling their chairs in our direction. I smile. My pancake makeup cracks. I would have been better off doing this in a ski mask under the cover of darkness.

"Okay, John. It's great to see you and you are always welcome in Research," Sharon says. "Connie's file is right over there in *S* for Sellecca. But the rule here is that no files leave this room. Understood?"

"Yes, ma'am."

"Also, if you want to make copies, the machine is right over there."

"Thanks, Sharon," I say, sufficiently chastened by her inviolable rules. "And hey, Sharon?" I whisper. "Can we keep this just between us?"

Sharon laughs as she quickly scans the faces of her workers around the room to be sure anyone who has been paying attention—which is everyone—knows what the score is. "Sure, mum's the word, John. Good luck."

Yep, she's *definitely* onto me.

On my knees in front of Sharon's file cabinets, I go right for *S*: Savalas, Schwarzenegger, Scott (as in George C.), Sedaka, Seinfeld, Sellecca. I reach for her file and it's rife with hundreds of clippings and AP wire stories. The magazine articles alone give the file most of its weight. I am instantly impressed and, to be honest, more than a little overwhelmed. The fear starts to creep back in.

I rush to the copy machine to make copies and carefully squirrel away the Sellecca loot back in my office desk drawer before I have to run down to the set to broadcast that day's show. There is no way I want to be caught thumbing through this dossier on the set. Still, I can't resist sneaking a peek at the bounty before I tuck it away. Right away I see that "Connie Sellecca" is not even her name. Her given birth name is Concetta Sellecchia. How Italian and supercool is that?

Later, back in my office, following the day's taping, I have my first real chance to experience the scope of the Sellecca file. In front of me is Connie on the cover of *TV Guide*s in three different languages and cover photos and feature stories about Connie in *Good Housekeeping*, *McCall's*, *Redbook*, and, be still my heart, *Mad Magazine*! This accomplishment is reserved for the celebrity crème de la crème, and there she is on the cover with my hero, Alfred E. Neuman. In the file there are stories about Connie's early years as a fashion model, dozens of television movies, the *Greatest American Hero* and *Hotel* series, *Beyond Westworld*, and a Golden Globe nomination. There are also several well-written stories of her journey as a single mom to her nine-year-old son, Gib, from her marriage to actor Gil Gerard. My journalist instincts kick in, and I think it'll be tough to share a drink with this woman without interviewing her. Then it hits me and I'm consumed by a flop sweat as I try to imagine my half of the conversation on Friday, just two short days away.

Well, let's see, I got my Eagle Scout award in 1968. Animal Husbandry was my most challenging merit badge. In 1976, I was the first reporter on the scene at the suspicious dumpster fire outside New York's Endicott Hotel, and later that year there was my two-part special report on disco. More wine, my dear?

In my head is the sound of bad brakes on a '62 Corvair. And when that clears there's another, much worse sound in my head. My own voice. And that voice is saying, *There's a reason Susanne Pickens laughed in your face when you asked her to the prom, a reason Janie Dillingham dumped you for your best friend in high school, and there's a simple explanation for why June Malitani called you Johnny Braces in the ninth grade.*

I try desperately to quiet the voice of doubt in my head, but it's winning the battle for my confidence and so by the time Chuck and I slip into our limo that Friday, bound, one more time, for Palm Desert and another IBM performance, I know it in my bones. I quit. I am resolved to bail on the date. The talk in the limo is not at all what Chuck was expecting—about picking out a diamond ring. I am preparing myself for the terms of surrender. I even convince myself that I'd never really confirmed the date.

This is the power of fear and doubt. Whether they come from within or they are foisted upon you from the outside, they have the capacity to erode your confidence, to turn any silver lining into a dark cloud, and, in my case at least, to take a courageous act that I was honestly proud of myself for having made and morph it into an exercise in futility. Fear and doubt can make anything seem like a total fool's errand. When you're in their clutches, it can even feel like they change your brain chemistry and erase your memory.

"Listen, Chuck," I say as our car hits cruising speed on the highway headed east. "I really want this to be a boys' night out after the IBM thing. There really never was a firm plan with Connie. Let's just hang out at a pub in town, away from the hotel. We'll throw back a few brewskis after the show."

I build my case and continue with even more conviction.

"I told Connie that we should play it loose on Friday anyway. And besides, she's obviously going to be with all of her actor friends from *P.S. I Luv U.* I'll end up as a fifth wheel. Plus, I'm really not interested in trying to keep up with a Hollywood actress. There's a 100 percent chance I'd be competing with every leading man in Los Angeles."

I'm certain Chuck feels whipsawed listening to what is coming out of my mouth. Three days earlier we were planning a wedding. Now, at the rate I am spouting doom, there is no opportunity for Chuck to bring me back to my senses.

I don't know if there exists a demon of self-doubt and self-sabotage, but if it does, then I am surely possessed by it on this drive out to the desert.

"Are you sure about this, John?"

"Yeah. C'mon. It's boys' night out!"

Chuck gives it one more shot, this time with a *Top Gun* pitch. "C'mon, Maverick. I really think she likes you. You've got this! Don't you feel the need for speed?"

"Shut up, Goose."

There isn't anything Chuck can do. He can tell I've psyched myself out and there is no chance I am going to connect with Connie.

At the pub that night, the Donna Summer song all barflies dread signals our last call along with the call for a last dance and one final round of shots. I stagger to my hotel room with the feeling that I made the right decision hanging with my buddy.

The next morning I pay the price for my cowardice with a blinding headache and a dose of regret. Initially, my self-talk sounds defiant in the face of the waves of regret that are starting to lap at the shores of my consciousness. *So I messed up a date. What's the big deal? Moving on.* But something is troubling me. It gnaws at my brain. The doubt that seized control of my faculties in the two days since I poured over Connie's research file has done such a complete job on my psyche that it has convinced me that I'm much better off playing it safe. Me. The guy who forged a professor's signature in a desperate attempt to change majors, who lived under a freeway and then fought back into a career against impossible odds. Where is this present cowardice coming from?

I have a sense that if these dragons are not slayed, if these self-reinforcing maladies are not cured, they will hobble me and then leave me crippled for the rest of my life. If you are wondering what the greatest enemies of relentlessness are, you've just met them: fear and doubt.

Chapter 18

Pity Party

August 2015–August 2016

When I was untethered from my catheter and told I was cancer-free, I believed that meant I was officially done. I was no longer a cancer patient. I could not have been more wrong. If I was no longer a "cancer patient," then why was I now hearing about the statistics on my "five-year survival rate" based on the virulent nature of the tumors they removed? Why did I have to report for regular nuclear scans to look at my pelvis and bones? And why were the doctors still taking my blood regularly? Don't get me wrong, I was shouting hallelujah every day and giving thanks to God. But this was clearly not Etch A Sketch done. Somebody definitely believed this wasn't over. Then there's that awkward experience when you run into an old friend who knows about your cancer battle.

Friend (with head cocked to the side): Hi, John, how *arrrrrrrre* you?

Now that I've been Sick—and it's always like that with a bad disease; it's a big scary word with a capital *S*, like it's a person with a name—I can see *it*, everywhere. Sickness, especially one that is originally diagnosed as terminal, can create and then galvanize a unique personality. I believe this is why some of us just cannot get healed. Or won't. Perhaps, sub-consciously, we don't want to be healed. It's just too darn comfortable being sick. You have all that attention; you get special meals; you can pretty much get any drug you want (antidepressants, antianxiety meds, would you prefer CBD oil?). You can be in any mood you want to conjure up. Who can blame you? You and your sickness are often the chief topic of conversation.

But then there are the times when the fear really sets in. It doesn't show up out of nowhere, don't misunderstand. It knocks on the door periodically from the very beginning, but once you get settled into this postsurgery recovery rhythm, that's when it decides to kick the door down and move in. Its favorite way of making its presence known to me was by waking me up at 2:00 a.m. and gripping me with doubt and unbelief. The daylight hours would be filled with attention from loved ones, with effort toward recovery, with broadcasting our radio show. And then the nighttime would come, the show would be over, the day's efforts would be concluded, the loved ones would go to sleep, and the void they left would be filled with the voice of fear and the sound of cancer cells multiplying inside me. Ruminations on recurrence would flood my tortured mind.

This struggle against fear and doubt was hard enough, but what made it worse was when I gave them the power to win and I resigned myself to being defined as a cancer patient. I owned that label; I claimed it. My battle became a huge part of my everyday conversations.

"Well, you know, we are hoping that my cancer . . . blah blah blah."

"I'm in the middle of my cancer treatments and let me tell you about the [insert inappropriate story about gruesome cancer tests here]."

"You know, I'm at the same age when my dad died of cancer."

"The doctors say there's only a 30 percent chance of being cured."

I was an awful dinner guest. Heck, I was an awful person. I started drinking more and more Scotch whisky at the end of the day. I found a way to make myself believe I deserved it. *After what I've been through,* I'd tell myself, *I should be allowed to have a few drinks at the end of the day!*

Connie was gentle with me but I could tell she was very concerned, not just about the drinking . . . about all of it. I looked disheveled and unkempt. I was devoured by self-pity. I was becoming more of a cancer patient every day. Even though *Gladiator*, *Warrior*, and *Braveheart* were my favorite, oft-watched films, I was neither a gladiator nor a warrior. I was a coward. So much of this book is about relentlessness but none of that was in evidence now, at least not from me. I had yielded to spinelessness. I had become less of the gladiator Maximus and more of the gutless, whiny Commodus.

Things finally came apart one day when Connie and I ended up in my studio toe-to-toe. It had been almost exactly a year from the day that we got the all-clear from Dr. Schaeffer at Johns Hopkins, and my self-destructive pity party had achieved full bloom. I cannot remember exactly what we were talking about, but I do recall that I basically put flesh on Satan. I could feel the devil in the room with us.

"The devil comes to kill, steal, and destroy" (John 10:10).

I cannot know what, exactly, you believe about the devil in the Scriptures, but I can tell you from personal experience that the devil is very real. Connie and I argued. It quickly escalated. Then I turned the conflagration around in my mind to mean that my wife cared not for my feelings and that I deserved more attention. I guess I felt I needed even more attention for everything, less accountability for anything. Whatever it was, it called for something dramatic. A tantrum, perhaps. Then I did something that no husband should ever do. I turned from the conversation and walked away.

A few hours later I had moved into a hotel by the beach and begun shopping for a touring bicycle. My plan was simple: put saddlebags on a road bike, pack them up with my radio-show microphone and portable production gear, then start riding south, out of Los Angeles. I wasn't entirely sure why I had picked a bike trip as my elixir/punishment. Renting a motorcycle seemed too predictable for a baby boomer. Hiking was not dramatic enough.

As it turned out I was utterly unprepared for the rigors of a three-day, ninety-two-mile ride down the California coast that included some very steep climbs. It was beautiful, obviously, but it was physically brutal and more emotionally draining than I ever could have imagined. How ironic that the guy who broadcast the twenty-four-hundred-mile Tour de France for seven years was now being tormented by a bicycle, barely able to balance in temperatures touching 100 degrees, with legs that had not been trained for this kind of daily punishment.

After the first fifteen miles, in the middle of a steep climb, it became clear that my choice reeked of self-flagellation. This trip wasn't about trying to get my head together; it was about playing the pitiful victim and trying in vain to outpedal the shame and fear that had packed themselves into my saddlebags.

Taking ownership of a sickness, a disease, is like sitting yourself down in the electric chair and then flipping the switch yourself.

—**Barry Bennett,** Charis Bible College

I was punishing myself. I begged God for forgiveness through each mile. If I reached the finish line, I knew it would not include a ribbon or a trophy. I knew I would still wake each morning with thoughts of a deadly disease that could be lurking inside my body, but what of my marriage? Of my family? Prior to my escape onto the road, I had tried to recruit family members into my pity party against my wife. My behavior made everyone uncomfortable and it would take hours of deep family therapy, tears, and reconciliation to put us all back together.

• • •

As night falls on that first day, another impossibly steep climb rears itself in front of me, and I punch Connie's number into the phone strapped to my handlebars. The heart rate monitor on my wrist reads 170 bpm. My lungs are on fire. I am now experiencing what I would describe as a metamorphosis. Much like a water baptism, I feel anger, pride, sin, depression, all being stripped from my body. Connie picks up. Her voice is stiff, cold. But she doesn't hang up on me. As soon as she hears that I am alive and safe, she cuts the conversation short. I'm grateful just to hear her voice.

We both believe in the God of forgiveness. This gives me hope. Hope that if God will forgive me, maybe she will too. It is hope that gives me chills to think about even today, just remembering how the Devil had used fear and doubt and unbelief to steal hope away from me.

• • •

I know now that underestimating the power of a satanic attack will make you very sick. I could have lost everything I held dear. It could've cost me my life. Don't get me wrong, I *chose* to walk out of our house and ride away on a bicycle. I'm not hiding behind "the Devil made me do it." I could see the prowler at my door. He was armed and dangerous. I made the decision to let him move into my brain, to let him live there rent-free. And his influence nearly robbed me of my precious Concetta, just as he had tried to do twenty-eight years earlier, before I even had her.

Chapter 19

Match Points

June 1991

Three months after blowing it with the most beautiful woman on the planet, I took a two-week vacation from *ET* and headed to London to host the nightly Wimbledon wrap-up show for NBC Sports. It was a plumb assignment that I knew, from experience, would draw harsh comments from more than a few sportswriters who were in short pants when I labored six years as a courtside reporter for CBS's US Open tennis broadcasts. The day before I was set to leave for England, I remember scribbling on my *ET* script the headlines I knew would be coming:

"Tesh? Wimbledon? Seriously?"
"What's the *ET* host doing at the Old England Club?"
"Get ready for 'Celebrity Birthdays at Wimbledon!'"

As always, from people like that, the unspoken message was one of intimidation through shame: stay in your lane and everything will be just fine.

I had bigger concerns than prophesying the barbs of sportswriters though. Flying eleven hours to Europe from Los Angeles, I found myself reliving my epic fail with Connie on an endless loop and trying to shake off this familiar feeling of regret, again realizing that I had dug myself another deep hole for reasons that didn't make any sense to me.

Call it insecurity, doubt, cowardice? Yeah, that sounds right. Let's call it all those things. They conspired to spoil a terrific opportunity to spend time with a fascinating, talented woman and compelled me to choose "boys' night out" instead.

I needed to spend this eleven-hour flight being more constructive than destructive. So at thirty-five thousand feet somewhere over the Canadian Arctic, I began to brainstorm ways to get back into Connie's good graces. I went through multiple British Airways cocktail napkins before finally arriving into London's Heathrow Airport with a three-part master plan:

1. Call my new friend Sharon Smith in Research.
2. Have Sharon and her team track down a contact number for Connie Sellecca.
3. Call Connie Sellecca relentlessly and ask her out again until she says yes.

• • •

It is a rudimentary plan, I admit, and there is probably a slim chance for success in any of it, but I fully intend to at least give it a shot. So while I get into a taxi and head to the Savoy Hotel, waiting for Los Angeles to wake up so I can organize my attack, I have some time to ruminate about what is ahead of me in London, at Wimbledon. And what is ahead of me, I am convinced, is a different kind of fight—one fought up close and personal with one of my broadcast partners on the nightly wrap-up show: my old nemesis Jimmy Connors.

Jimmy had been hired along with fellow Grand Slam title–winner Tracy Austin as an expert commentator for NBC's Wimbledon coverage. I already know from experience that Tracy will be as affable and approachable as Connors would be irascible and combative. Not just because that was his nature, but because that was my last, direct experience with him nearly a decade earlier, on *Center Court* after the 1982 US Open Men's Final.

• • •

That year Jimmy Connors met Ivan Lendl. As expected, from the start the match was a slugfest. It resembled, in retrospect, the final fight scene involving another Ivan three years later, that one named Drago in the classic *Rocky IV*. A comparison made even more poignant by the fact that Lendl had faced America's other great bad-boy tennis hero, John McEnroe, in the semifinals and had demolished him in straight sets to reach the finals.

In their history, Connors had won eight of nine previous matches against Lendl. Lendl only won his first match against Connors earlier that same year. On this day, Lendl, cast as the evil Czech foreigner, was playing perfect tennis. Connors, wielding his relic Wilson T-2000 metal racket, was doing the same, but he was also giving New Yorkers what they loved most—his larger-than-life personality. Grunting, gesturing, giving the finger to a linesman who disputed a call, Connors strutted around the court with the racket handle between his legs and, in his frenzy, yanked on the handle in a grotesque manner while his fans went wild. The louder the crowd got in Flushing Meadows, the stronger Jimmy grew. He absorbed the fan energy like one of my childhood Marvel Comics favorites, Galactus, who consumed planets to sustain his life force. Connors was that.

• • •

While Connors and Lendl are slugging it out, I stand at the ready, perched along the sidelines not thirty feet from the action, in my capacity as a sideline reporter for CBS Sports. This is a huge role for me. It will easily be my most-viewed appearance on the network to date.

Aside from offering updates to the producers in the booth between sets, the most important part of my duties will be asking the very first question of the day's champion. This will be broadcast live to a national TV audience while at the same time witnessed live, in the stadium, by twenty thousand fans. Right now those fans are watching a tennis match that's as much a street fight as anything else. Judging by the crackle of conversation in the production truck that I'm hearing in my earpiece, it's clear the producers are giddy with excitement.

Although I am not long out of the WCBS newsroom as a hard news reporter, these post-match tennis interviews are not intended to elicit *60 Minutes* "gotcha" moments. They are expected to be softball conversations, appealing to the average TV viewer at home. My job is to be more Mike Douglas, less Mike Wallace. Earlier in the week, in fact, I'd been kicked out of a post-match news conference by a US Tennis Association official when I'd challenged John McEnroe with a question about his verbal abuse of a linesman.

"Are you kidding me? Who is this guy?" McEnroe had shouted from the podium.

"No, Mr. McEnroe, I'm not kidding," I said.

"Why don't you get the hell out of here!" McEnroe replied.

I was led out of the press room to lots of muttering, boos, and head-shaking by my fellow reporters who wouldn't dare challenge McEnroe.

Perhaps inspired by this—or because of it—our team was cautioned during the broadcaster's meeting prior to Sunday's final to avoid asking questions that were too controversial or *confrontational*.

I had been conducting these post-match interviews for the last two weekends, so they were not unfamiliar exercises, and I knew I'd be taking strict time cues in my ear from the truck. I might be asked to stretch out my interview an extra four minutes to fill time, as I had been during the first weekend, or to keep it to a tight ninety seconds, as I'd been asked from the truck on the second weekend.

As I hear play-by-play announcers Pat Summerall and Tony Trabert wrap up Connors's two-hour-plus fist-shaking, finger-pointing, racket-abusing, obscenity-fueled four-set victory in my earpiece, I swallow hard and prepare for them to throw down to me, courtside, for the live interview. The crowd is stomping their feet and cheering. When Jimmy Connors steps off the court, the crowd and the international TV audience will be hanging on every word of the post-match interview. If you polled the crowd at this very moment, I'm convinced they would want to hear, in detail, what was going through Jimmy's mind as he delivered the knockout blows in this episode of *Bad Blood on Center Court*.

In my ear I hear, "Coming to you in five, four, three, two . . . Ready camera six annnnnnd . . . go, John."

"Congratulations, Jimmy," I say, "America's champion in America's tournament." The words echo twice inside the stadium, and then repeat one more time in my left ear with another delay created by the CBS production truck. Yikes, this is new. The audio delay on my voice gives me pause.

"Thanks, John," Connors replies.

"Well, Jimmy, it looked to me like there was a lot more than just tennis going on out there today. Tell me about that," I say.

The question hangs in the air for an extra moment as Jimmy thinks it over. I see his demeanor, his body language, shift a bit from sunny to almost sanguine. The pause between question and answer, between call and response, grows longer still. Mercifully, Connors leans into my microphone for his answer, but it's too late. The crowd has read his body language as being very put off by my question. Before he can say a word, twenty-thousand people answer for him and begin to boo. They're booing . . . *me*? And it's that inimitable, New York City, angry-mob kind of boo.

"Get outta here, throw da bum out," style of booing.

I'm baffled, disoriented. I'm in full panic mode. Jimmy turns from me now, as the victorious gladiator, playing to the crowd, and shows them his palms turned up in supplication, as if to say, "Can you believe this guy and his stupid question?"

They go nuts. The fans are screaming and stomping again. I'm in Marcus Aurelius's Colosseum and my head is in the lion's mouth. Finally, my earpiece crackles to life with the screaming voice of my producer Frank Chirkinian: "Tesh, Tesh, good God, Tesh, upbeat questions. Ask upbeat questions! What the hell are you doing?"

I try again. I know I can save the interview. I quickly change tack.

"Jimmy, after winning the first two sets, Lendl seemed to . . ."

I can barely hear my own voice over the raging crowd. Connors turns back to look at me. He's going to hang me out to dry, I can feel it.

"Hang on, John, you didn't let me answer your first question!"

The crowd erupts. Connors's condescending tone has triggered a blood lust. This is officially the Jimmy Connors Show. There's more shouting in my earpiece. I say a few more things into the mic that I can't remember. Jimmy smiles and then mercifully turns his back on me and heads back to center court for the trophy presentation and ceremony.

The CBS cameras to my left and right swish-pan off of me and follow Connors. The interview is over. And so, I'm convinced, is my brief career at CBS Sports. In less than two minutes, Jimmy, once more as Galactus, has absorbed me and the moment.

. . .

On Monday, as expected, sportswriters ripped me apart. Even the *New York Times* thought my debacle at center court worthy of a few painfully critical horrible paragraphs. As I walked off the elevator onto the thirtieth floor at Black Rock that morning, I was prepared to surrender my CBS Sports microphone flag and blazer. By lunch I'd already begun gathering up my personal effects from my office. Then network sports president Van Gordon Sauter summoned me to his office.

I knew Van would get right to the point. He was a brilliant communicator and his charm and wit in meetings was a big part of why the sports department was so popular with major advertisers. Sauter greeted me with a look that I was not expecting. Through his bushy beard and his red-and-white reading glasses, Sauter shot me a wide grin.

"Wow, if not for these guys, you'd be a goner, Tesh," Sauter bellowed as he held up the front page of the *New York Daily News* sports section.

The headline read, "Tesh Gets Right to Match Point!"

The thrust of the article was a defense of my approach to the post-match interview with Connors and an indictment of the way sports reporters often pandered to professional athletes. The writer went on to champion my hard news background and heralded CBS's decision to include me in the coverage. While the *Daily News* reporter had saved my job, Mr. Connors had still put a sizeable dent in my reputation as a broadcaster.

. . .

This was where I assumed my relationship with Jimmy had remained when, in the summer of 1991, I walked into the makeup room of the NBC Sports Wimbledon compound on the first day and there sat Connors, the two of us ten years older now and linked once more, this time both as sports broadcasters. I still saw us as adversaries and now we had been hired as broadcast partners.

"Hey, Tesh!" yelled Jimmy as I walked in.

"Oh, hi, Jimmy," I replied to the man who nearly torched my career a decade earlier.

"How ya been? I'm looking forward to working with you guys on this," he said.

The voice in my brain was so loud at this moment, I couldn't tell whether what I was thinking was already coming out of my mouth.

Here's the dilemma, says my brain. *Do we bring up the US Open thing and get it out of the way so it doesn't come flying out of our mouth while we're on the air, or should we just pretend it never happened? Maybe he doesn't even remember.*

I went with my gut.

"So, Jimmy," I said, "I haven't talked to you since that interview at the Open ten years back. I thought we could—"

"Oh my gosh, Tesh, that was hilarious! The crowd was going nuts. The look on your face! You gotta love that New York crowd, right?" he said, completely oblivious to the impact his antics had on my psyche. "I'm working on getting back there to play one last time this year, actually. I've been training hard. I'll be almost forty. Can you believe it?"

In fact, there was so much about our exchange I couldn't believe. But now was not the time to litigate all that. I had to decide how to respond: go right into "host rage" and give him a piece of my mind in an attempt to clear the air while indulging my ego, or take one for the team, chicken out, laugh like a hyena, and give him a high five?

I chose Door Number Two and went full Colonel Sanders.

"Yeah, that was crazy," I said. "Everybody was booing me and you looked like you were loving it."

"I know, right?" Jimmy chuckled.

That was it. Game, set, and match, Connors.

•   •   •

I won't lie; it helped that I had much more important things on my mind than Jimmy Connors. I had to activate Operation: Get the Girl, my battle plan for Connie's heart that I knew would require relentless determination.

Since the sun had come up back in Los Angeles on my first day in London, I had made some decent strides. I managed to reach Sharon Smith in Research, who armed me with the number for Connie's answering service and for her publicist, Richard Grant. I then immediately dialed Mr. Grant, and while I cannot remember what fiction I engineered, I do remember that it wasn't nearly convincing enough to result in a direct line to Connie. From there I evolved my plan into what one might call a message carpet-bombing strategy. I would leave two messages a day with Connie's answering service until I got a response from the woman herself.

I don't know about you, but when I think about engaging with an answering service, I expect a neutral party, like Switzerland, who tries to stay out of the particulars between the parties—the leaver and the receiver—on either end of a message. In the case of Connie's answering service, however, I felt very much like the saddest member of the Axis powers trying to establish a line of communication through a united Allied front. Each time I called the number Sharon Smith gave me, a human picked up the phone and offered increasingly condescending responses to my entreaties: "Yes, Mr. Tesh, we've given Miss Sellecca each and every one of your messages. I'm *suuuure* she'll call you when she can."

Still, I persisted in my singular purpose. Connie had agreed to a first date for a reason, so I had to believe whatever that reason was still held *some* sway in her heart. I had to have faith.

After a week of unreturned calls, I resorted to adding a pathetic post-script to my messages: "Please tell Connie I'm calling from Wimbledon, where I'm hosting NBC's television coverage. If I can't pick up the phone, because I'm on the air, have her leave her direct number and I'll get back to her the moment I'm off the air." (It still makes me cringe today that I said this.)

If my relentlessness wasn't enough to earn a returned call, I thought, maybe I could impress her with my professional bona fides.

Wimbledon lasts two weeks. So did my Connie Sellecca answering-service phone-barrage. I left twenty-eight messages—*two a day*. All of them unreturned. Ironically, in that time I'd managed to repair one relationship I thought was completely unsalvageable, while getting shut out completely from another that I was positive held great promise. I took the first plane home after my hosting duties were complete, battered and bloodied but not beaten.

The way through ultimately materialized thanks to two Los Angeles DJs, Mark and Brian from KLOS. The boys were heading out on a two-week vacation and they decided to invite various musicians and entertainers to fill in for them on the air while they were away. I got the call to host their three-hour morning show on August 29, 1991.

The program's producer, Nicole Sandler, suggested that the guest hosts "invite some of their 'famous friends' to come on air with them." That's when the light bulb went off. First, I invited my old Nashville co-anchorman, Dan Miller, to join me, knowing that he would make a great Ed McMahon for the broadcast. Then I suggested to Nicole that she call Connie Sellecca's press agent and schedule an interview with the Mark & Brian Morning Show to promote her new TV series, *P.S. I Luv U*, which was set to premiere on CBS in a couple of weeks.

"But don't mention that I'll be the one doing the interview," I told Nicole. "I want it to be a surprise. Trust me, it will be great radio."

From my research, I knew that Connie was still in Palm Springs shooting the series with Greg Evigan and Earl Holliman. I also knew that the powerhouse ratings of the Mark & Brian Show would appeal to a PR maven like Richard Grant, and that my pal Dan Miller would go along with whatever scheme I'd cooked up.

Sure enough, Connie agreed to the interview, which was set for that Thursday morning at 5:15 a.m. before her call time to the set of *P.S. I Luv U*. When Connie called in, it was Dan Miller who greeted her live on the radio: "Good morning, Connie, this is Dan Miller from the Mark and Brian Show. I'm here co-hosting the morning show with John Tesh."

"Oh, John Tesh," she said, with a coyness in her tone that broadcast a thinly veiled message to me over the Los Angeles airwaves.

I swiftly launched into a barrage of softball questions about the series premiere to try and keep the train on the tracks. Listening to her answers, with that hint of the Bronx occasionally slipping out, I was bewitched. She was classy, witty, and hilarious. She spoke in perfect radio sound bites. She was the ideal interview, which I hoped would, one day soon, translate to being the ideal conversation partner over dinner. Eventually, Dan came through with the smooth transition that only my master-interviewer-buddy could deliver.

"So, Connie, you and John have met before. Is that right?"

"Yes, we have," she said, letting each word dangle in the air so that I would know she still hadn't forgotten my disappearing act four months earlier. Dan picked up on it, too, and he immediately shifted into Cyrano de Bergerac mode, outlining the top reasons he thought Connie and I should go on a dinner date. It was a stunt straight from the morning zoo radio-show playbook.

There was coy banter back and forth between Connie and Dan. Then I pretended, as we had planned, to be outraged by Dan's unprofessional behavior and protested his lack of interview etiquette.

"Dan, this is neither the time nor the place!" I said into the microphone while giving Dan a huge thumbs-up.

Now Dan slid into the closer role and suggested that Connie stay on the line after the interview so I could get her phone number. The interview wrapped and as the commercials played, I picked up the studio line to find Connie still there. We spoke directly for the first time since April. She confided that in her fury over my disrespectful first date no-show, she had told Richard Grant not to give me her number. "If you give John Tesh my number, you're fired" were her exact words. And yet, after a few more minutes of conversation, I managed to breach her defenses and secure that ten-digit Holy Grail.

· · ·

This encounter—while not exactly face-to-face, more voice-to-voice—was a total reversal of my original mind-set (fear and avoidance). This time I was prepared to follow through, even in the face of possible rejection. There was something very special about this woman that had gnawed at my conscience long enough to reconnect my backbone to my brain and produce my natural tendency (in other endeavors) toward persistence.

I was on a mission to fix my original mistake. I had made a plan with Connie in that gym. A date. A *promise*. And I had broken that promise to mitigate my own insecurity. I even convinced myself that I hadn't really made a commitment in the first place. A fiction I held in my mind as absolute truth until years later when, at a dinner one evening, I was telling my version of this story and Connie produced the hard copy of my note on the hotel's stationery confirming our date as evidence to the contrary.

. . .

A week and a few phone calls later, Connie agrees to dinner in Pacific Palisades at Giorgio Baldi, a renowned celebrity-spotting restaurant known for its incredible Italian dishes and beachy atmosphere.

On the appointed evening I get there early, secure an outdoor table, and wait. Under normal circumstances, I would have picked my date up from wherever she asked and escorted her to dinner. But as a single mom, Connie had a practice of not letting her son, Gib, see her get picked up by a man for a date until she felt there was real potential there. I had not yet attained "potential" status. It was, after all, our first date, and I had not done anything to move myself out of relationship purgatory. I was still just elated that she'd said yes to our date.

Connie arrives wearing wings and a halo and floats out onto the patio. *Sorry, that's my memory.* Dinner is fantastic. The conversation is even better.

We talk for five hours. About our families, about being fellow New Yorkers, about her life as a single mom to her nine-year-old son. I have to be careful with my reactions and my facial expressions, though, because I already knew from the *ET* research dossier so much of what she was telling me. Still, it is awesome hearing her say it.

. . .

Then Connie spoke of something I had not read in the research: her faith in God. I told her I was raised in the Methodist church. She told me she was raised Catholic and then described herself as a born-again Christian. She told me she attended a Messianic service on Sundays and explained that her church combined Christianity—most importantly, the belief that Jesus is the Jewish Messiah—with elements of Judaism and the Jewish tradition.

I was intrigued.

I had been born into the church, but I had not attended church regularly since I enrolled in college in 1970. I'd gone to church camp every summer for five years and I'd studied for and completed my confirmation as a Christian. I had attended church three times a week with my family. I had memorized dozens of scriptures. I'd said the Lord's Prayer every night before bed. Then, as a freshman at NC State, I took a religion course that I expected to be a walk-through of the Bible but instead turned into a semester-long argument by the professor that Christianity was nothing more than man's desire to understand the things he could not explain through science. The professor was effective and had me questioning my own beliefs. I told Connie all of this. I spoke these words aloud for the first time in decades.

This was heavy conversation on a first date. But it felt right, natural. At this, Connie suggested I might like her church. She told me that this was how she spent her Sundays, so if we wanted to spend what little free time each of us had together, I might want to consider giving it a try. I liked Connie, so of course I was interested in her church.

As it turned out, I would fall in love with Connie and her church. Beth Ariel Fellowship would become a big part of my life. Led by a Vietnam veteran named Louis Lapides, the Sunday service at Beth Ariel was more like a Bible study. It was held in a tiny school gym that rarely held more than a hundred people. After my first couple of visits, Louis and a few other men in the congregation suggested I join them in the Los Angeles Coliseum for a men's-only conference called Promise Keepers. The following week I found myself among eighty thousand men singing "Amazing Grace." A month after that, I found myself serving as the music worship leader at Beth Ariel.

It was quite amazing, all of it. My new relationship with Connie. My renewed relationship with the Word of God. I cannot honestly say that this was what I was looking for when I left for London the previous June and concocted my plan to win over Connie. But I also cannot help but believe that it was God who led me back to Connie, just as it was Connie who led me back to God.

Chapter 20

The Whirlwind

There's no other way to describe it. Ours was a semi-long-distance, whirlwind romance. I was in Los Angeles working each day on *Entertainment Tonight*. Connie was in Palm Springs filming *P.S. I Luv U*. During the week we did one of two things. Either I would drive to her shooting location in Palm Springs after I finished *ET* in the early afternoon, or she would drive the two and a half hours to LA in order, at the very least, to be home two or three times a week when Gib woke for breakfast.

On the days I drove out, when Connie's work day ended, we'd sit and talk for an hour or two and then I would drive back to the Paramount lot, where *ET* was taped, around 2:00 a.m. I would sleep on my office floor until the producers called me to Stage 28 to shoot that day's show. On the nights Connie drove home, I would keep her on the phone while she was driving so I could confirm that she hadn't fallen asleep. I also used that time to play her pieces of a song I was composing called "Concetta," which was ostensibly my musical description of her personality. It grew over the days and weeks of our courtship, from verse to chorus to full orchestration.

Thanksgiving weekend 1991, mere months into our courtship, I suggested to Connie that we spend Thanksgiving weekend in Carmel, California. There was a great opportunity to serve the homeless that week and it was a very romantic area.

I also had another motive. I knew that I knew that I knew it was time to put a ring on her finger. I was not sure what her answer would be. Ours had been an intense, albeit hyperdriven, courtship. However, we had both been married before. We knew what we did and did not want in a partner. Still, I've never played poker with Connie for the same reason I was unsure what her reaction would be to an engagement ring. Italian girl from the Bronx. No tells. Hard to read? Yep.

. . .

When we arrive at our dinner destination, Spadero's Italian Restaurant on the Friday after Thanksgiving, there's a sign on the door of the restaurant, along Cannery Row, which Connie immediately spots.

"Oh no, it's closed for a private party," Connie says, disappointed.

"Let's go in anyway. Maybe it was from yesterday," I say to her, opening the door.

When we walk in, there is no party. The place is completely empty, save for restaurant staff and a string quartet in the corner. They are performing a song she immediately recognizes. It's her song, "Concetta." As the violins and cellos rise in crescendo, the maître d' escorts us to our seats by the window overlooking Monterey Bay. I grip Connie's hand tightly as we walk through the tables covered in white cloth. It's soon evident to her that no one else will be dining in the restaurant that evening. The room is ours. I'm hoping this Don Juan–esque gesture has not been too forward. She doesn't try to sprint for the exit, so I take that as a positive sign.

With the sun setting over our shoulders, we laugh and marvel at the velocity of our courtship. Dinner comes and goes, and before we know it, the dishes and coffee are cleared, night has fallen, and I'm hoping that what is about to happen next isn't too premature. My plan this entire time has been to conclude our dinner with the proposal. (Earlier that week I had phoned her widowed mom, Marianna, in New York to ask for Connie's hand. She was wonderfully flustered and gave her consent.) Suddenly the specter that Connie might say no taps my brain. I can feel the version of me from the limo ride back to Palm Springs barely six months earlier starting to surface. I quickly shake it off and get down on one knee. I reach into my pocket for the ring and formally ask Connie to spend the rest of her life with me.

She says yes. I ask her to repeat it. *Yes.*

There was one final coup de grace to cement the yes from Connie when I popped the question. I had planned a fifteen-minute fireworks display to be launched from a barge over the water. As weather would have it, however, a dense fog had rolled in over the bay a few hours before dinner and the fireworks company had called to tell me we'd have to delay the fireworks to the following day.

So the next night we return to the restaurant. I take Connie's hand and lead her out past the restaurant's deck and onto the sand at the water's edge. With a signal from a tiny flashlight I've pulled from my pocket, a small barge, floating just offshore, erupts in spectacular fireworks. Connie is properly awestruck and in that Bronx brogue, she screams over the explosions in the air, "These are mine? These are for me?"

People are now running from the street to the sandy shoreline, eager to enjoy the fireworks. Connie reacts again, smiling and this time screaming and claiming ownership of our public display: "Hey, these are mine! I'm sharing them with you, but these are for me!"

• • •

The following year on April 4, 1992, Connie and I are married, and a partnership is formed that nearly three decades later catapults us together as a couple into the world of supernatural healing.

Chapter 21

Newtonian Physics

Sir Isaac Newton's first law of motion states that "an object at rest stays at rest, and an object in motion stays in motion with the same speed and in the same direction unless acted upon by an unbalanced force."[1] Newton's second law of motion states that the acceleration of an object is dependent upon two variables—the force acting upon the object and the mass of the object.

Twenty years earlier, when I decided I'd had enough pup tent camping and backbreaking construction work in Raleigh, I created, with my demo tape and persistence and focus on finding purpose, a forward motion. In roughly thirty-six months that forward motion landed me a spot as a CBS television news correspondent in New York City at only twenty-three years old (the youngest reporter in the newsroom). The momentum of that force, combined with the acceleration of God's will, propelled me around the globe for CBS Sports by the time I was thirty and into the seven-figure seat next to Mary Hart on *Entertainment Tonight* when I was thirty-five. Yet I was still, at my core, a musician. I had enjoyed a supernatural path to success in the world of broadcast media, but music kept hijacking my attention.

· · ·

If you had asked anyone at *ET* to describe me during those years, they would likely have said that I was not "also" composing music, but rather that I was "also" doing a television show in addition to writing theme music and orchestrations. My work environment (and habits) would have proven them right. There was a practice keyboard in my office. There was a second keyboard, microphone, and multitrack recorder in my dressing room. Connie still tells the story about how I would come home from the set and go right into our recording studio. Then, as she was preparing dinner, a commercial would come on the TV with my voice promoting what was coming up on *ET* that evening. Connie would page me in the home studio, anxious for details about the lead story, and invariably I couldn't remember a single detail. Often, I couldn't even remember *reading* the story. I was clearly off in some other music netherworld while I read the teleprompter. Connie was the first person to fully affirm that my heart really was in my music.

Early in my tenure at *Entertainment Tonight*, Mary Hart and Lucie Salhany gave me some insight into my focus too—or lack thereof. They helped me see that I wasn't fully committed to my role as a television host.

I'd barely been co-hosting with Mary for a month when Lucie called me into her office to inform me that she had decided to send me for "body language" training in Dallas.

"What? I'm not doing that" was all I could find for a reply.

She continued. "Our focus group research studies are telling us that viewers feel you don't like Mary. You're not reacting to her comments during the host chat. You're even rolling your eyes at times. Plus, your body language comes off as condescending. John, Mary is the franchise of *Entertainment Tonight*. Her Q-rating [recognizability and likeability] is through the roof, and you're not doing yourself any favors by treating the star of the show like this."

My mouth was agape. I will admit that I tried to project a "newsier approach" on the set. I also occasionally and intentionally delivered my copy tongue in cheek. But I certainly didn't think I was being mean to my partner. Nonetheless, Lucie and Frank Kelly required that I spend three days in Dallas working with a body language coach.

When I arrived for the training, the coach was armed with dozens of clips showing transitions on the set where I was being a terrible co-host. I couldn't believe my eyes. The evidence was clear. I was being a jerk. It was right there on the screen. It *wasn't* surprising that viewers noticed.

And so, with a stack of fifty old *ET* scripts and the coach pretending to be Mary, we set about "fixing" Mary's co-host. After about three to four hours, I settled into the process that was both demoralizing and enlightening. You know when your spouse says, "Stop being a jerk" and you think they are nuts? Well, now I can tell you that it's probably a good idea to take a closer look at yourself. I gained even more respect for Mary during this process because when I watched those clips, I realized that she had been putting up with a lot of petulant behavior, the kind perpetrated by someone who deep down didn't want to be there, even if he didn't know it consciously at the time.

Ultimately, I was able to swallow my pride. Of course, if I had refused to go to "host school," I probably would have Mr. Cool-ed myself right out of that job, a job that eventually led me to the IBM gig in Palm Springs, which led me to Connie, which led me back to music where all of my available focus was now trained.

I had been professionally composing music since the opportunity arose with CBS Sports. I composed and recorded hours and hours of original music during the Tour de France coverage and had hundreds of letters from bike racing enthusiasts asking how they could get the music from the TV coverage. I had duplicated a few thousand cassette tapes—and I bought an advertisement in *Bicycling* magazine—then sold a few hundred tapes. Since I also had fifteen to twenty million viewers watching me on *ET* six days a week, I didn't need a whiteboard and a brainstorming session to come up with my pitch to the record companies.

I assembled a demo tape of three songs. Then I laid out all of my promotional assets and the reasons why the project, *John Tesh: Music from the Tour de France*, would be a huge success and sell millions of records. Unfortunately, a stack of rejection letters began to form on my desk. A&M Records: "Thank you for your submission. This is not for us right now." Columbia Records: "We are not accepting unsolicited recordings at this time." Warner Brothers, Geffen Records, Polygram, Arista, Island, Virgin—all said thanks but no thanks. Finally, the fledgling label Private

Music agreed to release the "Tour" record. To *where* they released it, I do not know, because it barely made it into record stores. The project bombed and I was quickly dropped from the label. The problem was, while I was equally a sports announcer and music composer in the eyes of bike racing fanatics, my connection to everyone else began and ended with my role as commentator. When millions of viewers see you introducing TV clips each night, that's who you are to them.

I was not all that surprised by this turn of events. Nobody but me (and, thankfully, Connie) cared that I wrote "musician" on my tax returns. It was enough, for a while, that I was blessed with a schedule at *ET* that ended each day after we delivered the show to our syndicated stations at 1:00 p.m. via satellite. I could then rush home from the Paramount Studios to work on my music, with the full support of my wife, who even got behind the construction of a small recording studio behind our house from which we would eventually start our own record company, GTS Records (Gib. Tesh. Sellecca).

I realized that trying to slowly bludgeon my way out of my current talking-head job description was not much of a strategy. I needed a unique and powerful way to create the good ol' paradigm shift.

Then, in the spring of 1994, two things occurred that, on their own, didn't mean much to me. But taken together they would obey both Newtonian laws of motion and send me hurtling toward three gold albums and two Grammy nominations.

First, in March, I stumbled upon *Yanni, Live at the Acropolis* and *The Moody Blues, A Night at Red Rocks* airing back-to-back on PBS. These were epic performances. Spectacles. Amazing.

Second, *ET* producer Bob Flick handed me an advance copy of *Life Is a Contact Sport* by super-manager Ken Kragen, who had worked with entertainers Lionel Richie, Kenny Rogers, Trisha Yearwood, Olivia Newton-John, the Bee Gees, Burt Reynolds, and the Smothers Brothers to help them move to the next levels in their careers. In 1985, he secured the talent that appeared on the fund-raising single "We Are the World" and album of the same name.

I devoured Kragen's book in one afternoon. In it, using his artists to illustrate the theory, he makes the convincing argument that in order to introduce an artist to the marketplace, or to reinvigorate their career, you had to create a huge event. The event had to be epic in scope and differentiate itself and the artist simultaneously. Having mounted the legendary *We Are the World* project, and later *Hands Across America*, Kragen had cemented his reputation as a public relations genius. He knew of what he spoke.

And like a flash, my revelation for life as a concert pianist materialized from the pages of Ken Kragen's book and the PBS pledge programs. I had to create an epic concert event. It was the only way through.

Connie and I brainstormed the concept. The show would combine five key elements: my original music, the Red Rocks Amphitheatre, the Colorado Symphony Orchestra, Olympic gymnasts Bart Conner and Nadia Comăneci, and David Michaels and his production team.

It would be called *John Tesh: Live at Red Rocks with the Colorado Symphony.*

Chapter 22

"How Dumb Can You Be and Still Breathe?"

Fall 2016

After three long days, I'd returned home from my bicycle trek purged of my self-pity and touched by what I like to call Connie's "Italian compassion": "I'm keeping you alive so I can deal with you later."

That night at dinner Connie declared, "I've been listening to this guy on the radio and I love his teaching. His church is fifty-eight miles away and I'm going on Sunday. You can come if you want."

I wanted.

So that Sunday we piled into the car in the predawn darkness and drove an hour to the church of a man named Jack Hibbs, whose message that day was not only brilliant but guided me to this powerful, very appropriate scripture:

> Let all bitterness, wrath, anger, clamor, and evil speaking be put away from you. . . . And be kind to one another, tenderhearted, forgiving one another, even as God in Christ forgave you. (Eph. 4:31–32)

Several months later, our doorbell rang in the middle of the afternoon. It was a friend we had not seen for years: Cha Cha

Sandoval-McMahon, a Hollywood stuntwoman and comedian whose daughter had gone to preschool and then high school with our daughter, Prima. I thought it odd that she would just show up without calling. I soon understood why.

Cha Cha had been attending Jack Hibbs's Calvary Chapel and heard through the grapevine that we were now regular attendees. She had also fought cancer. Worse still, in the middle of her treatments, Cha Cha's husband got sick and died. It was a heartbreaking story.

This unlikely reunion soon evolved into frequent Sunday-morning carpools to Calvary Chapel (Connie, me, and Cha Cha) and regular after-church cups of coffee where we'd talk about life and the Word and, not infrequently, our cancer journeys. One of those Sundays, after a particularly engaging conversation, Cha Cha handed us a CD.

"Hey, I think you two should listen to this guy's teaching. His accent is a little wonky, but if you can get past that, there is some amazing teaching on here."

Oh, terrific, another CD-website-book-DVD-meditation technique-raw-food-cancer-fighting strategy, I thought. I may have also said that out loud, which earned me a well-deserved eye roll from Connie.

Nonetheless, on the hour-long drive home, Connie shoved the CD into the car stereo. Cha Cha was right. The voice coming out of the speakers belonged to a preacher named Andrew Wommack and was reminiscent of TV's Gomer Pyle dialed up to 11. Wommack was telling me that I had been praying incorrectly for sixty years. He was telling me there was *A Better Way to Pray*—the title on the CD.

. . .

With Connie behind the wheel, I lean my head against the side window for a nap. Then, half-awake, I hear this: "How dumb can you be and still breathe?"

What did he say?

"Why don't you try using your head for more than a hat rack!"

My uncle Jake was a pastor in Tulsa, Oklahoma, but he'd never preached like this.

Andrew Wommack says he's "killing sacred cows," the ones many churches have created. He sounds frustrated—even angry. He has my attention, mostly because he's quirky and rebellious and because what he is saying is starting to make a lot of sense, eighteen months removed from my initial diagnosis and just recently on the other side of a personal and spiritual crisis.

If I bottom-line what I am hearing, it is essentially this: Wrong teaching, specifically religious doctrine, makes God's Word ineffective. Freeing ourselves from religious traditions will reveal the simplicity of God's Word and get me healed.

Wommack is using dozens of examples from Scripture to support this message of divine healing. He's explaining how Jesus gave us full authority over sickness and pain. We already have it, Wommack says. We don't have to beg God for it. I reach to raise the volume. Connie smiles. Wommack's next salvo is like plutonium. It's Mark 11:23. Wommack recites it slowly: "For assuredly, I say to you, whoever says to this mountain, 'Be removed and be cast into the sea,' and does not doubt in his heart, but believes that those things he says will be done, he will have whatever he says."

Boom. The words detonate inside me. He speaks the next verse: "Therefore I say to you, whatever things you ask when you pray, believe that you receive them, and you will have them" (v. 24).

"Get this," Wommack says, "and you get everything."

. . .

To someone who had been begging God for a healing, these words were, literally and figuratively, a revelation.

From the time I was a child, growing up in the Westbury Methodist Church, I was always taught that "God is a good God" but that He also acts in *mysterious* ways. When a young child would die, our pastor would often say that "it was God's plan to take this child" and "God could have healed her if He wanted. But we have to accept God's will." We would hear that oft-used phrase "God won't give you anything you cannot handle" (that's not in the Bible, by the way), and naturally figure that whatever hardship we were facing was there for a reason. It was somehow a test that God had put before us.

I was also taught that the only way to get God to do something for you was by bombarding Him with prayer. I had done that a lot, in fact, throughout my life. There were the desperate nights in my attic bedroom as a boy, begging Him to intercede on behalf of my sisters as my dad directed his ire at them. There were the long nights pleading from my pup tent after I had been thrown out of school. That's certainly how I approached my cancer, even as a sixty-three-year-old man, beseeching God from my hospital bed for deliverance from this deadly disease that I was sure He'd allowed to happen to teach me perseverance.

Not knowing what God had on His mind, and recalling plenty of reasons why He had cause to teach me a lesson, manifested terror in me. I found this spiritual healing lottery to be chilling. But as we drove home from Jack Hibbs's church, I was becoming convinced that prayer is not trying to twist God's arm to make Him do something. It is becoming settled in my heart that God wants me healthy and well. That He wants me to prosper in all things. And that it has always been this way. That's why Jesus went to the cross. He took our sins. He took our sicknesses.

"By whose stripes you were healed" (1 Peter 2:24).

Chapter 23

The Multiple Miracles
of Red Rocks

As a kid, I often visualized myself in live musical performances. Thanks to my ignition in elementary school at the hands of Dr. Wagner and the hustle required to keep up with my older sisters, my earliest visions were grand ones. They were of me, seated at a gigantic grand piano, with an orchestra at my command, playing my original compositions. I went to bed nearly every night wrapped in this recurring dream. I awoke, recalling that same dream. At nearly every point in the process, almost from the moment I conceived of the idea to create *John Tesh: Live at Red Rocks with the Colorado Symphony*, things could have fallen apart. A few times they nearly did.

When I took the idea to PBS, they were not entirely thrilled with the idea, not that I could blame them. At that point, I had no distribution for my recordings. I had been dropped as an artist by my record label. My live concert experience was mostly small jazz clubs. Even if I wrote a song that would produce significant air play on the radio, there was no guarantee that it would generate the kind of emotional, almost spiritual response that successful pledge specials on public television were generating.

The Three Tenors Live in Rome. Yanni: Live at the Acropolis. These were not merely concerts; they were giant symphonic events, staged in exotic locales. These concerts, edited down into thirty-minute program segments and separated by twenty-minute pledge pitches, generated millions of dollars in revenue for PBS. And then, with their proven track records on PBS, Yanni, the Tenors, and later Riverdance and *Les Misérables* could command hefty license fees to defray production costs.

Could my Red Rocks special be the next *Three Tenors in Rome*? I'm pretty sure their programmers bottom-lined it like this: *Let's see . . . the guy who hosts* Entertainment Tonight *performs his sports music with an orchestra and gymnasts? Uh, maybe not.* I'm certain, given the circumstances, I would have come to the same conclusion, especially after one particularly awkward final conference call.

PBS: So, John, how many concerts did you perform last year?
Me: Uh, three.
PBS: How many records did you sell that year?
Me: Maybe a thousand.
PBS: How extensive will your concert tour be to support the Red Rocks TV special?
Me: Well, I have a full-time job at *ET*, so I'm not sure how that would work out. Why do you need that information now?
PBS: It's really not possible to offer you a commitment of production funds right now. We will be happy to have a look at the concert special after it's done. If a station wants to test it, that will be up to them.

PBS's approach to its pledge drive broadcasting was atypical in the world of network television. PBS corporate supported their local stations by purchasing the broadcast rights directly from the artists so their stations could then use it in fund-raising. However, at the same time, the local affiliates were empowered to make their own decisions when it came to scheduling those shows. For example, if Long Island's WLIW was airing Yanni's concert on Wednesday evening, and it generated more pledge dollars than Riverdance, WLIW could make the decision to replace already-scheduled airings of Riverdance on Thursday with multiple showings of the Yanni program. The local programmers were playing quarterback, reading the defense at the line of scrimmage, and then making quick adjustments, calling an audible, in their programming.

The beauty of this system was that it was, at its basic level, a meritocracy. Compared to the world of commercial television, this was an honest, respectable business model. Plus, the money the local stations raised with their pledge programs promoted the production and broadcasting of programs families could actually watch. In the end, PBS's idiosyncratic paradigm opened the door for me as an independent producer/artist to become an outlier in both the public television universe and the recording industry.

But first, I needed to find a way to get this special made. The budget for the Red Rocks special, as it currently stood, was pushing $800,000, and Connie and I had no commitment from PBS to put it on the air. This would be an *enormous* risk and I could not take that gamble alone. I needed to persuade Connie to sign off on this creative moonshot, but I had to be sure that this was more than just the realization of a singular childhood dream. There needed to be real long-term purpose behind it.

To her credit, Connie is naturally risk averse, so I knew I needed a strategy, a vision. Fortunately, we'd been down this road together before, when we started our tiny, independent record company to produce and distribute my music after every major record label had rejected it. When Connie and I discussed it, she ultimately gave her support for the Red Rocks special, and it deepened, even more, the love and affection I had for her. From the moment I'd met her, Connie had been my muse for creativity and a touchstone for all my career decisions. She understood that a bold statement like this could materialize a lifelong dream for her husband to become a professional musician.

Not everyone agreed with our risky blueprint for realizing this dream, however. My entertainment attorney pleaded with my business manager, Steve Callas, to dismantle our plans. He insisted that Connie and I should not be using our own money to invest in such a risky venture. He believed that the only sane way to produce a show of this magnitude was to use someone else's money. I knew he was right. I knew the risk bordered on recklessness. It was horrible stewardship of finances. But I still felt a supernatural pull in my heart to put my head down and forge ahead to produce the show. And besides, we had already passed the point of no return after Connie was officially all in. Our costs continued to rise, and we would lose at least a quarter of a million dollars if we bailed out now.

I knew I had no choice but to remove all doubt from my subconscious and replace it with visions of victory. I began to see the album at number one. I imagined millions of viewers watching on PBS. I rehearsed each song in my head. I filled my entire being with positivity and prayers of thanks.

Anchored by real belief, it was ultimately Connie's yes to the Red Rocks wager that galvanized my resolve to make it happen. Her commitment to the idea, and to me, lightened my spirits, but it also added weight to the responsibility I already felt to properly manage the risk we were about to take. Because, in addition to no major record company support, no commitment from PBS, and gambling an enormous amount of money on my music career (which did not even exist yet), our home was still in shambles after having just barely survived the 1994 Northridge earthquake. Shards of glass were everywhere and, oh, by the way, Connie was also four months pregnant with our daughter, Prima, and she was starring in another CBS show, *Second Chances*, alongside then little-known actress Jennifer Lopez.

Eventually, everyone was fully on board, and we got down to work. David Michaels set about selecting his handpicked dream team of crew members for the production, and I began the process of working out the orchestrations for my songs with Charlie and John Bisharat. These brothers possessed enormous talents. Charlie had been playing solo violin and co-writing with me for a few years. He is that rare talent who possesses both perfect pitch and virtuoso skills on his instrument. Charlie suggested his brother, John, as orchestrator and conductor. In the weeks and months leading up to Red Rocks, the three of us would meet for hours at a time, going over each song and expanding the arrangements to ensure that the orchestra would be featured in the performance and not just background support. John Bisharat's orchestrations were brilliant from the beginning, and when we began rehearsals with the orchestra members in Denver, his sheet music required few changes.

Then, on the evening of May 26, 1994, barely two and a half months before the concert, everything nearly came apart for reasons wholly unrelated to and infinitely more important than the music.

• • •

It was the day after Connie's birthday. As we prepared for bed, Connie said, "John, there is something wrong. Something is wrong!" She was thirty-six weeks pregnant and having already been through a previous pregnancy and birth with Gib, she knew what she was feeling was not typical. I felt helpless. Her rising stress level began to concern me. With terrible Neanderthal-esque advice, I gave her the only counsel I could think of in the moment: "I think you need some protein, honey," I said and left our bedroom for the kitchen. A few minutes later, I returned and said, "Here. Have some cheese." She looked at me like I had just suggested she eat worms.

"You want me to eat cheese?!" she said. "That's it?"

What came out of my mouth at that moment has become a long-standing family "Dad Guffaw" that gets pulled out whenever someone in our family is not feeling well, but I swear I read about the healing benefits of cheddar somewhere. I still can't produce a medical journal to support it or to defend myself, though.

That night was a restless one, but Connie awoke feeling more stable and with less concern, so we started our day like normal. Connie headed off for an early meeting for her skin-care line with her business partner, Sheree LaDove, in Beverly Hills. I pointed my car toward Paramount Studios to begin my day at *Entertainment Tonight*. As we were about to begin taping, I got an urgent message in my earpiece that Connie was on the phone. She was calling from the ob-gyn's office at Cedars-Sinai Medical Center to tell me she was being admitted. I tore off my microphone and bolted from the set. In the middle of her business meeting, the odd feeling had returned, and Connie's intuition was now signaling that she needed more than camembert or cheddar.

By the time I arrived at Cedars, Connie was already hooked up to telemetry monitoring both her and the baby. It turns out, Connie was almost completely out of amniotic fluid. While I was at her bedside, she revealed to me that the doctor basically said, "I don't know what it was you were feeling, but thank God you're here. You made the right choice to come in!"

The prescription was immediate bed rest in the hospital. The challenge was to keep the baby inside Connie for as long as possible and, to that end, to figure out where the amniotic fluid had gone since her water had not broken. Most importantly, the doctors wanted to let Connie's body replenish the amniotic fluid to ensure that the baby stayed in the womb long enough for her lungs to be fully developed when she was born. Over the next week, several amniocentesis procedures were performed to give doctors an idea of the baby's lung maturity. Following a week of bed rest, including a drug to stop the progression of contractions, which had begun, Connie's physicians finally had the confidence that the baby's lungs were sufficiently developed for the birthing process to proceed.

Except there was another challenge: Prima was in the breech position. Her legs and buttocks were facing down toward the vaginal canal. This typically means birth by Caesarean section. Connie had delivered Gib in natural childbirth, so she wanted to know if this baby could also be delivered naturally, without serious risk. Her team of doctors suggested an ECV—or external cephalic version. The procedure, performed by two or more obstetricians, is designed to turn the baby head down by manipulating the baby from the outside. The problem with this idea was that with a lack of amniotic fluid, it would basically be like trying to move a six-and-a-half-pound baby dolphin along the bottom of a dry pond bed.

We agreed to try the ECV along with extensive monitoring to ensure our baby's safety. The medical team began to push and pull on Connie's stomach with brute force. Connie groaned in pain. I felt weak. I saw the outline of what looked like a little foot pressed against Connie's stomach like a relief map, looking like it might explode out of her skin. I was watching a horror film. The foot would move and then snap back to its original position. After five or ten minutes of the doctors trying to push Prima's little butt and head in opposite directions through my wife's giant pregnant belly, I had had enough.

"Stop! Stop!" I said. These were brilliant physicians, and Connie was showing incredible bravery. She wanted to do the work. She wanted to push our baby out into this world. But now it was *my* intuition telling me we were about to snap off one of the kid's little legs. My courageous wife would need a C-section. In a short time, I was in the operating room and struggling to hide my fear and trepidation. As I drew another breath through my hospital mask, I listened intently to the sounds of the monitoring devices and the commands of the surgeons and the anesthesiologist. And then I heard something else. Singing. Connie was holding her giant belly and, with a "jolly ol' Saint Nick" look on her face, was belting out the lyrics from the Paul Anka song "Having My Baby." Except she had replaced *my* with *your*. "Having YOUR baby!"

It made me laugh. I told her Paul Anka wouldn't mind the ad-lib.

It was vintage Concetta. Any other patient in this situation would have been a tad bit apprehensive. My wife was serenading us with a 1963 pop song.

The singing stopped when the anesthesia kicked in and the surgeon made his incision. Not long after, Connie called out from the operating table, "Hey, guys, I think you're losing me here! I feel like I'm going to pass out."

The surgeon looked to the anesthesiologist, who nodded and then administered a drug known as a "presser" to raise her blood pressure. Her vital signs went back to normal. Mine were now pretty much fried.

Up until this moment, the gender of our baby had been kept secret. We had decided if it was a boy, he'd be Primo, after Connie's dad. If it was a girl, she would be Prima, also after Connie's dad. (My mom's name was Mildred. Case closed.)

When all six pounds, seven ounces of Prima Tesh emerged from Connie's tummy, she was all legs and a head. *No wonder they couldn't turn this kid.* Heck, Connie had just delivered a baby giraffe! What added even more emotion to the event was that Gib, at only thirteen years old, had been permitted in the operating room with us. His job was to videotape the entire procedure. Talk about a bonding experience! When the doctor lifted Gib's little sister up by her ankles, our son reverentially lowered the video camera and proclaimed, "Wow, it's purple!" Everyone laughed. He spoke the truth. It was a miracle. A beautiful purple baby girl.

What happened next still makes me shudder. Baby Prima was not crying. She was grunting. It was a deep, low-pitched, haunting sort of noise that sounded nothing like any of the babies in birthing-class videos. It turned out, a nurse said that grunting sound meant that she wasn't breathing normally.

Prior to our arrival at the hospital, our family had decided that if mother and baby were separated for any reason, I would stay with the baby and Gib would stay with Connie. So as the doctors sutured Connie's midsection and attended to her recovery, they positioned her body strategically away from the action that was unfolding around Prima. When facing critical medical challenges, doctors and nurses are trained to control their emotions around patients and families, but this operating room team could not disguise what appeared to be an intense intervention on Prima's behalf. They suctioned her tiny throat and after placing her briefly on Connie's chest, they announced that the baby needed to be transferred to the neonatal intensive care unit (NICU). Prima was laid in a plastic incubator, which was then placed onto a cart. I followed the cart to the NICU while Connie and Gib headed to the recovery room, one floor down.

. . .

I am still wearing my mask and gloves when I enter the NICU and see a long row of isolettes lining both sides of a fifty-foot corridor. Still numb with apprehension, I begin to wonder if I've been transported to a world that resembles a kind of suspended animation for infants. Inside these twenty or thirty plastic rectangles are newborns, most no bigger than my fist. Their isolettes regulate temperature, humidity, and oxygen levels. Each has armholes through which adults can reach the infants without disturbing their controlled environment.

My daughter, in her isolette, is between two infants one-fifth her size. Taped to the side of her mouth is an endotracheal tube—a small plastic tube that leads into her mouth and travels down her windpipe to her lungs. On her left index finger is a pulse oximeter to measure the oxygen in her blood. The nurses have also run an arterial line—a thin tube inserted into Prima's artery—to check her blood pressure and measure blood gases. There's nothing comforting about seeing your child in this condition, and I'm in a room surrounded by them. My knees are weak, but Prima is no longer grunting. She appears to be in no distress. She is stable, so I head down the elevator to see Connie.

The physical pain she was in previously is nothing compared to her frustration over being separated from her newborn. A physician, nurse, and hospital administrator arrive at Connie's bedside and tell us, "Your little girl is very sick." They diagnose her with "wet lung," a fairly common condition in babies delivered by C-section, in part because their lungs don't benefit from being squeezed the way they are during a vaginal birth. "She is getting the best possible care in the NICU," they reassure us. I am terrified. Connie, however, thinks they are overreacting.

"She's going to be okay," Connie says. "I want to see her now."

The doctor is smiling but insists that Connie stay where she is and recover from her surgery. He promises that she can visit Prima in the NICU the next morning. Then, in a move that is quintessential Concetta, this bold, Italian mamma-bear pulls herself into a sitting position on the hospital bed. She grabs my arm for support, and with her other hand she grabs the IV stand that still connects her to her recovery hydration.

"I want to see her now," she demands. And she marches toward the elevator, with nervous hospital staff trailing behind.

Connie knows instinctively that a mother's touch along with nursing her baby will provide a powerful dose of healing therapy. Inside the isolette, Prima's little arms are restrained by cloth ties, one to each side, so that she won't reflexively pull on the endotracheal tube that is supporting her breathing. Connie reaches into Prima's isolette and touches her daughter's tiny palm. Prima's fingers curl around mommy's pinky. My face is soaked with tears.

Connie is right, I think. *She is going to be okay.* Indeed, it's wonderful to watch our Prima today in the light of those first scary moments and minutes and days. It turns out God planted a full measure of fight inside her that we all enjoy today. Relentless. Hard worker. Incredible talent. She dances on stage with us at concerts, and while audiences often remark at her incredible technique, the thing they notice most is the palpable joy that seems to leap from the stage. But Prima's very first concert would be at one of God's natural wonders as her tiny body is held in the arms of her mother.

Chapter 24

John Tesh: Live at Red Rocks with the Colorado Symphony

It was 2:00 p.m. on dress rehearsal day for *John Tesh: Live at Red Rocks with the Colorado Symphony*, and from my position at the piano—which is wrapped in a silver space blanket to reflect the sun's rays and protect it from the drop in temperature that will occur between now and the dress rehearsal, which could throw the piano out of tune—my view of the legendary Red Rocks Amphitheatre was framed by giant rocks that looked as if they had exploded from the earth. "Creation Rock" on the north end, "Ship Rock" on the south, and "Stage Rock" to the east reminded me of family trips I'd made to Utah's Monument Valley and the Grand Canyon. Like those places, Red Rocks inspires feelings of awe.

The walls of the amphitheater contain records dating back to the Jurassic period 160 million years ago. There are dinosaur tracks on the property as well as fossil fragments of the forty-foot sea serpent plesiosaur. Impossibly, these natural formations looked even more majestic in the midafternoon sun than they did when I was in this exact spot several months earlier during the site survey. We would film the PBS concert special the next day with a five-piece core band (drums, percussion, bass, guitar, electric violin) and the Colorado Symphony.

During the site survey I'd walked into the venue with my old friend

David Michaels to find a beautiful nine-foot Steinway piano in the middle of the giant stage. In a wonderful gesture of encouragement and inspiration, the amphitheater management had rented it for the day so that I could experience the legendary Red Rocks acoustics as our production team went about their work: picking camera and lighting positions, plotting sight lines and crane positions, and planning for the huge logistics challenge ahead of them. Our crew would need two full days just to load in all the equipment.

I sat at the Steinway, playing for an empty amphitheater and listening as each note was first amplified by the giant rock wall behind me, and then projected forward and propelled toward the rear of the amphitheater. There was no slap-back echo on a back wall that would normally be present in a conventional concert hall. From the stage, the sound of the Steinway piano strings entered a massive rock funnel created by the monolithic formations on each side. In that canyon between the rocks, the music gathered three seconds of natural reverberation and then vanished at the rear of the amphitheater. No sound system. No amplification. I imagined the powerful sound that the symphony would make in this supernatural place. As the sun set on Stage Rock behind me that day and we wrapped up the site survey, I felt the presence of my favorite artists in this ancient amphitheater. Jimmy Hendrix, 1968. Jethro Tull, 1971. U2, 1983. The Moody Blues, 1992. The Beatles, 1964. Each of these artists was, in their own way, responsible for why I felt like Red Rocks was the only place I could make a big enough musical and visual statement that I might finally come into my own as a professional musician.

Later that night, David and I returned to the venue to see what it would look like during a live concert. ZZ Top was performing. Their unmistakable Texas blues–driven guitar sound ripped through the Colorado night air like lightning. This was only to be surpassed, midway through the show, by *actual* lightning that descended on the venue with an earthshaking crack and a fireball bolt of static electricity that struck the left speaker tower suspended from the metal scaffolding. The band, seemingly oblivious to the event, continued to play on, even as smoke poured from the speaker tower and with only the right speaker array still in service. The crowd roared with delight.

• • •

The only thing that could match the impossibility and unbelievability of that moment is the one I'm experiencing right now, on day two of our rehearsals before the actual event. I'm realizing I'm going to be playing my music on the same stage as my favorite band, the Beatles, the band I had watched on television as a twelve-year-old boy.

It feels like a dream come true. But not just any dream. A specific dream brought forward from my childhood years—much of it spent alone creating things in my head—that has been so vivid and so graphic for so long, it has never not appeared to me in living color when I think about it.

I look halfway up the audience seating area to where there is a twenty-foot-by-twenty-foot carpeted platform with a pommel horse and a balance beam bolted to it. Gymnastics apparatus. Two cameras on cranes are tracking the movements of Olympic champions Nadia Comăneci and Bart Conner as they rehearse separate routines that have been choreographed to three of my songs. Oblivious to the production crew that surrounds them, Nadia and Bart are deep in a creative process using jargon only they can understand.

Nadia is on the beam. Bart is calling out choreography ideas in a series of eight-counts, barely heard above the recorded playback of my "April Song" from a boombox at the base of the platform. Next, Bart takes his turn on the pommel horse. With Nadia now looking on, Bart's legs are whipping back and forth across the pommel horse in world championship form. His hands, at full speed, are indistinguishable from one another as he reaches between his legs in movements that are synchronous with "Group 5," a frenetic composition of mine with three different time signatures. The song was originally created as the underscore for the death-defying downhill segments of the Tour de France. It's a rush of nostalgia for me. I had worked as a sports commentator with both Bart and Nadia, of course, and before that watched them grow up together on the world stage and become Olympic champions. Now they are a couple who just recently become engaged to be married.

I go backstage to my dressing room, which is framed by walls of rock.

There are even rock benches. I should be nervous. I should be a mess. But the hundreds of hours of rehearsal, the overwhelming amount of details swimming in my head, and the fact that my wife and baby girl will be in the audience tonight have created an odd calmness in me.

I close my eyes, meditating on the truth that I have memorized every note, every phrase that each orchestra member is about to play. I can tell you the width of the piatti cymbal and the hourly rental cost of the Sony PCM-3324 digital recording machine. I know the distance of Nadia's balance beam to the keys of my grand piano, and I can tell you the weather report at this exact moment. It is not good.

I open my eyes.

My dearest wife, Concetta, is standing in front of me with an oxygen mask on her face, fighting off the effects of altitude sickness. Red Rocks resides at nearly seven thousand feet. Our brand-new daughter is in her arms.

"Okay, John. It's time to pray, and it's time to go out there and focus on one thing. Just play piano, my love," she says.

She's right. The weather. The audience. The orchestra. The risk. Her altitude sickness. They are all in God's hands now.

Walkie-talkies continue their distorted crackling, and the stage manager walks over and hands me his unit. It's Michaels. There will be only one final conversation before downbeat. When conductor John Bisharat lowers his baton, David and I will be in this together without further communication, connected only by the drama that is unfolding on my stage and in his TV truck. We have been all over the world together creating the sports version of this kind of television, but we have never been "here" before.

Decades later, when I read that Mel Gibson spoke encouragement over himself during challenging shots for his film *The Passion of the Christ*, I related to his combination of bravado and loneliness. Gibson's recurring mantra on location was simply: "I can do this. I know how to do this." When you've jumped off a cliff hoping to fly, you must believe that God will help you build your plane—or your wings—on the way down.

I know in my heart I can do this. I just need to focus on the one thing I can control, which my wife has reminded me: "Just play piano."

I hear the unmistakable sound of seventy world-class musicians tuning to a concert C. Then I find myself pulled into a circle of band members, standing hand in hand. They have joined me on a six-month journey of rehearsals and live concert performances, preparing for this very moment. Violinist Charlie Bisharat. Bassist Tim Landers. Drummer Dave Hooper. Percussionist Brian Kilgore. Guitarist Paul Viapiano. We hold hands and say prayers of thanks. Then I repeat the words of Martin Luther King Jr., which my bandmates have heard many times before: "You don't have to see the whole staircase, just take the first step *in faith*."

One song at a time.

As we approach the stage, I remind Tim and Dave not to "go with me" if I push the tempo. I knew that the tension of the moment, further exacerbated by the altitude at Red Rocks, would increase our heartbeats significantly, and when performing an instrument, it's human nature for the clock in your brain to be driven by the beat of your heart. So, for example, if a song is designed to be played at 80 beats per minute, but my rapidly beating heart tells me that's slow, I might push the tempo. My resting heart rate at sea level is 48 bpm. It was now 90. The orchestrations created by John Bisharat were complex enough that even a 5-beats-per-minute push could create a train wreck of mistakes. Though it's common for the engine room—the drums and bass—to follow the tempo of the featured artist (me on piano) for continuity, it is crucial that Tim and Dave hold the line on tempo and force me to stay with them. Thankfully, Dave has created a metronome click track that will play in his earpiece to ensure we start each song at the right tempo. All I need is a few raised eyebrows from Tim, and I'll know I am playing on top of the beat and should back off. This is one concert where I cannot trust my instincts. I am performing in a unique paradigm.

As I step onto the stage, it's all I can do to hold back a flood of tears. I am not ready for the roar of nine thousand people and the burst of five hundred high-intensity Vari-Lites in my face, heralding the beginning of the concert. The crowd is already on their feet. A cameraman, dressed in all black, is on his knees, inches from my left hand. Out of the corner of my eye I see a giant camera crane swoop down, inches above the crowd and speeding toward the stage. I realize that I've been holding my breath and exhale with a long sigh (which is audible on the recording later). I smile, quickly scanning for the readiness of each band member. One final nod from maestro John Bisharat. Then he raises his arms high over his head. The musicians lift their instruments . . . and . . . downbeat!

The stage shakes beneath me with a synchronized eruption of tympani, orchestral bass drum, and piatti cymbals. The fifty-foot-tall pillars on either side of the stage explode on cue with fiery pyrotechnics. The crowd erupts and I have to strain to hear Hooper's hi-hat to dig out the tempo. Now, with the strings and brass all playing triple-forte unison lines, the fanfare for "A Thousand Summers" unfolds. This is one of the biggest songs on the set list, with no less than five different time signatures and four separate themes. I originally composed the piece to describe the vast scope and pageantry of the Tour de France. It's our opening theme, and along with maestro Bisharat's wonderfully bombastic orchestrations, it sends the message to the Red Rocks audience that they are witnessing an epic event. I'm drunk with emotion and in the heat of the moment, I again hear Connie's encouragement in my head: *Just play piano!*

In another twenty minutes, though, I would need more than encouragement to overcome an unexpected obstacle.

Chapter 25

Obstacles

―――――――――

As often happens, when we are struggling inside our obstacles, they tend to present themselves as insurmountable, but Ryan Holiday writes:

> Overcoming obstacles is a discipline of three critical steps. It begins with how we look at our specific problems, our attitude or approach; then the energy and creativity with which we actively break them down and turn them into opportunities; finally, the cultivation and maintenance of an inner will that allows us to handle defeat and difficulty. It's three interdependent, interconnected, and fluidly contingent disciplines: Perception, Action, and the Will. It's a simple process.[1]

Perception, *action*, and *will*. I'd practiced these my whole life prior to this evening, yet when I look up and feel raindrops on my face, my old foes of doubt and fear begin to creep in. I am facing a brand-new obstacle unlike any I've encountered before.

At first I think the loud cracks of thunder I am hearing are a triple forte orchestral bass drum or more fireworks from those prankster production geeks. But when I see the entire violin section stand up and run offstage, shielding their heads with their sheet music, reality sets in. I turn to look at the crowd. Many are frantically moving; some are grabbing parkas and umbrellas. Then I feel the pouring rain on my hands as

I play and I feel certain that if I look to my left, I will see thousands of fans, like the orchestra, running for the exits. Game over.

But when I do, the thousands of faces in the audience are obscured by a sea of colorful umbrellas. I look back toward the stage. The entire string section has vanished; violins, cellos, and basses have run for cover because their instruments will be quickly destroyed by the rain. They leave behind fifty empty seats that are reflected in the water now covering the stage. We had performed only four songs with the symphony before they had exited stage left.

At that moment, I believe my vision of a hit PBS special will be reduced to a two-minute "Concert Mishap at Red Rocks" video report on Denver's 11:00 p.m. newscast. Thoughts of losing my house are front-of-mind.

Thump, thump, thump. THUMP-THUMP-THUMP.

I look across the stage at Hooper, still perched on his drum throne. His shrug of confusion telegraphs, "It ain't me."

THUMP-THUMP-THUMP.

The sound continues to grow. With their feet, the audience is stomping out a message: *"Do something! We aren't going anywhere!"* Because most of the crowd are holding umbrellas, they can't use their hands to clap. They are using their feet.

THUMP-THUMP-THUMP-THUMP.

In a sonorous, basso-frequency range, the rhythmic thumps continue to rise in volume as thousands more join in. The sound is amplified by the two massive rock walls and then bounces back into the amphitheater. This is not in my playbook. It stands to reason that when the orchestra left, the show was over. Then I also see that my band has not moved from their assigned spots onstage. Bassist Tim Landers, violinist Charlie Bisharat, guitarist Paul Viapiano, percussionists Dave Hooper and Brian Kilgore are standing their ground in the soaking rain. It's all too much emotional data for my brain to process.

Charlie brings me back to reality: *"C'mon. Let's just play! Listen to them. They want us to play!"*

I would later learn that these downpours were an acknowledged part of the Red Rocks charm by the locals. In the Rockies, they were accustomed to the capricious weather. Why else would concertgoers carry an umbrella or tie a rain parka around their waist?

Water is now streaming out of my piano. Charlie is wearing a maniacal grin. I call across the stage to Hooper for a downbeat. "Road Made!" I scream. "Count us in!" As Dave strikes the snare drum, a spray of rainwater is launched into the air. "Road Made for Animals" is a rock-and-roll piece that was also written for the Tour de France. Here and now, it explodes like a music cue from a fight scene in *Raging Bull*. The wind is whipping raindrops into my face. We are on a *Stage* Made for Animals. I see Charlie running . . . then skidding . . . across the stage to stand beside me. Playing an electric violin in the rain while hydroplaning on a concert stage—*That's new*, I think.

With the promise of a live TV special gone, all that's left is the music, this compelling moment, and a crazed bunch of madmen, furiously playing their instruments in the pouring rain. And when we hit the chorus of the song, I hear something else. Trumpets, trombones, and tubas have joined us. Water is running off their bells and their sheet music is matted to their stands, but they have not deserted us. Brass players? They were veterans of their high school marching bands with a US Post Office credo (neither snow nor rain nor . . . Red Rocks). We are performing for these nine thousand stomping fans who are giving us an inexplicable gift.

When we reach the middle section of "Road Made for Animals," Charlie and I tear up the arrangement and there's a flurry of hand signals between us and the band. It's time to extend the solos and stay connected with the audience as long as possible. There's no telling when the rain will reach a transformer or two and we will lose power.

As we near the end of the song, I spot our stage manager, Victor Frank, in my eyeline. He's gesturing wildly from the wings to stage right, and he now has my attention. He points to our second stage in the middle of the audience. Bart Conner has appeared on the stage and the boom camera is repositioning toward him.

"Bart wants to perform!" shouts Vic.

Bart's performance had been scheduled for later in the program but we all realize that "later" is not likely. More shouting and hand signals across the stage, and we prepare to perform "Group 5." Given the weather conditions and my stress hormones, I do not have the luxury of thinking this through. If I had, I would have concluded that this Olympic champion performing on soaking-wet equipment could be seriously injured and I would have nixed it. But in the flow of the performance, I stand up from the piano and grab the microphone:

"Ladies and Gentlemen . . . performing, I do believe, for the very first time in the rain . . . please welcome Olympic champion Bart Conner!"

The crowd goes nuts as Bart performs his choreographed routine, perfectly synchronized to the song. A blast of rainwater explodes off the pommel each time he grabs it. When we finish the piece, the audience erupts with more stomping and shouting and pumping of umbrellas. From the stage, the thousands of colorful umbrellas rise and fall in unison. Mary Poppins comes to mind. Just as quickly as this bizarre image reaches my retinas, it's gone.

Then people begin retracting their umbrellas and looking up at the sky. Over Red Rocks there is now a sliver of a crescent moon surrounded by stars. Not a cloud in sight. I lean back, arms in the air, and thank God for this blessing. I shout something at Charlie, but he cannot hear me. The roar from the audience has become deafening as they see that, behind me, the orchestra is retaking their positions. My brain is processing snapshots. Someone is wiping down the piano. Vic Frank is smiling from the side of the stage. John Bisharat is walking to his position as conductor, baton in hand. A cameraman once again kneels beside my piano, his lens inches from my fingers. Once more, John raises his baton. This is happening. The orchestra responds and lifts their instruments. Downbeat!

. . .

In the dressing room following the performance, my brain and legs are Jell-O. The rain, the crowd, the risk, and the emotional whipsaw of what had transpired in that ancient arena are a dizzying blur. I plop down onto a couch in the corner of the dressing room, aware, for the first time, that my three-piece purple suit is soaked through to my skin. If you've ever run a marathon, then you know this feebleness. No will, no stamina, no legs beneath your torso. If a fire broke out, you'd be the last one out of the building.

Through the door of the dressing room walks my Connie. She is cradling Prima in a nursing pose. As she strides purposefully toward me, I can't help myself. I break into hysterical laughter. I have just emerged from out of all that earthly lunacy onstage as a drowned rat. And now here's a gorgeous woman standing over me with our eight-week-old baby attached to her breast.

"I spoke to Michaels. He says he's got it. Every bit of it."

It takes a moment to register. "What? How is that possible? The cameras and the equipment in that huge rainstorm? They kept shooting?"

Connie replies with enthusiasm. "He says they got it. He was smiling when he said it." She is moving so much as she talks that Prima's mouth keeps popping off her breast, and I feel a bond with our newborn. Prima can't believe her mom won't hold still so she can finish her dinner and I can't believe what her mom is telling me.

"What about all the microphones? The wind? There was a flood coming out of my piano!"

"Ross says he lost a few mics and that there are times when he could hear the rain on the piano, but he says it's not bad at all."

Sound engineer Ross Pallone and David Michaels had spoken the truth to Connie. Not one of the fifteen cameras went down in the rain and all forty-eight tracks of audio made it to the digital audiotape machine.

. . .

On an early Monday morning in March of 1995, a wonderful lady named Linda Taggart left me a message on my answering machine. As the program director for a local PBS affiliate in Maryland, she had received a copy of *John Tesh, Live at Red Rocks with the Colorado Symphony* in the mail (from me) and said that she had watched the VHS screener tape. She "enjoyed it very much," she said. She was especially taken by the segment where "you and your band played in the rain." I loved the matter-of-factness of that statement—like we had planned to play in a torrential rainstorm all along. She said she thought the show was inspirational, so going on intuition she decided to test my ninety-minute concert special on her Maryland Public Television station. There were no meetings with her programming staff or with PBS corporate in DC; she just decided that she wanted to see if her viewing audience shared her strong feelings about the concert.

If that wasn't encouraging enough, as someone who had taken a huge creative risk that had yet to pay off—literally or figuratively—Ms. Taggart then delivered the real news: the show had pledged well Sunday evening and had actually surpassed *The Three Tenors* and *Yanni, Live at the Acropolis* in fund-raising dollars that night. And this had happened despite airing my show close to midnight. She said she would pass her results along to PBS corporate and to the rest of the local PBS stations across the country and wished me luck.

The phenomenal success of the Red Rocks concert that Sunday night on Maryland Public Television instantly caught the attention of the PBS brass in Washington and producer Jim Scalem, who was a veritable genius when it came to promoting and packaging PBS programming. He soon became my mentor and guide.

The Red Rocks special began airing throughout the PBS station universe on March 1, 1995. My seventy-six-day live concert tour was scheduled to kick off the first week of May that same year. In between recording segments for *ET*, I would dash off the set to call local PBS television station managers directly, promoting airings of the Red Rocks program and just to say thank you. Little did I know that in less than a month I would face a lawsuit that would simultaneously threaten to derail the concert tour, destroy my television career, and bankrupt my family.

· · ·

By the time our special made landfall on PBS's national schedule, I had added three key members to my team: producer Mary Mueller, recording industry veteran Ken Antonelli, and public relations expert Dan Klores. Ken used his connections to beat on record-store chains to place early orders for the CD and VHS of *John Tesh: Live at Red Rocks with the Colorado Symphony*. Klores had connections of his own with *Newsweek* and the *New York Times*. Three weeks into PBS's broadcast of our program, *Newsweek* ran a story with the headline "The Teshing of America." It read, in part:

> Pavarotti, Domingo, Carreras . . . Tesh. The Three Tenors may not know it yet, but they've got company. . . . Known to millions as the booming blond anchorman on TV's *"Entertainment Tonight,"* he's now reached millions more as the star of *"John Tesh: Live at Red Rocks."* The No. 1 fund-raiser during PBS's besieged begathons this month featured Tesh at the piano, the Colorado Symphony Orchestra behind him, and gymnastic accompaniment by ex-Olympians Nadia Comăneci and Bart Conner. So popular was the 90-minute spectacle that Judge Lance Ito requested it for the O.J. jurors.[2]

In the twenty-five years since this concert, we have met hundreds of fans who were with us that night at Red Rocks. They show up early at a sound check. They call out from an audience, "I was at the Red Rocks show!" They wait outside the stage door just to share the memory with us. We are forever joined by the experience.

Still, what puzzled many of the journalists and reviewers at the apex of the mind-boggling success posted up by PBS, performing arts centers, and record stores was that I would frequently collaborate with the late-night television producers and writers in their Tesh-bashing comedy bits. If the concept was creative, I had no problem diving in. Search "When Teshes Attack" on YouTube. Or "John Tesh and Triumph the Insult Dog." Even today, when you attend one of my concerts, you'll see bits and pieces of these comedic vignettes as an introduction to the show. During my broadcasting career of forty-plus years, reporting on and interviewing thousands of creative professionals, I've often cringed as I watched more than a few artists get eaten alive by their knee-jerk reactions to criticism. In some extreme cases their anger and hurt caused them to take the critics to heart and actually change their creative process.

Don't get me wrong. I view self-deprecation as something of an art form. Too much of it can easily come off as goofy and slavishly submissive. The wrong concept or lousy writing will demean your personal brand. On the other hand, unbridled self-aggrandizement is a losing strategy.

Chapter 26

And Then This Happened

A nd then this happened: Paramount Television vice president Frank Kelly called me in for a meeting in March 1995. In my haste and eagerness to announce my first major concert tour, I thought it appropriate to place a full-page advertisement in the industry paper *Daily Variety*, thanking PBS and listing all of the concert tour dates. This proved to be a move that harkened back to the impetuous, drop-add forgery fiasco that, twenty-two years earlier, landed me in a pup tent under an overpass. Except the stakes were higher this time around.

With my close friend and attorney Chuck Kenworthy by my side, Paramount TV president Kerry McCluggage and Frank Kelly outlined their position. I had nearly a year left on my contract to co-host *Entertainment Tonight*. It was Paramount's position that it was not possible for me to fulfill that obligation with a four-month nationwide concert tour beginning in June. Kelly went on to say that if I didn't cancel the tour, or at least, somehow, cut it into pieces, Paramount would be forced to not only sue me personally but they would get injunctions against all of the concert venues, legally preventing them from presenting my concert.

Chuck and I refused to cancel the shows, but instead suggested that I leave *ET* and sign a noncompete, agreeing that I would not appear on a rival show for the next five years. A red-faced Frank Kelly then informed me that if I didn't cancel the tour they would be forced to hire a trial attorney and take this before a judge. Within twenty-four hours, Paramount had hired independent trial attorney Patty Glaser.

Two days after that, it was Paramount, Glaser, and three of her associates standing in a courtroom opposite me and Chuck. When I'd asked Chuck the night before if he knew anything about Patty, he said, "Trust me, you don't want to know."

"No. You have to tell me."

"Well," Chuck said, "a colleague of mine looked concerned when I mentioned that Patty was representing Paramount."

"What did he say?"

"He said she is known for ripping opponents' jugulars out of their neck and then leaving them to bleed on the ground."

My mouth dropped to the floor. "Seriously?"

"That's what he said. He said that—"

I put up my hand. "That's enough. Thanks."

Have you ever been pulled over by a police officer or been called on to give your book report in front of the class? Then you know the feeling produced by the body's fight-or-flight hormones. The sudden flood of epinephrine, norepinephrine, and dozens of other hormones cause a chain reaction in our body. Heart rate and blood pressure increase. Pupils dilate to take in as much light as possible. Veins in skin constrict to send more blood to major muscle groups. Your muscles tense up, energized by adrenaline and glucose. All of these physical responses are intended to help us survive a dangerous situation by preparing us to either run or fight for our lives.

Not all that long before the hearing, I had been floating through a colossal measure of success that I had worked to manifest my entire life. It had taken hard work, risk, and focus, of course, but there are plenty of artists who do the same and still come up short. The success of the show was a lightning strike. And now I could only watch the horrifying picture in front of me: Chuck and Patty arguing my fate before Judge Diane Wayne in Los Angeles Superior Court.

Patty sought to legally block the fifty-six performing arts venues from presenting my concert. As she put it to Chuck by phone earlier in the week, "We will send a letter to each venue, threatening a lawsuit if John Tesh appears on their stage." If she won that argument, if Judge Wayne granted the injunctions she requested, it would trigger a chain reaction that would demolish my music career. Not only would the tour be over, but I would likely be sued by each venue for the damages they incurred by having to refund all of the ticket money to fans (tickets had been on sale for eight weeks).

Without a tour and tickets to generate pledge dollars, PBS stations would likely remove my program from their schedules and replace it with another show. Record stores, encouraged by the promise of hundreds of airings of the concert special, had placed orders for more than fifty thousand CDs and videos. If there was no sales demand, the stores would return the product to us for a refund. Moreover, it seemed likely to me that if Paramount was victorious, there was no way they would renew my contract that was up for renegotiation in six months.

Lest I mistakenly present Paramount Television as the Galactic Empire's Death Star, I would like to pause a moment for an admission of grandiosity. Having the luxury to reflect here, I now have a wholly different perspective on how I dealt with my situation. When the Red Rocks special blew up on PBS; when record stores responded by placing huge orders for CDs; when the concert tickets approached sell-out, I did not handle my rising tide of fortune with any measure of grace and maturity.

That moment when I leaned toward Kerry McCluggage in the Paramount TV executive offices, emphatically declaring that I would not cancel my tour, I showed him deep disrespect. I gave Kerry no room to maneuver, no ground on which to walk back his threat. I was fatuous to a fault. Arrogant. Uncompromising. Paramount had invested heavily in me and Mary Hart. Paramount's local TV stations were counting on them to deliver the syndicated *ET* show with the hosts they had been promised in their syndication contracts. Additionally, if Paramount just let me walk off the set for three months, what dangerous precedent would that set for their future dealings with other *ET* employees?

• • •

From my seat in the courtroom, I heard Patty Glaser's voice rising in volume and intensity as she outlined for the judge why "Mr. Tesh is in substantial, material breach of his contract. Mr. Tesh had no right to do this and Your Honor has every legal right to stop the tour and put Mr. Tesh back in the *ET* chair."

I remember thinking, *This is why Xanax was created.*

My heart was beating through my throat.

What happened next was wiped out of my memory by what must have been "Courtroom PTSD," but the transcript shows that Judge Wayne told both Chuck and Patty that she was not inclined, during this court appearance, to order an injunction "preventing Mr. Tesh from performing his concerts," and that instead she would set a hearing for two weeks later to hear further arguments, "if the two parties cannot work this out on their own."

There would be no further arguments.

The next day, in a move that both shocked and thrilled us, Kerry McCluggage and his in-house legal counsel opened negotiations with Chuck to put together a plan for a calm and civil exit from my *ET* hosting job. Apparently, from a PR perspective, fighting one of their employees who just wanted to play music and help PBS raise money was a lose-lose situation for Paramount. My exit, we decided, would be timed to coincide with the launch of my first-ever concert tour.

. . .

I remain grateful to Kerry McCluggage and Paramount for calling off Patty Glaser. I am forever indebted to my pal Chuck Kenworthy* and I am fully repentant regarding my vainglorious behavior during this time. A few days before I departed on my tour, *ET* threw me a wonderful going-away party. They let me make a heartfelt goodbye speech on the air and then, for the next decade, broadcast reports on my album releases and concert appearances.

---

* Chuck's career as a trial attorney and negotiator continues to flourish. He currently represents several multibillion-dollar companies that specialize in cancer research. Chuck often hires outside attorneys to handle litigation for him. One of his regulars? Patty Glaser.

Thankfully, there was much to report on. The PBS broadcasts of *Red Rocks* over the next three years translated into millions of records sold, more than a quarter of a million concert tickets sold each year, a DVD/VHS that reached triple platinum status, and most importantly, millions of dollars in pledge contributions to PBS's 350 local stations. My band, the orchestra, and I traveled the country for two and a half months on that first tour. We taped my next PBS concert special, *Avalon*, on Catalina Island in Southern California. It, too, became a gold-certified recording. Next was *One World*, where the band and I traveled to Italy, Austria, Ireland, and Monument Valley, Utah, to collaborate with local artists. Following each TV taping we supported the PBS specials and recordings with aggressive touring.

Departing *Entertainment Tonight* and the media world for life as a full-time recording and touring artist was the realization of my lifelong pursuit. But after three tours and spending many months at a time living in a tour bus, I missed my wife and family. I'd left Connie, quite often, home alone to raise Prima, the toddler, and Gib, the teenager. It was a less than equitable relationship for a couple, and the kids were growing up without me. I was in love with performing live music, yet I was desperate to be with my family. I needed to figure out a way to make those two loves—music and family—work together.

The answer came during a chance encounter at a restaurant in New York City's theater district in 1996. The legendary record producer Quincy Jones was seated at the table nearest to ours. He smiled at me, leaned in, and said, "Hey man, how ya doin'? You're the hyphenate, right?"

I couldn't believe Quincy Jones had just spoken to me! "I'm sorry, Mr. Jones, I don't understand. I'm John Tesh. It's an honor to meet you."

"Yeah man, I know who you are. You're the hyphenate. TV-and-Music, right?"

"Yes, sir."

"Well, John Tesh, it's great to meet you. Keep it up!"

It didn't dawn on me at the time, because I was too deep into the touring lifestyle, but the answer was in the hyphen. I didn't have to be one or the other, even though Paramount had unwittingly put me in that position a few years earlier; I could be both. I could be any combination of things I wanted, God willing, as long as I found balance and created a schedule I had control over.

It was time to try and put the hyphen back into my life. Could there be a way to continue performing in concerts, help support my family, and still be around enough for them to know I was a husband and a father? Getting back into television was not the answer. Hosting a daily TV show would leave no room for live touring. I realized the answer for balance was much further back in my history. It was my old friend . . . radio. What if I could create a radio program that would enable me to broadcast in a studio and then also remotely when I was out on the road? But did the radio industry need another morning show, another "love songs at night"? Probably not.

Chapter 27

Intelligence for Your Life

I was on the phone with Scott Meyers, and for the first time in a long time he was nearly speechless.

"You're going to be the affiliate relations guy on this," I told him.

"What's that?" he asked.

"Well, you're already calling stations to promote my music," I said. "Just call them and tell them we've got this new radio show that we are launching."

"What's the show called?" he asked.

"It's called *Intelligence for Your Life*."

"Seriously? Wow, that's a very long title," he said. "What's it about?"

"It's the 411 so your life never becomes a 911. It's home improvement for your brain!" I was spitting out slogans like a madman. I was on fire.

"Wait, John? This is a radio show? Intelligence for your life? It sounds like a seminar or something."

Scotty and I had been working together for nearly three years. During that time he had been doing a masterful job of promoting my music on radio stations. Scotty had grown up in the radio business. He had strong connections with stations around the country and across the dial. His specialty was getting artists' songs played on the radio. Promoting my songs was one of his more difficult tasks. And now I was asking him to do the radio version of the impossible.

Just think about the landscape from his perspective: First, the host of

Entertainment Tonight declares to the world that he's really a songwriter and performer at heart. Then he announces that he is leaving the program and giving up his seven-figure salary to pursue a music career. And now he's decided he's going to launch a syndicated radio program . . . without a corporate syndication partner.

"You want to do this as an independent? You know that's impossible, right? Do you have a demo?" asked Scotty.

"Uh, no. No demo. Is that a problem?"

"If stations are even going to consider putting a radio show on the air, they need to know what it will sound like. That's the way this works."

"Scotty, I don't have a demo but you can just tell programmers about the concept. We can get on the phone together and pitch the idea."

"Also, John, delivering a weekly radio show is a huge amount of work and a lot of these programmers have become wary of celebrities catching the radio bug, launching a show, and then losing interest and quitting after a few months. It's going to be a hard sell, but you know me: I'm in if you're in. Let's give it a shot!"

I'm certain Scott Meyers had his fingers crossed behind his back when he committed himself, and I wouldn't have blamed him, as in that moment only one of us should have been committed.

My vision for the *Intelligence for Your Life* radio show was birthed in 1997 when Connie and I were retiring for the evening. I'm a maker of messes. I like to be surrounded by my creative stuff. Often times *where* I surround myself is wholly inappropriate.

"John, this is our bedroom. Your side of the bed looks like the clearance aisle at Radio Shack!"

She was right, of course. Connie was looking at a stack of wires and chargers and a plastic music keyboard and two dead iPods. It looked like someone had emptied their junk drawer by the side of my bed. Then, like a good spouse, I looked to her side of the bed, trying to find something to cross-complain about. I had it!

"Oh yeah, what's all of this on *your* side of the bed?"

Neatly stacked on the floor beside Connie's bedside table were dozens of magazines including *Prevention*, *O* (Oprah's magazine), *Reader's Digest*, and more. Poking out of each issue were yellow sticky notes. It was all very organized, but it was all I had if I was going to get some complaint-parity.

Connie smiled. "These are some of my favorite magazines. The sticky notes mark the articles that I want to read." I do have to admit they were all in alphabetical order and collated according to release date. The disorganized should never challenge the organized. Why? Because they're already prepared for what you're going to say.

That was the end of my feeble complaint. It was also, however, the nexus of an idea that started to germinate in my mind and would eventually grow into a global media brand.

Make stuff you love and talk about stuff you love and you'll attract people who love that kind of stuff. It's that simple.
—**Austin Kleon,** *Show Your Work!*[1]

This was a familiar feeling. It had been years since I had felt it. It was the "light bulb over the head" feeling that is often spoken of by entrepreneurs who have developed ideas that they know are going to work before they've even tested them out in the market.

When you know that you know that you know, you have only two choices. One of them is to take action. Knowing what I now know about the Spirit world, I am fully aware that nudges like this are a gift from the Holy Spirit. We ignore them at our peril.

However, when He, the Spirit of truth, has come, He will guide you into all truth . . . He will tell you things to come.
—**John 16:13**

At the moment I faced my bleak future in that pup tent in 1973, I knew that I knew that I knew that my only way out was to create that crazy demo tape and beg my way onto a radio station.

In 1991, when I destroyed a huge opportunity at the hands of my gross insecurities, I knew that I knew that I had to hatch an inventive strategy to sweep the girl of my dreams off her feet.

I knew that I knew in 1994 that only an epic PBS concert event in the legendary Red Rocks Amphitheatre could give me the foundational event from which to launch the music career I had only seen in my dreams. And so now, in 1997, the knowing was upon me once again.

To this day I believe that one of the big reasons for the success of the *Intelligence for Your Life* radio show is that I knew very little about the business of radio. Connie, Scotty, and I had dozens of people trying to warn us. We were told that self-syndication was suicide. Launching a show without the support of one of the big radio station conglomerates— Cumulus, Clear Channel, Westwood One—was considered impossible.

We were told the show would be too expensive. The idea that was birthed from Connie's stack of magazines would require eight to ten researchers as well as pricey satellite time to feed the show and a computer audio infrastructure to distribute it. Syndicating a show is expensive; it's important to realize that syndicating to five stations costs as much as it does syndicating to 305. The economies of scale happen quickly. Still, if we wanted to take the leap, Connie and I would once again have to self-finance the venture like we did with Red Rocks, which more than a few people believed was way too risky. I believe the words "dumb move" were uttered by someone at some point.

Twenty years later, I had to smile as I read author Steven Pressfield's *Do the Work*:

> Stay Stupid! The three dumbest guys I can think of are Charles Lindbergh, Steve Jobs and Winston Churchill. Why? Because any smart person who understood how impossibly arduous were the tasks they had set themselves would have pulled the plug before he even began.[2]

At my request, Scotty, a man who never sees the torpedoes in the water, dutifully started calling stations and promising "the next big thing" on the radio. This would not be a fast-paced-comedy morning show. This would not be love songs at night. Scotty promised program directors "purpose-driven radio." When they were unsure of my commitment to the idea, Scotty would put them on hold, call me wherever I was, and then conference me in to complete our dog-and-pony show. (We still perform that rodeo at least twice a week when pitching new stations.)

Now, keep in mind that in the beginning we were selling a show that did not exist. There was more of a radio show on Connie's sticky notes than there was in the conversations Scotty and I had with programmers. It became clear after enough of these calls that it was time for a demo. I had to create something, anything, so station managers could get a flavor for what we were up to. And this time it had to be a little more involved than faking helicopter traffic reports by pounding my chest into a microphone. I figured I would start at the source: the sticky-noted articles. The articles Connie had marked were, as usual, just what I was looking for:

The latest study on weight loss and interval training.
How probiotics can improve your gut health and cure depression.
The three signs that he or she is "The One."

In preparation for recording the demo, Scotty told me that the music-intensive stations we were targeting would not like content that was any longer than two minutes. That posed a bit of a problem. The magazine pieces I was pulling from were long, some as long as three thousand words. I would have to condense them down and rewrite them into three-hundred-word capsules to stay under two minutes and still leave room for my comments and ad libs. To give program directors a sense of what the show would feel like on their airwaves, the demo would also include snippets of the songs their stations had in regular rotation. To add a special touch (Scotty's idea) we customized each demo to include the station's call letters as well.

This was twice as much work, but it paid off. Within a week, Scotty had signed up six stations. Within a month, stations were getting phone calls from listeners asking about the segments they had heard. In six months, the stations were getting feedback from listeners who were pulling over during their commute to jot down the tips. Scotty was still burning up the phone lines, but this time he was recruiting help from stations that had signed on early. Program directors who were seeing positive ratings from our show were calling other stations to help Scotty pitch *Intelligence for Your Life*.

In the middle of all of this I was still going out and performing live concerts. I needed help with the research. That's when producer/writer Betsy Chase joined us. I had met Betsy at Westwood One Radio when I did a guest appearance for the vacationing Casey Kasem. Betsy was an experienced radio producer (she had also been on staff at the Rick Dees morning show). I knew if I could talk her into coming to work with us we could create even more great content. When she came on board we worked together to build our research team. We also added Christina Rasch as our head of production.

. . .

As it turned out, this little sticky-note light bulb of an idea was made for this exact time in radio, for two main reasons.

One, in 1998 we had begun living in the internet age. We began choking on information. Twenty percent of Americans were getting their news from the internet at least once a week already by 1998.[3] By 2002, that number had grown to 58.5 percent of the US population. There was more information available than ever before in history. There was also plenty of dangerous and false information at our fingertips. Our business model was curation. We vetted research studies from hundreds of sources. Our focus was health and longevity, relationships, finances, workplace, pets, and travel. Our researchers verified the information and then I broadcast it in two-minute bursts between pop songs.

Two, we were a safe bet for big brands. We were delivering a radio program into a radio environment that had become risky for many advertisers. You had controversial, profane morning shows on the FM dial, and you had screaming liberals and conservatives on AM-talk radio. There were very few places a multinational consumer brand could make a big ad spend and not have to worry about turning off a major portion of the public simply by virtue of advertising there. For years, advertisers had specified "No Howard Stern," for example. But now Howard was not the only controversial personality on national radio. The proliferation of politically charged programs in a growing PC environment was giving big brands heartburn.

I remember marveling at the early success of the show and asking Scotty, "I don't get it. How is it that no one else has done a show like this?"

His answer? "Probably because it's way too expensive to produce and it's too much **** work."

He was right.

• • •

As we started to get real traction in the marketplace, we hired a respected radio consultant named Mike McVay. Mike suggested right away that we expand our three-hour weekend show to a daily five-hour show. He insisted that there was nothing like what we were doing on the radio and that it was a great fit for female listeners—the key advertiser demographic on the stations most likely to syndicate our show. I'll never forget the look on Betsy's face when I told her we'd be generating five times the weekly content. Even with powerhouses Betsy, Scotty, and Christina we didn't have the personnel or enough manpower to launch the daily show. Those were some seriously sleep-deprived days and nights.

The next step was line extension. Our most popular pieces were health related, so that was the obvious choice. *Intelligence for Your Health with Connie Sellecca* was launched in June of 2002 as a three-hour weekend radio show. Connie always jokes that I asked her to be the host because she was "the closest warm body with a voice." In reality, it was because she had always carried a fascination for the latest wellness and longevity intelligence—a curiosity that would prove to be a lifesaver for her husband fifteen years later.

If you had told me at any point during the 1980s or 1990s that the story of my professional life as a broadcaster would begin and end in radio, I'm not sure what my response would have been, because back then it might have felt like I had gone backward, rather than come full circle, which is how I feel today. Because of my family, because of technology, because of my music—and my persistent, purpose-driven faith in all three—radio was my evolution, not my devolution.

Together, the *Intelligence for Your Life/Health* radio shows have prospered greatly over the last twenty-two years. Ten million people each week listen to the programs on three hundred stations across North America and on Armed Forces Radio. Like me, the show has evolved and grown. Gib has now joined me for special segments on the show and the three of us—me, Connie, and Gib—host the video version of *Intelligence for Your Life* on Facebook.

Thankfully, though, at least one thing has not changed at all: Connie still uses sticky notes . . . on just about everything.

Chapter 28

Mark 11:23

January–June 2017

O ver the years we've shared tens of thousands of personal development tips on our radio programs. When you are bathed in that
much "intelligence," you start to recognize patterns that can produce
pathways to success. One of the common pieces of advice is to frequently
look back on your life—at your successes and failures—and connect
the dots to see how you ended up at your current destination. Writing
this memoir required much personal *dot-connecting*, especially when it
came to tracking my growth in the world of divine healing. That process
enabled me to see, from altitude, this incredible timeline of my cancer
journey and, ultimately, divine healing. Take a look.

- The demonic spirit of infirmity (cancer) attacks my body.
- Satan begins to prowl and devour my mind. He attacks me with
  doubt, unbelief, and anger.
- Then Connie finds Jack Hibbs on the radio.
- Connie announces she's headed to his church. I tag along.
- Cha Cha Sandoval-McMahon shows up on our doorstep. She later
  hands us the Wommack healing CD.
- The true promise of Mark 11:23 is then revealed to us: "For assur-
  edly, I say to you, whoever says to this mountain, 'Be removed

and be cast into the sea,' and does not doubt in his heart, but believes that those things he says will be done, he will have whatever he says."

- Our revelation on healing begins.

The Holy Spirit had set Connie and me along a path of understanding supernatural healing. And just in the nick of time, because in January 2017—eighteen months after the all-clear from Dr. Schaeffer—during a routine quarterly MRI scan, something lit up among the lymph nodes in my pelvic area.

A two-hour biopsy revealed that there was likely cancer present in the chain of lymph nodes near the surgical site (formerly known as my prostate). Schaeffer, who had become head of urology at Northwestern in Chicago since becoming my doctor, recommended that I see an oncologist.

I knew enough about prostate cancer at this point to know that my cancer had likely matriculated into a candidate for what was known as systemic treatment—treating your entire system, your whole body—which made my heart sink.

Would it be chemo? Radiation? More surgery? I was gripped by a more intense fear than any I had faced even in the darkest moments of my cancer battle in 2015. It was a fear that would regularly test my faith in the path of divine healing that I had just recently set upon with Connie. It would also test my faith in the medicine that, to date, I had relied upon and given credit to for saving my life.

We were again on the hunt for another specialist. This time, an oncologist dedicated to diagnosing, treating, and researching cancer. The indefatigable Connie was able to make a connection to MD Anderson in Houston and a world-renowned specialist in prostate cancer named Dr. Christopher Logothetis, "Logo" to his team. Logo quickly recommended another robotic surgery to remove an entire section of lymph nodes in my pelvis—a "lymph node salvage." The plan was to harvest nodes that Dr. Schaeffer's team regarded as possibly cancerous. Then Logo would study the nodes to determine what kind of cancer I had and what treatment I should receive.

Mine was a rare, non-PSA-producing metastatic prostate cancer. It was prolific and aggressive. By now you may have guessed that when cancer moves from its epicenter in the body, when it metastasizes, it will likely continue to move until it is stopped by chemotherapy or radiation or both. That's why Logo prescribed four rounds of chemotherapy and something called ADT (androgen deprivation therapy). The drug used for ADT is designed to remove all of the testosterone from your body because prostate cancer thrives on that hormone. The idea is to suck out all your male hormone, thus weakening the cancer cells, which are then killed by the chemotherapy.

I'd faced terrible side effects in my first battle with cancer. However, I was not at all prepared to hear the grisly side effects manifested by the ADT this time, which included muscle loss, overall weight loss, and extreme fatigue. My violent reactions to the chemotherapy treatments were so horrible that every means used to ameliorate the nausea were virtually useless. On the rare occasions I would feel well enough to go out to a restaurant, Connie would cheerfully say, "Oh no, let ME cook tonight."

I had lost so much weight she knew I would be a shocking image in a public place.

Soon enough, I found myself slipping back into a familiar headspace, that of a cancer patient. I spoke like a cancer patient. I even referred to the disease as "my cancer." I was a terrible patient. I would go from feeling pitiful and feeling sorry for myself, to experiencing the guilt of costing my family so much of their lives. My thoughts often drifted into plans for suicide (perhaps my exercise kettlebells strapped to my ankles and a quick jump into the pool would do the trick). Then I would show up at the hospital for more treatments and there would be little kids walking the halls with five more IVs than I had, and they would be smiling, fighting for their lives. It only made me feel worse, because I was weak. Suffering is personal. You don't really care where you are on the spectrum, or who is there with you.

A man's suffering is similar to the behavior of a gas. If a certain quantity of gas is pumped into an empty chamber, it will fill the chamber completely and evenly, no matter how big the chamber. Thus suffering completely fills the human soul and conscious mind, no matter whether the suffering is great or little. Therefore the "size" of human suffering is absolutely relative.

—**Viktor Frankl,** *Man's Search for Meaning*[1]

_____

Fortunately, Connie and I had acquired new weapons for this fight, and we had received serious training for how to use them. We had learned that most people, in attempting to exercise the authority of Jesus as Scripture describes in Mark 11:23, speak to God about their mountain instead of speaking to their mountain about God. So we had begun to think and act differently. We understood that there was a *better way to pray.* We exercised our authority over the thoughts that came into our minds, and we spoke to the ailment itself. For example, if the problem was pain, we said, "Pain, in the name of Jesus, I command you to leave my body."

I was learning this lesson firsthand, from my own experience, because even though I was walking further and further down the path of divine healing, I was still periodically trying to twist God's arm to force Him to take this cancer from me. And if it wasn't God Himself I was begging, it was the god of modern medicine to whom, in the first half of 2017, I was giving more (or most) of my faith.

I knew that I could pray the better way. I could speak to the pain, to the cancer, to the infirmity, in the name of Jesus. I also felt I could not give half of my heart to science and half to the Word. As they say, when you sit in the middle of the road, that's when you get run over.

At some point, I was going to have to make a choice. The question was not *if*, only *when.*

Chapter 29

Get Uncomfortable

On December 26, 2004, a magnitude 9.1 earthquake struck beneath the Indian Ocean near Indonesia. The quake was so big it made the entire planet vibrate and changed its shape. It shortened the day and shifted the North Pole a couple inches to the east. But worse than all of that was the tsunami it generated. The massive rupture in the seabed dragged rocks weighing millions of tons as far as ten kilometers across the sea floor, displacing trillions of cubic feet of water in all directions, and sending multiple waves, some as high as one hundred feet, crashing into the shores of developing nations as far as five thousand miles away. In the end, the tsunami claimed more than 230,000 lives in fourteen different countries. It was one of the deadliest natural disasters ever recorded.

At the moment the earthquake struck and the waters began to move, Connie and I could not have been in a more opposite place. It was the day after Christmas (Indonesia was thirteen hours ahead), and we were in snowy Idaho to witness the proposal of our son, Gib, to his girlfriend, Janeé. Back in our hotel room, we were cozy and warm and comfortable. Life was good.

Then we switched on the television, and we watched in horror as half a world away, life for millions was turning into a watery, debris-ridden hell. Newscasters, backed by the terrifying footage of floodwaters and destruction, tried to give us a sense of the magnitude of what occurred as reports from on the ground rolled in. As they waited, they encouraged us all to "send thoughts and prayers" to the victims and their families.

I was way ahead of them. I had plenty of prayers and many thoughts for those unfortunate souls. But the thought I had the most, the thought that only grew as the news became more bleak, was that I was helpless. I just remember feeling so utterly helpless! There had to be something else we could do. But it was so far away.

Over the next several days, I remember organizations big and small calling for donations of all kinds—money, blood, clothing, canned goods. But I couldn't help wondering if there was something else we could do. The answer came from our friends at Operation Blessing, the boots-on-the-ground relief organization whose mission is to demonstrate God's love by alleviating human need and suffering around the world. The messenger was the group's COO, Bill Horn.

The phone call from Bill went like this:

> John, we are sending a container ship of supplies and a relief crew to Sri Lanka. We need your help. If you and Connie could go with us, you could raise awareness on your radio show and your listeners could perhaps get involved with the fund-raising for supplies and medical aid. There are some tiny towns in Sri Lanka that have been wiped out and they are desperate for help.

This was the "go" opportunity we had been praying for. We wanted to do more. We wanted to *act*. We just weren't sure what to do. How would we get there? If we somehow managed to find our way to one of the affected nations, would we just be in the way? Or could we actually make a difference? Bill's call answered all those doubts. Without much discussion, Connie and I knew what we needed to do. We had to go. It is, after all, one of God's first commands:

> Now the LORD had said to Abram:
> "Get out of your country,
> from your family,
> and from your father's house,

To a land I will show you.
I will make you into a great nation;
I will bless you
and make your name great;
And you shall be a blessing." (Gen. 12:1–2)

This idea is deep. We cannot miss it. It is fundamental. We must go. Yes, it's important to meditate on big decisions, but not without always remembering that we are commanded to *go*. Particularly in service to others, and especially to new frontiers, which are always in front of us and so never disappear. The internet or friends and family will give you a hundred reasons to remain where you are. Comfortable. We must get uncomfortable. The land that's beyond the land that we know is always where we should go.

I've since learned that the thing that beckons you forward is the Holy Spirit. Indeed, some of the smartest people I've known, interviewed, or studied have been compelled, led, inspired—you choose the word—by the power that is available to us courtesy of the Holy Spirit (also known as the Spirit of Truth). It is what led not just Connie and me but Gib and Prima also to accept Bill Horn's offer and to join the intrepid volunteers at Operation Blessing on their ten-thousand-mile journey to Sri Lanka. It would become one of the most profound experiences we ever could have imagined.

Make voyages. Attempt them. There's nothing else.
—Tennessee Williams[1]

But first, a trip to the doctor's office to get all the required shots, which tested our faith and our resolve, if only for a moment. As we watched the inoculations go into Prima's arm, I shared a look with my wife that said, "Are we really taking our ten-year-old to ground zero of this disaster?" We would be traveling to Maruthamunai, a coastal village along the eastern coastline of Sri Lanka where the waves killed 922 people and displaced

11,086. Fourteen hundred houses were completely destroyed. Before the tsunami there were 341 fishing families in Maruthamunai. Among them, 113 people were killed. They all lost most of their boats and fishing nets. Knowing all that, Connie and I remained steadfast, and we set a course—physically and spiritually—for the other side of the world.

When we pulled up to the village in the Operation Blessing jeep several days later, it looked like the town had been leveled by an atomic blast. Two hundred and fifty meters inland there were boats on top of the few houses that still remained. Yes, that means that when the water receded, it dropped the boats on top of the homes. The majority of the survivors were crammed into a church property at the far end of town. And yet, when Connie, Gib, Prima, and I piled out of the jeep, it wasn't the devastation that captured our attention. It was the giggles and smiles of the hundreds of children running toward the jeep. We were immediately taken.

Gib had been trained as a camp counselor at the Kanakuk Christian leadership camp in Missouri, and within minutes he had a four-year-old on his shoulders and two others hanging off his biceps. When he took off running, he would have a trail of thirty kids chasing him.

Prima, who was quickly surrounded by little girls her age, resembled an alien life form to them, someone their own age who was so tall and blonde. She began teaching them how to break dance. What a scene. These kids were so sweet and full of joy that it made us weep.

Connie shared tears with a woman who had lost her two children and her husband. There was no common language between them. It wasn't necessary. We were surrounded by unimaginable pain and suffering with the surreal punctuation of laughter and squeals from the children, desperate for a diversion.

We knew from our earlier briefing that many of these children had lost their entire families. Moms. Dads. Aunts. Uncles. Brothers and sisters. Hundreds of their family members had drowned when the ocean swelled and consumed them. Gone in an instant. And now the children were homeless, sleeping on the ground in this makeshift shelter, looking wherever they could, you would assume, for moments of relief and possibly even joy, just as we were looking for a way to be of service on this newest of new frontiers.

The question was *how*, exactly. We weren't sure what we were supposed to be doing. It was the ol' "jump off the cliff and build the plane on the way down" decision. I remember distinctly Connie looking like Lieutenant Colonel Bill Kilgore in *Apocalypse Now*: hands on hips, surveying the battleground.

"I have an idea," she said. "Let's have these kids do artwork of the experience of the tsunami. They are still having nightmares."

Huh?

It turns out, it's classic PTSD therapy for young children, but at the time, as a former newsman, I thought it was a classic way to be incarcerated in a foreign country for practicing psychology without a license.

Connie seemed awfully serious as she devised her plan on the fly, so the crew was sent inland for paper and crayons. Within a few hours these kids started creating masterpieces. Connie later would say in an interview, "I knew enough just from being a mom that they needed to get these images out of their heads." There was only one problem—we didn't have enough blue crayons. Nearly every single child wanted one so they could draw the water. "That's what they wanted to do," Connie said in that same interview. "They wanted to draw the water that had engulfed their homes."[2]

That moment, that entire experience watching these young orphaned children express themselves so brilliantly, so beautifully, with the most rudimentary of supplies, was both humbling and revelatory.

It was humbling because these kids, who had just survived the inconceivable, used scraps of paper and the worn ends of crayons to create works of incredibly personal art that moved everyone to tears.

It was revelatory because it sparked an idea. A way for us to help beyond thoughts and prayers, beyond even our time with boots on the ground in Sri Lanka. After the trip, we published a book full of the children's drawings that described the people we met, the stories they told, how we tried to help them, and how this trip ultimately gave us, as a family, more than we gave. We called it *Shades of Blue: The Tsunami Children's Relief Project*.

Eight months later, that little book had raised $336,000 for the Tsunami Children's Relief Project. Operation Blessing made sure the money was used to build hundreds of new fishing boats to replace those that had been destroyed. Without boats the men were jobless. Without boats the families could not feed themselves.

Give a man a fish, and you feed him for a day.

Teach a man to fish, and you feed him for a lifetime.

Give a man a boat, and he can feed an entire village.

Every now and then someone will show up at one of our concerts carrying a copy of *Shades of Blue*. It takes me right back to the moment we first met those children. What if we had talked ourselves out of going? What if we had remained comfortable, treading the familiar ground of our own known frontiers? It would have been understandable. Prima was only ten! What made us think that it was safe?

At the time, we didn't know that we were fulfilling God's command given in Genesis 12:1–2. I wasn't familiar with the scripture at the time. Nor did I have revelation of the force that compelled us to go. It's now clear that we had, indeed, experienced the tugging of the Spirit. The Spirit of the living God had asked us to go somewhere and do something we wouldn't normally want or choose to do. It gave us the power to get uncomfortable.

I have tried life with and without this power. I much prefer operating with high octane fuel in my tank. You will too. And when you learn to "pray in the Spirit," perhaps in your own special language, it will be jet fuel to your life.

The truth is that the Spirit of the living God is guaranteed to ask you to go somewhere or do something you wouldn't normally want or choose to do. The Holy Spirit of God will mold you into the person you were made to be. This often incredibly painful process strips you of selfishness, pride, and fear.

—Francis Chan, *Forgotten God*[3]

One of the functions of the Holy Spirit is to bring to our hearts a revelation of the future. If we need to know things that are to come to pass, and the ways in which they will come to pass, the Holy Spirit is the One to reveal them. We need not go to a fortune-teller or to an astrologer. We can go directly to the Holy Spirit.

—**Lester Sumrall,** *The Gifts and Ministries of the Holy Spirit*[4]

But the Comforter, which is the Holy Ghost, whom the Father will send in my name, he shall teach you all things, and bring all things to your remembrance, whatsoever I have said unto you.

—**John 14:26** KJV

The power evident in these words, the power derived from the Holy Spirit, is available to us all. The wiring is done. Flipping the switch is our choice. With Connie's help, I flipped mine. I hope I can help you flip yours, so that you may feel what Connie and I continue to feel as the Holy Spirit of God continues to mold us into the family we were made to be.

For as the Spirit tugs at our hearts, enlivens our spirits, and fills our minds with possibility, wherever it pulls us, we should *go*!

Chapter 30

Instant Dad

W hen Connie and I first started dating, it quickly became clear to me that, as a single mom, she was very protective of her then-nine-year-old son, Gib. It wasn't until Connie and I had been seeing each other for a couple of months that she was even willing to introduce me to him. It was a beautiful moment. I pulled up to Connie's house, jumped out of the car, and Gib was already running toward me from the house. He threw his arms around me for a hug. It was apparent to me that Connie must have said a few nice words about this guy she was seeing. Connie later told me that she told Gib I was someone important to her.

Gib and I became fast friends. I'm sure it was awkward for him at the time. He already had a dad, so he eventually decided he would call me Dada. And that's been my name ever since . . . except when he made me a grandpa three times. Now I'm Pop Pop.

When Connie and I got married on April 4, 1992, Gib was a big part of the ceremony. He made a speech. It was a three-ring ceremony, so he got a ring to wear as well. It was the perfect way to celebrate our new, blended family. When Connie and I were on our honeymoon in Hawaii, she was offered a starring role in a movie that was filming in Budapest, Hungary. The shoot schedule was four weeks. Two days after we got back, she left for work. That meant Gib and I would be home alone together for *a month*.

While it seemed like a terrific opportunity for some Dada-son bonding, I also found it to be intimidating at first. Instant-Dad would now also be driving carpool and trying to help with homework. Gib, who was ten at this point, was a math whiz and even at that age he could solve a Rubik's Cube in minutes. I did my best. He laughed a lot.

The first weekend we were by ourselves together, Gib asked if we could go to Raging Waters outside of Los Angeles. It was the second week of April and still pretty chilly in Southern California. We arrived to find very few people at the water park and the attendants wearing parkas. Two hours and forty-five tube rides later, I was suffering from what felt like hypothermia. When Gib saw that I had turned blue, he agreed to leave. We drove home with our seat heaters on, listening to "Bohemian Rhapsody" at full volume.

At some point, Gib and I decided that we needed to make a movie every week to send off to his mom in Budapest. My favorite was when we dressed up as Wayne and Garth from *Wayne's World*, complete with wigs. I was Wayne. We pretended we were live on TV and even rewrote the theme song to serve our purposes: *Connie's World . . . Connie's World. Party time. Excellent! Party on, Wayne. Party on, Garth.*

Twenty-seven years later, during the taping of our seventh PBS special, Gib performed with me on stage and I replayed that clip. The audience loved it. Prima was born when Gib was thirteen, so he became a "third parent" as we raised Prima. At times during family meetings, he would act as Prima's legal counsel and try to ameliorate her situation or her sentence for breaking the family contract. She paid him in chore hours.

When I was suffering mightily during my cancer journey, both of my kids were by my side during surgery, chemo, recovery, healing, all of it. Today I get to perform with them all over North America on the concert stage. Gib, playing music and performing comedy; Prima, dancing jazz and modern. Connie, as producer and director, somehow makes sense of it all and turns it into a PBS event.

I cherish the times when we work on a project together as a family. It's a powerful combination of creativity and purpose. And whether it's cancer or a tsunami, my family are warriors. And when a family member is in trouble, we are in the fight together.

Chapter 31

The Crack Den

I met Connie's brother, Vincent, for the first time on the phone in December 1991, shortly after Connie and I got engaged and four months before we were to be married. Vinny had been absent from the family for a while. He had battled with addictions, mostly drugs, since he was a young teenager and those addictions followed him into adulthood. Families can naturally drift apart simply because of geographical challenges, but lengthy estrangements are not the normal paradigm for a New York Italian family, drugs or no drugs, so I wanted to try to include him in the wedding party and perhaps bring him "back into the flock," so to speak.

"Let me call Vincent. I'd like for him to be one of my groomsmen," I said with my usual blind-faith, "full speed ahead" exuberance.

"That would be great," Connie said. "Here's the number. But make sure you don't refer to him as 'Vincent Sellecca.' Use Sellecchia. He's not a big fan of the shortened version."

In 1973, Connie's agent decided that her last name, Sellecchia, needed to be shortened, removing the *hi* to make her name more agency-friendly and less obviously ethnic.

"With a name like Concetta Sellecchia and coloring like yours," her agent said, "I'm going to get phone calls asking, 'Can this Concetta Sellecchia even speak English?'"

To this day Connie regrets she didn't respond, "Well, just say yes!"

I love the name Concetta. I have it tattooed on my right forearm (the full name would have been too painful).

Vincent Sellecchia had already survived two decades of serious drug use and run-ins with the law that should, at the very least, have landed him in prison and most certainly would have put an average human in the ground. Vinny was the quintessential Italian stallion: thick black hair in a long mullet with the optional ponytail; classic, stocky build; and a focus on bicep development. He wore a crucifix on a chain around his neck. When Vinny spoke, his voice rang out like a character from *Scarface.* That was the voice I heard on the telephone when I called him on my way to work at the *Entertainment Tonight* studios.

"L-oh?" the voice said.

Whoa, I thought. *I'm speaking to Tony Montana!*

I had heard only one syllable, but it was enough to send a shiver up my spine. *What's coming next? Is he going to ask me if I think he's a clown who is here to amuse me?* I wasn't going to wait to find out. I needed to spit out my pitch and get it over with.

"Hello, Vincent, this is John Tesh calling. As you may have heard, your sister Connie and I are engaged to be married and we'd like you to be in the wedding."

Silence.

No wonder. I had sounded like a cross between Dudley Do-Right and the Fuller Brush man. I imagined Connie's brother gagging on my mawkish opening. I continued.

"It's really important to your sister and me that you be a part of our celebration. I'd like you to be one of my groomsmen. Can you make it? The wedding is on April 4."

"Let me talk to my sista," he said. "Maybe tahmarrah."

No cursing, no threats of bodily harm. Wow, Vincent Sellecchia said yes! I mean, maybe not yes *technically*, but at least he said, "I gotta talk to my sista!"

"That's great, Vinny," I said. "We'll let you know the details as soon as we have them. Thanks again, man."

Vinny attended our wedding on April 4, 1992. He was a great addition and was quite dashing in his rented tuxedo. We didn't see much of him after that, though. We visited him a handful of times in Florida, but the visits were predictable, given the history. Vinny would be mostly lucid, stable for a day or two. But forty-eight hours was his willpower limit. In the middle of a conversation, he would suddenly be overcome by cravings and need to leave. Those few times we were with him, we saw a progressive decline in his appearance.

Vinny was in a serious relationship with a girl named Kathy. They were living together, smoking crack cocaine together, but after the daily investment in their drug habit, they could barely scrape together enough money to feed themselves. By scraping, I mean they were, by their own admission, working intricate shoplifting schemes to rip off supermarkets for food. They had also engineered more serious scams for generating cash. Vinny is not sure about the statute of limitations on these more felonious wrongdoings, so I'll leave that part of the story alone, for now.

When we were with Vincent while he was using drugs, we felt like we were speaking with a POW who had been held in captivity for decades. He had that "thousand-yard stare" that comes with chronic suffering, malnutrition, and sleep deprivation. Given his self-inflicted predicament, I could only marvel at his superhuman efforts to connect with his family, even if for only one or two days a year. If we were lucky enough to catch Vinny in his rare moments of clean and sober, it was easy to believe he was a pastor, a motivational speaker, the leader of a motorcycle gang, the mayor of Little Italy, or Thomas Edison. Connie believed there was never going to be an average, small life for her brother. "Fortune 500 CEO, or life in prison," she would say. "Inventor, or drug lord."

As I write this, Vinny and Kathy are stone-cold sober, over-the-road truck drivers who, in their spare time, run a mission called Intelligent Kindness that feeds the homeless and takes care of war veterans. Ask any expert on addiction and they'll tell you, it's a miracle. One that began to take shape at the dinner table on Thanksgiving 2003.

• • •

We're all seated before an Old World Italian feast. On the table are minestrone soup, three types of homemade pasta, clams oreganata, and, oh yeah, a turkey dinner with all the trimmings. Connie's mom, Anna, and all the women are still wearing their embroidered, flour-stained aprons as we bow our heads and proceed clockwise around the table to give personal prayers of thanks and gratefulness.

Before I take my turn, I'm struck once more by the absence of Anna's only son. By then Vinny and Kathy's circumstances had turned critical. Pieces of information would drip in from various sources. The consensus is that the two of them are in very bad physical and financial shape. For Anna's part, she's held out hope for Vinny's healing and homecoming for almost two decades.

My table prayer quickly becomes a conversation with God.

"Thank you, God, for our health, our family, our opportunities. God, I have one prayer today. Please bring Vincent back to us. Let Vinny hear that we love him and that we will always save a place for him at this table. And give us the strength to do what we can do to bring him back home."

I lift my eyes and see Connie's mom, widowed at fifty-nine years old by her husband, Primo. Heart attack. Her sad eyes now focus on nothing at all. You can tell that she has little room left in her heart for any more loss.

Then, before I take my first bite of the antipasto, I take a deep breath and give my best version of Maximus Meridius's booming voice while a Roman general in the movie *Gladiator*: "We cannot celebrate another Thanksgiving without Vincent seated at this table!"

I go on. "I think we should fly to Florida, do an intervention, get Vinny into rehab, and then bring him back home. It's that simple. Who's with me? Faith without works is dead!"

The battle cry divides the room.

Gib, now twenty-two, is right there with me from the start. We are both fans of the *Braveheart* and *Gladiator* movies and we are always spouting lines from both films. That happens spontaneously now at the table.

Gib: Every man dies, not every man truly lives.
John: What we do in life echoes in eternity.
Gib: Strength and honor.
John: Strength and honor.

I look over at Connie and she gives both father and son the Italian eyebrow, her eyes underneath it saying to us: "I'm not so sure about this, guys. I'm willing to think about it, but there must be a plan!"

The rest of the table explodes in protest.

"Are you ***** kidding me!?!"

"Already three failed rehabs. It's not going to work with Vincent this time either."

"We tried this with him before. It didn't work then. It won't work now."

Wow, I'm thinking, *maybe this is a bad idea after all.*

But it could also totally work and end up being an awesome, testosterone-fueled, father-son climb up to the summit of Mount Everest.

The protests soon evaporate, mostly because the dissenters view this as pure nonsense and because Connie, mercifully, has changed the subject. Gib and I, seated next to each other, can't help whispering about our evolving plan for the "Raid on Uncle Vinny." We think better of having T-shirts printed up and, instead, calm ourselves enough to embrace the wonder of what's immediately at hand: the Sellecchia Thanksgiving Feast.

. . .

The Learjet 35 is a mini rocket ship of an airplane that was once commissioned by the US Air Force. In more recent times it serves as a charter aircraft for thousands of CEOs who want to travel quickly between small-town airports with short runways. It's a very "mission specific" airplane. Lifts off quickly. Lands almost anywhere. The Lear 35 can fly at forty-five thousand feet, five hundred miles per hour. That's where Gib and I are, forty-five thousand feet up, somewhere between Los Angeles and Delray Beach, Florida.

Connie had insisted that before we got on the plane, we would all work together to determine the rehab program and destination. She knew that before she put two borderline ADD family members on a Learjet (me and Gib) bound for a Florida crack den, there needed to be a plan.

Following a few more days of research and recommendations, we had decided that Pastor Steve Arterburn's New Life facility in Arizona would be a good fit for our needs. Our basic plan is for Gib and me to spend as many days as required convincing Vinny that he needs to come with us and start his life over. We will then get him onto the plane and all three of us will fly to the New Life Treatment Center for Vinny's month of drug rehab. Connie will establish a command center in Los Angeles, remaining behind with Prima. She will maintain contact with us and with the New Life counselors. Together they will suggest strategies for Gib and me, based on our moment-by-moment experiences at Vinny's place.

Private air travel is, of course, more expensive than commercial, but we know there is not a chance that Vincent will get on an American Airlines commercial flight, change planes in Dallas, wait out a two-hour layover, take one more flight to Phoenix, and then get into a rental car for the drive to rehab. We have to remove as many barriers, as many potential objections as possible. With the private plane, we can take Vinny with us with only a thirty-minute heads-up for the pilots. We are able to fly directly to Phoenix with no change of aircraft, even if it's three in the morning. The less time Vincent's body is in withdrawal, the safer we'll all be in the air.

When Gib and I land in Delray, a car will be waiting for us at the private terminal and then we'll head toward Vinny's house. Connie made contact with a local friend of his (we'll call him Angelo) who knew the location of the crack house where Vinny will likely be. Angelo will drive his car ("The lead car!" says Connie), which we will follow, until we got too close to Vincent's house for Angelo's comfort level. He is not interested in being a snitch who gave up the location of Vinny's crack house.

As we begin closing in on Delray, I get a big dose of stage fright. Without any experience or basic training in interventions, except for watching a Dr. Drew promo on cable, I might as well have been preparing for an exorcism. I don't know how to do this. What if I say something that makes things worse? What if we fly all this way and Vinny won't let us in the house? What if the house is filled with drugs and the cops pick that time for their sting operation? Prison time for all, for sure.

"John, Gib, we are about fifty miles east of Delray Beach Airport."

The Lear PA system is loud enough to restart my prefrontal cortex and end most of my rumination. I have less than an hour to put the finishing touch on my "We Miss You, Uncle Vinny" slideshow. The purpose of the photo montage I'm creating is, if the conversation stalls, becomes awkward, or if guns are drawn, I can pull out the family photo montage on my laptop and show Vincent all the family events and milestones he's missed. It will be an inspiring distraction that should hijack his mind for a while. I agree with Gib's strategy that the photo presentation should be our secret weapon that we only activate if talks get stalled. Gib can sense my nervousness and, in typical Gib fashion, he gives me one of his dark, double-edged pep talks.

"Hey, Dada, if Uncle Vinny gets really mad, remember that he probably won't kill you . . . in front of me."

"Great speech, Gibber."

. . .

Ninety minutes later, Gib and I are parked just south of Vinny's driveway, far enough away that he can't see us.

"Let's go," Gib says.

"Hang on a second. I'm not ready yet. Turn on the radio. Let's sit for a while."

What happens next is one of Gib's favorite family stories. I've turned the volume up, and I suggest that we guess the name of each song that goes by on the radio. Since it's XM Radio the song title is displayed on the screen. So I hold my hand over the screen and we each take turns guessing the song. Wink Martindale would have been impressed.

This goes on for twenty minutes until Gib finally says, "Hey, Dada, we just flew across the country on a Learjet. Mom is sitting on pins and needles in Los Angeles, and an entire team of doctors and psychiatrists is counting on us to walk into that house, grab Uncle Vinny, and take him to Phoenix. We can't sit here forever and play 'Name That Tune.'"

Gib drags me out of our foxhole and we head for the entrance to Vinny's home. Along the walkway the smell is overwhelming. There are huge piles of dog poop covering the weeds and patches of grass on either side of the walk. There are four video cameras mounted on either side of the door.

"Who's there?!"

Vinny is bellowing through his massive front door, covered with four Kwikset deadbolt locks in a vertical array directly above the door knob. No one is getting in to see Uncle Vinny without an invitation or a battering ram.

"Uncle Vinny . . . it's your brother-in-law, John Tesh, and your nephew, Gib."

This time I sound like Charles Durning in *Dog Day Afternoon*. All I need is a bullhorn. I'm reminded why the Navy SEALs actually go through a few weeks of training before a secret mission. Proper planning prevents piss-poor performance, as they say.

There's silence. Then . . . an explosion of dog barking. And then: *CLICK, CLICK-thwack, CLICK . . . CLICK-thwack.*

The door swings open and there, standing before me, is Vincent Sellecchia, cigarette hanging from his mouth, wearing a Yankees T-shirt with the shoulders cut off. It resembles a tank top that's been mangled in the dryer.

"Tesh! What the hell? And *Gib!*"

Moving quickly past me, he embraces Gib with a bear hug.

"Gib!"

"Come in. Come in!"

At that moment it seems like German Shepherds are everywhere, barking, climbing, sniffing.

Through the fortified front door to Vinny's home we have stepped down into a great room that is spartan except for a giant wooden desk in the middle of it. The desk is positioned roughly six feet from a large-screen TV. It resembles Geppetto's workbench. There's a soldering iron, some copper wiring, two hot glue guns, bits and pieces of electric motors, a few large magnets, half a dozen screwdrivers, and ash trays. Let's disregard the Pinocchio reference because what was on Vinny's desk was eerily similar to the forensic evidence you would discover following terrorist activity.

Vinny's girlfriend, Kathy, is standing at the kitchen sink. I had met her a few years earlier, but I remember her with a very different hair color. She offers a smile and a nod and turns back to the sink. There is what appears to be a half inch of water covering the kitchen floor. Water or film. I can't be sure.

A movie, *The King of Comedy*, is playing on the big screen at full volume. Vinny motions for us to take seats in a BarcaLounger and a bench to the left of the big desk, where he now takes his position. With his ponytail, beard stubble, and hypertrophic arms, Vincent presents as a captain on the bridge of a pirate ship. Behind Vinny there has begun a slow parade of bizarre, slouchy characters. They are moving back and forth down the hallway, in and out of a room I'm guessing is a bedroom or office. The walkers are doing a credible impression of the illustrations you'd find in my *The Walking Dead* comic books. There are so many of them that it resembles a macabre version of that clown-car gag you see in the circus. *Where are they all coming from?!* Vinny is not reacting to the scene behind him, so I can only assume that it's normal crack-house activity. It's certainly nerve-racking. I'm trying to maintain eye contact with Vinny, while keeping an eye on the cavalcade of zombies. Zeus, one of the three German Shepherds, lays his monstrous head in my lap. Zombies. Wolves. Crack. Hot glue guns. This is the part of the film where you're screaming at the actors from your seat. *Get out of the house! Can't you see what's happening? Get out!*

I panic. I pull the pin and throw the Hail Mary.

"Hey, Vinny. I want you to see this slideshow I made for you on my computer."

I glance back at Gib, whose shocked expression is saying, "What the hell, Dada? You get one quick look at the waterboard and you spill your guts?"

I continue, "Vin, I've put together a montage of all the photos from our family get-togethers that you may have missed!"

I hit Play on the slideshow. He's completely into it. The family photos hold Vincent's attention for a full forty-five seconds. Then my Hail Mary pass is picked off in the endzone. Vinny lifts a three-foot stick off his desk and shouts, "Gib, Gib, check this out," neutering my feeble "this is your life" movie screening.

"I took this motor here out of a hair dryer," says Vinny, "and I glued the tongue depressors together to make a propeller."

He is speaking with inventor's pride. He goes on to detail how, to complete his invention, he hot-glued the propeller and the motor along with a D-cell battery to the scratching end of a three-foot back-scratcher.

All I could think is, *Who has an itch on their back right now?*

Now with Gib's full attention, Vinny flips the power switch on his "miracle back-scratcher fan." It revs up to deafening weedwhacker buzz level.

"Check this out!" he shouts over the ear-splitting racket. "I've invented a battery-powered fan back-scratcher. I'm going to apply for a patent. I want you to have it, Gib!"

Gib is thrilled and immediately takes the opportunity to use the contraption to cool me down. I'm sweating. I'm not sure why I'm so nervous. Oh wait, maybe it's because this is my first field trip to a crack den. Perhaps it's because there is a six-foot gun safe over my left shoulder. Or it could be because there is an umbrella caddy next to the gun safe that has four Japanese swords in it. What's the scenario where you suddenly need a sword? And what are the zombie clowns behind Vincent up to? They look harmless, but I feel like I still need to keep an eye on them.

(Vinny would later tell me that the group of zombies included a guy named Duck who was, at the time I had spotted him and the others, hiding all of the drugs in the backyard. He said it was so Gib and I wouldn't be in any danger. Vinny said it was a big job.)

"Hey, Kathy," Vinny yells to his girlfriend, who is still at the sink. "Make my nephew and my brother-in-law BLTs, will ya?"

From the big screen, De Niro declares, "Better to be king for a night"—Vinny joins him—"than schmuck for a lifetime!"

Vincent is in hysterics. "Tesh, do you love this movie?"

"Yes, it's awesome, Vin."

It's now 9:00 p.m. *The King of Comedy* has gone around one and a half times. Gib is grinning ear to ear and whispers to me, "Are you getting all of this? If we make it out of here alive, we have to write a book. What a scene!"

I'm certain that there's little chance that Gib and I will be able to make an intervention pitch in this noisy, toxic environment. If we don't take control of the conversation, this will end up as nothing more than an all-night, one-film movie marathon. It's clear from the look on Kathy's face that she knows something is up. She keeps looking us over, while standing in that half inch of kitchen water.

Where did the water come from?

I excuse myself to take a walk outside and place a frantic phone call to Connie to fill her in on our dilemma. After my update, she suggests Gib and I get Vinny out of the house and make the intervention pitch to him one-on-one. I can also tell, by her follow-up questions, that she is very concerned about Gib's safety. I don't blame her. I probably should have left out the part about the swords.

. . .

It turns out that a venue change is just what we need. It's now 11:00 p.m. as we grab a table at the only place in town that's still open. Delray's Ugly Mugg sports bar.

Generally speaking, anyone who is still in a bar after 11:00 p.m. on a Monday is very serious about being in a bar, and that's what this crowd appears to be. Serious. Gib and I, dressed head-to-toe in Lululemon athleisure-wear, with $120 sneakers, look exactly like two out-of-town family members attempting their first intervention. Mercifully, now that we're alone with Vincent, the shadow-boxing and zombie railroad at the house are history and Gib, to my relief, launches into an incredible monologue detailing what Vincent means to the family. I knew that as soon as Gib and Vinny were able to have a conversation, we'd have our best shot at making some serious headway. The odds of success are just not all that great when your brother-in-law shows up and tries to talk you out of decades of drug dependency. It just wouldn't look good at all on Vinny's bio:

For decades, I was a hopeless crack addict, but then my brother-in-law took a break from interviewing Pee-wee Herman and came to my rescue!

See what I mean?

I sat quietly and watched Gib go to work. For years, when Gib was in elementary school, he and Uncle Vinny had played chess together over the phone. They had that bond, and Gib speaks of it now. Both Vinny and Gib had always shared the distinction of possessing whip-smart brains and a love of strategy. At the table, Gib continues with his monologue, which now includes hilarious memories of Uncle Vinny attending Gib's Little League games. In one story Gib, age eleven, was at bat, and from the moment he stepped up to the plate, Vinny was eviscerating the young pitcher. Vinny had brought the Bronx with him: "Let's go, Gib! This guy's got nothin'. Home run, baby. Home run!"

First pitch. "Strike one," shouted the umpire.

"C'mon, Ump, that pitch was way outside," screamed Vinny. "Go back to LensCrafters and get a refund, you bum."

By this time, the parents seated in the bleachers were growing visibly uncomfortable, but none were interested in confronting the burly, snarling Italian. The diatribe of trash talk rose with each pitch, now directed, ad hominem, at the pitcher himself.

"You got nothin', little man, you're going down. Look, Gib, his arm is like a noodle!"

The pitcher appears visibly shaken and then:

THWACK!

Gib connects with the very next pitch, driving it over the pitcher's head. It loops into the outfield and he's headed for first base. That's it for the pitcher. He bursts into tears. And that's it for everyone else. The umpire has removed his mask and is turning toward the stands. Two of the dads, now resembling villagers with torches, have jumped to their feet from their bleacher seats and are staring daggers at Vincent. Whispering in her brother's ear, Connie frantically summarizes the rules of conduct for Little League baseball. This matters little to Vinny, as Gib is now smiling at his uncle from second base and the pitcher is with his mommy. From Vincent's point of view it was, simply, mission accomplished. He was happy to remain mute for the rest of the game.

As the three of us share the laugh at the Ugly Mugg, you can see the wave of understanding cross Vinny's face. He misses his family. And so the time is right to make our pitch for rehab. I'm stunned by his swift resignation to our plan, and I have the palpable feeling that he might, indeed, get on the airplane and travel with us. But then Vincent starts laying out all of the obstacles. Basically, he doesn't see how he can leave his house for a month without putting his motorcycle, the gun safe, and other valuables into storage in the meantime. He's convinced that without doing this, his valuables will most certainly be sold for drug money (I'm assuming by members of the zombie brigade).

Ultimately, Gib and I agree to rent a U-Haul truck and move his belongings to a local storage unit. Back at the crack house, we grab some blankets and settle into our chairs next to Vincent's desk-colossus and try to grab some shut-eye before the U-Haul office opens at 7:00 a.m. *The King of Comedy* blares once more from the big screen. Jerry Lewis is now duct-taped to a chair. Sunrise won't come soon enough.

With his Harley-Davidson, giant entertainment center, gun safe, swords, and three power washers safely locked away at the Delray Public Storage, the three of us are ready to jump in the rental car and head for the private jetport. I'll never forget the departure scene and it haunts me to this day. Gib and I are already seated in the rental SUV with the engine running; Vinny and Kathy are in the driveway, locked in a farewell embrace. It is the look on Kathy's face, as she and I briefly lock eyes, that breaks my heart.

I'm not proud of the fact that, up until this moment, I had operated under the preconceived bias that everyone in that house, other than Vincent, was a crack addict, and as such should be regarded as collateral damage. Kathy was silent for much of our visit in the house. That could have been because she was high or because she was anticipating an outcome that would be bad for her. In any case, the demure woman I saw now was materializing as a loving, caring human being.

What transpired next has been a source of regret for me for nearly a decade. It's one of the reasons I am today more apt to trust the tug of the Holy Spirit, the nagging human conscience, when faced with a big decision. That day I'm ignoring the tug and we leave Kathy behind. All I need to do, as Gib steps on the gas, is yell "stop," and we could put Kathy on the plane with us and get her some help as well. Instead, I do nothing.

Gib and I are both nervous. Vinny looks ragged and is chain-smoking. I reach over and hit the child-safety locks on the SUV. I'm sleep deprived and paranoid enough to envision Vinny throwing himself from the vehicle. It's 7:00 p.m.

We had alerted the pilots, so they are standing by on the tarmac. The Learjet has been fueled and the engines are idling. Vinny grabs a blanket and curls up in one of the seats in the back of the plane. He's asleep. Like soldiers in a bunker, guarding the front line, Gib takes first watch and I enter the deepest sleep of my life.

. . .

Researchers will tell you that it's nearly impossible to gather data on the success rate of drug and alcohol interventions because there are just too many variables: the type of drugs, the length of the addiction, the relationships that exist between all parties, to name just a few. Psychiatrists are quick to point out that it is even possible to make matters worse and to permanently damage family relationships. Once we got Vinny on the plane, my blind faith and naïveté had me believing, with certainty, that Gib and I had emerged victors and had only to return to Rome and to Caesar (Connie) to be crowned victorious.

Thirty-five thousand feet in the air and Vinny had been in the air-plane lavatory for an hour. He would later tell us he was smoking crack one last time before we landed in Phoenix for his rehab. We're lucky he didn't start a fire.

Vinny wasn't in treatment very long. He left New Life's rehab program after five days. Connie, Gib, and I were crushed. When we got the call from the facility's program director, it sucked the air out of the room. When we created our plan, we knew there was a very good chance it wouldn't work. We also knew we would never give up on Vincent, despite the nagging realization that somewhere out there was a family member saying, "I told you this would never work. It never works."

We proceeded anyway. Our *why* was bigger than all the noise about the likelihood of failure. Sure, when we looked up at the scoreboard, it showed a loss. But our journey, our planning, our dedication to intervention drew us closer together as a family. It created an even deeper bond between my wife and me as we joined together to save her brother. That's now written in our book of life. The journey further connected Gib and me as father and son: gladiators in lockstep for a common fight (while generating hilarious stories that we still laugh about today).

It's my belief that, as Lin-Manuel Miranda once said on *60 Minutes*: "If you pick a lane, and you stay in that lane (with focused intensity over time) you cannot help but produce greatness."[1] However, sometimes we slip on a wet field. The ball takes a bad bounce. You end up in a pup tent in a park. Sure, the losing score is up there in lights, but the score always comes down before next season.

Nearly a year after our intervention attempt, Connie and I received a call from Kathy and Vinny. They said they had gotten sober and asked if we would loan them $5,000 and give them one more chance. They wanted to enroll in truck driving school together and become an over-the-road big-rig driving team. Their thinking was that, since the trucking company had random drug tests, it would be the best way to keep themselves clean and sober. We agreed to give it one more shot, knowing that we might never see the money or Vinny and Kathy again.

At this writing Vincent Sellecchia and his girlfriend, Kathy Banning, have been clean and sober for sixteen years. They've remained free of drugs. Their gratefulness for this new life has caused them to start a ministry called Intelligent Kindness. While traveling across the country, they seek out homeless people and veterans and they intervene for them with food and supplies.

We're not sure what exactly broke the cycle of addiction. Perhaps our intervention wasn't a failure after all. Maybe it was just enough of an interruption in their cycle of darkness. A show of love. I've always thought that our trip might well have sent up a flare that shone just enough light on their path, revealing its undeniable, suicidal ending. Connie, Gib, and I sat down to speak with Vinny and Kathy just prior to this writing. I recalled for them the image that has always stuck in my brain. That ghoulish procession of addicts and drug dealers behind Vinny's desk. The zombie parade. Vinny set his jaw and looked down at his feet.

"Those people, Tesh? They're dead. All of them. Everyone that was in that crack house when you and Gib came to see me? They're all dead. Every last one of them."

Chapter 32

To Live and to Fight
Under the Word

September 2018

As Connie, Gib, and I step into the hospital elevator and push the button for radiology, the display above the doors reveals that we are headed somewhere below the basement level. I'm not sure if it's protocol for all hospitals, but it makes sense to me that best practice for machines that produce radiation would be to keep them underground.

As we step out of the elevator into the waiting room, I hear myself suck in a deep breath of air. I don't remember ever releasing it.

Connie senses my inability to speak and checks me in at the desk. We grab three seats in what can only be described as a ghastly waiting area. I feel as if I'm looking at scenes from all my favorite postapocalyptic Hollywood movies: *Riddick*, *Book of Eli*, *Godzilla* (the original). There's a man in a wheelchair to my left who has either passed out, fallen asleep, or worse. He has what appears to be a simple black tattoo on his neck, which resembles a target. The flesh on his legs, exposed beneath an oversized hospital gown, is hideous shades of gray and magenta. Connie has seen my expression and gives my leg a squeeze, offering reassurance. For the first time since we met twenty-eight years ago, her touch startles me and produces a terrible uneasiness. She squeezes again.

"Honey, please stop. I can't . . . I'm sorry," I say.

After two surgeries, chemotherapy, and ADT, the follow-up protocol up to this moment had been to travel from Los Angeles to MD Anderson in Houston every three months for scans. These always included a CAT scan and MRI of my pelvis and a bone scan (using a radioactive isotope). The first two trips were all clear. During the third, the doctors believed they saw one, maybe two, lymph nodes light up in my pelvis, signifying disease. This triggered yet another nuclear scan that, according to the radiologist, "confirmed" the two nodes as possible cancerous metastases.

The recommendation? Go back into my pelvis with another twelve-inch biopsy needle and try to pull out a sample of the nodes. I said no.

The next idea was to schedule a meeting with a top radiation oncologist back in Los Angeles and have him create a plan for treatment, and that's what we did. We are now in his waiting room, which is filled to capacity with poor souls who look like survivors of some global disaster.

The radiation oncologist presents an aggressive treatment plan. He would "carpet-bomb" (my words) my pelvis with thirty-seven focused radiation treatments over a seven-week period. They would start with a 3-D scan of my pelvis, and then the machine would circle my pelvis and irradiate my entire pelvic region, destroying all of the lymph nodes in that area along with any healthy tissue within range.

When I ask about contraindications (collateral damage), I once again hear a doctor's voice soaked in reverb as he goes through the list: nausea, diarrhea, possible incontinence, and possible permanent loss of sexual function; a chance of damage to the bowel and bladder and potential neuropathy. As usual, my subconscious mind offers me a metaphor courtesy of an epic movie. This time it's a scene from the movie *300*.

A Persian messenger has arrived in Sparta to tell the Spartan king, Leonidas, that the Persian god-king, Xerxes, wants an offering from the Spartans. Leonidas is resistant and the messenger can sense this. "Choose your next words wisely," says the messenger, "for they may be your last." As Leonidas ponders the certain annihilation of his people that will come with declining the messenger's demands, he glances back at his queen for her counsel. Her nod is nearly imperceptible, but it's enough for Leonidas. He and his queen are of one mind. Leonidas slays the messenger and sets in motion one of the greatest underdog battles in history, the Battle of Thermopylae.

The familiar scene is playing out once more, in real time, for Connie and me. Because what none of these doctors know is that while Connie and I agreed to undergo the tests upon which the aggressive treatment plan is based, we had actually begun a more effective way to cure the disease and were set to go down that path with full faith and total resolve. How could we not? We were sure in our hearts that I was healed.

In the exam room, Connie, Gib, and I listen intently to the doctor go over his plan one more time. We hear and catalog all the risks. Then I turn from the doctor and find Connie's eyes. In an instant we measure the challenge brought by this messenger. With an eyebrow flash and a nod, we are done. The biggest decision of our lives passes between us in seconds and lands with a firm conviction. Connie and I had not only been mated for life, we are now equally yoked with our stand on the Scriptures' promise for my healing.

. . .

Faith in God presents a fascinating conundrum. So many of us have faith, but when doubt and unbelief creep in, our faith is the first thing to be compromised. Protecting your heart from the sinister attacks of unbelief takes practice. Training. It's a constant struggle during normal, daily challenges, but it can be a more desperate, pitched battle when the stakes are high. Life-and-death high.

That's where I am in my mind. I'm in the bunker along the front lines with night-vision goggles, straining to spot the enemy. Like Captain Kirk, on the bridge of the USS *Enterprise*, barking out the command to divert all of his ship's power to the shields. My faith is my shield. My scriptures are my phasers, set to more than stun.

So, what do I have faith for? Is it faith for what will come out of the doctor's mouth, what the machines say? Or is it faith for what's in Psalm

118:8: "It is better to trust in the LORD than to put confidence in man"? Or maybe 1 Peter 2:24: "By [his] stripes you were healed." Or perhaps for what Jesus promised in Mark 11:23–24:

> For assuredly, I say to you, whoever says to this mountain, "Be removed and be cast into the sea," and does not doubt in his heart, but believes that those things he says will be done, he will have whatever he says. Therefore I say to you, whatever things you ask when you pray, believe that you receive them, and you will have them.

Connie, Gib, and I all have that scripture tattooed on our bodies. But do we wholeheartedly believe its promise? Yes, we do. When we got my first terminal prognosis three years earlier, we had faith for the plan the surgeons and oncologists had put together. We had faith that God trained brilliant physicians and that they had removed the cancerous tumors. But when the first biopsy came back from the lab at UCLA, I didn't have enough faith or understand enough scriptures to conjure up a healing back then. At that point, my faith was in the doctors. That's where most of us land in the natural world. But my cancer kept coming back. If we were to manifest God's healing, Connie and I needed to fully understand the meaning and the scope of Mark 11:23, John 14:12, and even Psalm 118:17: "I shall not die, but live, and declare the works of the LORD."

Once we did, we became different people.

Connie and I now pray differently. We do not beg God. We accept the healing and the authority already given to us. We do not plead our case. Rather, we express our gratitude for the gift that is promised in the new covenant. Understanding the nature of Jesus was a revelation. We are communicating daily with the Holy Spirit and meditating on the authority given to us in the scriptures specific to healing.

Connie and I had witnessed miraculous healings. We were encouraged. We became committed. Steadfast. We had renewed our minds and connected to the supernatural promise of healing. We know that God's wish and desire is that we prosper and be in health (3 John v. 2). God wants us to be world overcomers (1 John 5:5).

As powerful as the healing power that resides within the Word is, equally powerful is our ability to neutralize the promise of health and wellness when we speak death over ourselves. Our words are powerful. With our words we can release life or we can release death. There is an awesome, positive power in our words. There is also the potential for negative power. When we whine and gripe and complain, we release the negative forces of unbelief into our bodies and out into the world. That's why we believe and live by Mark 11:23: "Whoever says to this mountain, 'Be removed and be cast into the sea . . .'"

The mountain is our problem. If you are sick, speak to your sickness. Command it out of your body in the name of Jesus. As Andrew Wommack has so brilliantly put it, "The Bible says to speak to your problem, yet most people speak to God about their problem." Amen.

. . .

My process during the writing of this book has been to complete a rough draft of each chapter and then, rather than send it to the editor, have Connie read the chapter aloud to me while I take notes. It's incredibly revealing and helpful to hear the words you've had in your head read by someone else. Someone you trust.

One evening, late in the writing process, Connie and I were enjoying dinner in New York City at one of our favorite Italian restaurants, Il Gattopardo. Connie was reading this very chapter to me at whisper-level from off my phone. At the very moment she spoke the words, "Whoever says to this mountain, 'Be removed and be cast into the sea,'" an Italian waiter stopped in his tracks, smiled, and said in his thick accent, "Mark 11:23!" and then moved on. Our mouths fell to the floor.

"Wait! Hello? Come back?" Connie called after him.

Tazianno was his name. He returned to our table with a smile, and for the next forty-five minutes he erupted in conversation with his love for the healing scriptures. He prayed with us and agreed with our belief that I was healed. He told of his experiences speaking in tongues. Time stood still. It was a divine meeting. We had decided to come to this restaurant at the last minute on our way to our hotel. My phone had 2 percent of its battery remaining when Connie began reading. It shut down moments after she finished. And Tazianno was not even our waiter! He had to pass the table at the exact instant Connie whispered those life-affirming lines.

Tazianno told us, "My life changed forever when I unlocked these powerful scriptures: 1 Peter 2:24 and Mark 11:23."

. . .

"Thank you for your time, Doctor," I said as Connie, Gib, and I rose and headed toward the door of the radiation oncology exam room. "We truly appreciate your time and all the detail on the radiation protocol. We have plenty to think about."

"Of course," he said. "I'll get with your oncologist on the phone and fill him in on our meeting. We will need to have you come in for a pre-liminary CAT scan prior to your first round of radiation. We want to be able to map your pelvis for the future treatments." I nodded and let the door close between us. Moments later we were rising in silence together in the elevator, out of the sub-basement and into the hospital lobby.

Connie spoke only one line of scripture. It was 1 Peter 2:24: "By whose stripes you were healed."

And in that moment faith was born, in earnest, from our hearts and our minds into our actual physical lives. Faith in divine healing.

I stepped out onto the street. The California sunshine poured merci-fully down on my face. The only kind of radiation I would expose myself to ever again. Because I knew that I knew that I knew, with the deepest conviction, that I was healed.

I shall not die, but live,
And declare the works of the LORD.

—PSALM 118:17

Acknowledgments

I am eternally grateful to my relentless editors: Nils Parker, Connie Sellecca, and Jenny Baumgartner. My profound thanks to the most awesome warriors of faith and love—my family: Connie, Gib, Prima, Janeé, Uncle Vinny, Kathy, and my three amazing grandchildren. I am grateful for Dad, who made the tough decisions that shaped my life.

Thank you to Ann Sellecchia for showing me what true grit looks like. Thanks to my mom, who, along with Dr. Tom Wagner, taught me persistence and process. Thank you, Chuck and Terri Kenworthy, for your steadfast love and support.

To my radio families who have partnered with me toward a purpose-driven life: Scotty Meyers, Betsy Chase, Jason Burns, Elizabeth Negoski, Ben Harris, Jack Maatman, Lisa Guzetta, Christina Rasch, Jen Boller, Mike Drolet, Chris Shannon, Scott White, Bill Leslie, Max Powell, Steve Cohen, Andrew Heyward, Ed Joyce, Peter Kosann, Hiram Lazar, Jeff Warshaw, Spencer Brown, David Landau, Mike McVay, and Grace Carrick.

Thank you, Mike Atkins, for your vision for this project. I am grateful to Matt Baugher and Jenny Baumgartner and everyone at HarperCollins and Thomas Nelson.

I am grateful for my composition and performance professors: Dr. Thomas Wagner, John Diehl, and Harold Danko.

A big shout out to the Red Rocks Amphitheatre staff for sharing my vision and for supporting my music. My thanks to the Red Rocks crew, including David Michaels, Victor Frank, Ken Woo, Chris Chandler,

Acknowledgments

Allen Wollard, Mary Mueller, Charlie Bisharat, John Bisharat, Ross Pallone, Bart Conner, Nadia Comăneci, Lee Rose, BB Jewett McLeod, and Brett Steinberg.

Thanks to my *Entertainment Tonight* family: Mary Hart, Ron de Moraes, Robb Weller, Bob Goen, Lucy Salhany, and Kerry McCluggage.

To my current live-concert team: Scott Meyers, Rick Farrell, Gib Gerard, Prima Tesh, Mark Visher, Tim Landers, and Blair Shasky—your work has enriched the lives of thousands.

Thank you, Steve Callas, Layth Carlson, and everyone at Callas, Carlson & Associates.

Thank you to the original GTS records crew: Ken Antonelli, Bill Sobel, Cynthia Sissle, Candace Hanson, Dan Klores, Arthur Indurski, and Chris Roberts at Polygram. Thanks to Jon Small and my creative pals at PictureVision.

Thank you to my early mentors and bosses: Max Powell, Mike Kettenring, Ed Joyce, Ken Lowe, Scott White, Walter Windsor, Steve Cohen, Peter Lund, Peter Tortorici, Neal Pilson, and Van Gordon Sauter.

I'm grateful to the awesome teachers in my Divine Healing journey: Andrew Wommack, Jack Hibbs, Curry Blake, and Barry Bennett.

Thank you, Dr. Marshal Matos, Dr. Ronald Moskovitch, and Dr. Steve Galen for your brilliance and devotion to our family.

Randomly, and in no order, thanks to the many lifelong friends and colleagues who have been a part of this crazy and relentless ride: Steve Thomas, Mark Templeton, Ariel and Laura Bagdadi, Matt Thompson, James Sammataro, Ron Anteau, Dawn James, Dan Miller, Jim Scalem, Linda Taggert, Dine Bliss, and Dr. John Hart.

I want to express my deepest gratefulness to Dr. Patrick Walsh, Dr. Ted Schaeffer, and all the nurses at Johns Hopkins. Thanks to Dr. Christopher Logothetis, Dr. Brian Chapin, Claudette Mendoza, Alycia Hughes, and the incredible nurses and staff at MD Anderson. I am also grateful for the guidance of Dr. Chris King, Mel Kline, and Mac Dunwoody.

Thanks to Larry Zampino, Scott Varga, Carter Cathcart, Jay Madigan, Lee Rainie, Ed Goodwillie, David Koenig, and all of my fellow garage bandmates.

Acknowledgments

And a huge measure of gratefulness goes out to my live-concert fans who have filled the jazz clubs, performing arts centers, and amphitheaters to support my music for all these twenty-five years. You keep coming; I'll keep playing.

Notes

———

Introduction

1. Allison Stewart, "John Tesh: 'Anything Can Happen,'" *Chicago Tribune*, December 6, 2012, https://www.chicagotribune.com/entertainment/ct-xpm -2012–12–06-ct-ott-1207-john-tesh-20121206-story.html.

Chapter 1: Mentors in Persistence

1. Pat Conroy, *The Great Santini* (New York: Bantam Books, 1976).
2. Ryan Holiday, *The Obstacle Is the Way: The Timeless Art of Turning Trials into Triumph* (New York: Penguin, 2014), 68.

Chapter 2: Deadly Paradigm

1. Stephen Covey, *The 7 Habits of Highly Effective People: Powerful Lessons in Personal Change* (New York: Simon & Schuster, 2013), 39.

Chapter 3: True Grit

1. Steve Kroft, "Will Smith: My Work Ethic Is 'Sickening,'" *60 Minutes*, November 30, 2007, transcript, https://www.cbsnews.com/news/will-smith -my-work-ethic-is-sickening/.
2. Angela Lee Duckworth, "Grit: The Power of Passion and Perseverance," TED Talks, April 2013, https://www.ted.com/talks/angela_lee_duckworth _grit_the_power_of_passion_and_perseverance/.
3. Scott Davis, "Former NBA Coach Byron Scott Reveals the First Moment He Knew an 18-Year-Old Kobe Bryant Was Going to Take Over the League," *Business Insider*, December 18, 2017, https://www.businessinsider.com /byron-scott-kobe-bryant-take-over-nba-2017-4.

4. Tim S. Grover, *Relentless: From Good to Great to Unstoppable* (New York: Scribner, 2013), 43–44.

Chapter 5: Buried Alive

1. Betty Friedan, *The Feminine Mystique*, 50th anniv. ed. (New York: W. W. Norton & Co., 2013), 62.

Chapter 6: Walk On

1. Robert Greene, *Mastery* (New York: Penguin Books, 2012), 203.

Chapter 7: Burn the Ships!

1. Daniel Coyle, *The Talent Code: Greatness Isn't Born. It's Grown. Here's How.* (New York: Bantam, 2009), 97.
2. Jordan B. Peterson, *12 Rules for Life: An Antidote to Chaos* (Ontario: Random House Canada, 2018), 63.
3. Rebecca Leung, "Larry David: Curb Your Enthusiasm," *60 Minutes*, January 19, 2004, https://www.cbsnews.com/news/larry-david-curb-your-enthusiasm-19-01-2004/.

Chapter 9: Dream and Become

1. James Allen, *As a Man Thinketh* (n.p., Chump Change, 2017), 21.

Chapter 10: Be Found Ready

1. Greene, *Mastery*, 67–68.
2. FOX was still more than a decade away from existing.
3. Benjamin P. Hardy, *Slipstream Time Hacking: How to Cheat Time, Live More, and Enhance Happiness* (n.p.: Benjamin Hardy, 2015), 35, emphasis original.

Chapter 12: Homeless Once More

1. Jimmy Breslin, "The Horror of 'Sam,'" *LA Times*, July 1, 1999, https://www.latimes.com/archives/la-xpm-1999-jul-01-ca-51797-story.html.
2. Jonathan Mahler, *The Bronx Is Burning: 1977, Baseball, Politics, and the Battle for the Soul of a City* (New York: Picador, 2005), 6.
3. "Homelessness Is a Shared Experience in New York City," The Bowery Mission, https://www.bowery.org/homelessness/.

Chapter 14: My Worst Nightmare

1. Charles Q. Choi, "Why Time Seems to Slow Down in Emergencies," Live Science, December 11, 2007, https://www.livescience.com/2117-time-slow-emergencies.html/.

Chapter 21: Newtonian Physics

1. "Balanced and Unbalanced Forces," Physics Classroom, https://www.physicsclassroom.com/Class/newtlaws/u2l1d.cfm#balanced.

Chapter 25: Obstacles

1. Holiday, *Obstacle Is the Way*, 9 (see chap. 1, n. 2).
2. Staff, "The Teshing of America," *Newsweek*, April 2, 1995, https://www.newsweek.com/teshing-america-181686.

Chapter 27: *Intelligence for Your Life*

1. Austin Kleon, *Show Your Work!: 10 Ways to Share Your Creativity and Get Discovered* (New York: Workman Publishing, 2014), 132.
2. Steven Pressfield, *Do the Work: Overcome Resistance and Get Out of Your Own Way* (North Egremont, MA: Black Irish Entertainment, 2011), 12.
3. "The Internet News Goes Ordinary," Pew Research Center, January 14, 1999, https://www.people-press.org/1999/01/14/the-internet-news-audience-goes-ordinary/.

Chapter 28: Mark 11:23

1. Viktor Frankl, *Man's Search for Meaning: The Classic Tribute to Hope from the Holocaust* (1959; repr., Boston: Beacon Press, 2006), 44.

Chapter 29: Get Uncomfortable

1. Tennessee Williams, *Camino Real* (New York: New Directions, 2008), xii.
2. Tatiana Morales, "Don't Forget Tsunami Victims," CBS News, July 22, 2005, https://www.cbsnews.com/news/dont-forget-tsunami-victims/.
3. Francis Chan, *Forgotten God: Reversing Our Tragic Neglect of the Holy Spirit* (Colorado Springs: David C Cook, 2009), 50.
4. Lester Sumrall, *The Gifts and Ministries of the Holy Spirit* (New Kensington, PA: Whitaker House, 2005), 22.

Chapter 31: The Crack Den

1. Lin-Manuel Miranda, interview by Charlie Rose, *60 Minutes Presents: A Front Row Seat*, February 5, 2017, https://www.cbsnews.com/news/60-minutes-presents-a-front-row-seat/.

About the Author

For the past forty-five years John Tesh has been internationally recognized as a journalist, composer, broadcaster, and concert pianist. His *Intelligence for Your Life* radio show currently airs on 350 stations and reaches 14 million people each week. John's highly successful and varied career path also includes six years as a correspondent for CBS News, a ten-year run as anchor on *Entertainment Tonight*, broadcast host and music composer for the Barcelona and Atlanta Olympic Games, induction into the National Radio Hall of Fame and the North Carolina Music Hall of Fame, and the unique distinction of composing what critics have hailed as "the greatest sports theme in television history" for NBC Sports basketball. John's live television concerts, including the seminal "Live at Red Rocks," have raised millions for Public Television. John and his wife, Connie Sellecca, live in Los Angeles, California.

Visit JohnTeshRelentless.com for photos and
videos related to stories in this book.